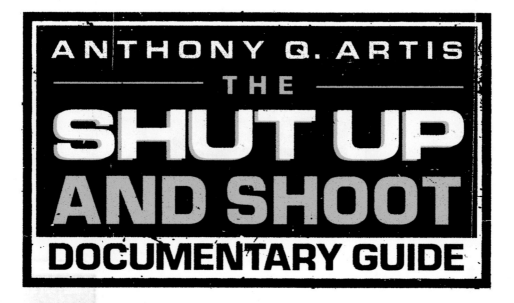

ANTHONY Q. ARTIS

THE

SHUT UP AND SHOOT

DOCUMENTARY GUIDE

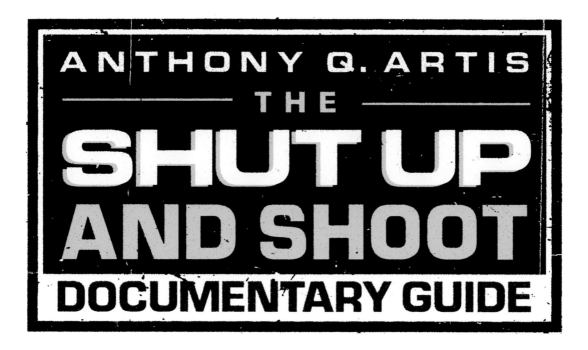

ANTHONY Q. ARTIS
THE
SHUT UP
AND SHOOT
DOCUMENTARY GUIDE

A

PRODUCTION

ELSEVIER

AMSTERDAM · BOSTON · HEIDELBERG · LONDON
NEW YORK · OXFORD · PARIS · SAN DIEGO
SAN FRANCISCO · SINGAPORE · SYDNEY · TOKYO
Focal Press is an imprint of Elsevier

Focal
Press

Publisher: Elinor Actipis
Associate Acquisitions Editor: Cara Anderson
Publishing Services Manager: George Morrison
Senior Project Manager: Dawnmarie Simpson
Assistant Editor: Robin Weston
Marketing Manager: Rebecca Pease
Cover Design: Dutton and Sherman Design
Interior Design: Dutton and Sherman Design

Focal Press is an imprint of Elsevier
30 Corporate Drive, Suite 400, Burlington, MA 01803, USA
Linacre House, Jordan Hill, Oxford OX2 8DP, UK

∞ Recognizing the importance of preserving what has been written, Elsevier prints its books on acid-free paper
whenever possible.

Library of Congress Cataloging-in-Publication Data
Artis, Anthony Q.
  The shut up and shoot documentary guide : a down & dirty DV production / Anthony Q. Artis.
    p.   cm.
  Includes index.
  ISBN-13: 978-0-240-80935-9 (pbk. : alk. paper)   1. Documentary films−Production and
direction.   2. Video recordings−Production and direction.   I. Title.
  PN1995.9.D6A78 2007
  070.1′8−dc22

                                                                        2007009360

British Library Cataloguing-in-Publication Data
A catalogue record for this book is available from the British Library.

ISBN: 978-0-240-80935-9

For information on all Focal Press publications
visit our website at www.books.elsevier.com

07 08 09 10 11 5 4 3 2 1

Printed in China.

Working together to grow
libraries in developing countries

www.elsevier.com | www.bookaid.org | www.sabre.org

ELSEVIER   BOOK AID
            International   Sabre Foundation

This book is dedicated with love and gratitude

To my son, Tai, let this book stand as a testament that you can do anything you set your mind to, whenever you're ready to do it.

To my wife, Sonya, who always has my back, front, and sides and keeps my feet on the ground. Without all of your sacrifice, encouragement, and faith I would have never even started, let alone completed, this project.

And to my elementary teachers Ms. Fletcher and Ms. Klein, who many years ago told a skinny little Black kid from Baltimore that he could write . . . and he believed them. Your faith in me gave me faith in myself and the heart to help others discover and nurture their own talents against the odds. I'm forever grateful to you both.

To Pete who helped to water this seed and to Maxie who helped to plant it. Watching you both do your thing up close gave me the courage to step out on a limb to do my own thing. (First one to the top, reach back.)

To Mom, Gwen, and Sharon, who all believed in me before I believed in myself. Thanks to my Dad for my twisted sense of humor. It's become an effective tool in my teaching toolkit.

I'm very thankful to all my filmmaking colleagues who agreed to be interviewed for the Down and Dirty DV Project. Thanks for sharing your expertise, wisdom, and time on this project. I learned so much from all of you in the making of this project. I know that so many others will do the same.

A big thanks to the entire NYU Tisch School of the Arts Production Center, faculty and administration, and the Doc Committee. Everyone's constant support, enthusiasm, helpful answers, and candid feedback inspired me to make this book a better tool for students. To Lou LaVolpe, your encouragement and advice have been invaluable. Thanks to all the filmmakers and fans who crewed and modeled for the video and DVD. I couldn't have pulled any of this off without you all watching my back and making me look good.

To my oldest friend, Darren Hackett, the man who introduced me to the film game and who was brave enough to take the first crack at editing this book in its roughest, self-published incarnation. Not only did you introduce me to filmmaking, but you showed me how to actually *be* a writer. (Shut up and write.) I will be eternally grateful for both.

To Dan "The Man" Shipp, we've come a long way from those all-night edit sessions for *Storybook Theatre*. Thanks for still having my back and still making me look good all these years later. I promise, the best is yet to come . . . and this time we're getting paid!

To Dave DiGioia, who taught me half of what I know and didn't even know he did. You've had an incredible impact on how I shoot, direct, and produce video. Not only did you school me to the video game, but you taught me how to be a video professional. And no, I ain't giving you any royalties, but you'll always have my eternal gratitude. Much love.

And of course I gotta thank my Focal Peeps for helping me pimp this book and get it out to the masses of the Down and Dirty DV Nation. Elinor, Rockin' Robin, Cara, Dawnmarie, Joanne, Dennis, Becky, Sheri, Big Jim and company, you guys are aaalllright! I appreciate the trust you gave me on this project and your putting up with all my changes and additions to additions. To my literary agent, Jan Kardys, your sincere generosity, guidance, and support helped make this the best possible publishing experience. You're one of the people that give agents a *good* name. Thanks to all of you for pushing me to take this from a little, homemade, self-published book to a bona fide, worldwide, live publication. (This is why *we're* hot!) Much love and guerrilla gratitude. Let's do it again sometime soon.

So many other people have contributed to this project in ways big and small, tangible and spiritual, that it'd be impossible for me to name and thank them all here (although you wouldn't know it from the long book and DVD credits). Please forgive me if I overlooked any of you in my rush to press. My coworkers, friends, and family have all been so incredibly supportive through the years that I've been *living* this project. I'm truly grateful and blessed to have such a film-family and family-family behind me.

Lastly, a special thanks to all the students I've instructed over the years. I've learned as much as I've taught. And I've been inspired as much as I've inspired. You help me remember why I got in this crazy business in the first place. (I had no clue what I was getting myself into.) So many of you have such a creativity, passion, and sincerity about filmmaking. It's been my main inspiration in writing this book and it's contagious. Hold onto that whatever you do. If you ever get lost along the way, just go back to the mindset you started with and take it from there. I hope this book helps you somewhere on your journey.

I love and thank each and every one of y'all. No joke.

CONTENTS

CHAPTER 6—COMPOSITION AND COVERAGE............153

THE CRAZY PHAT BONUS DVD

BONUS PAGES AND FORMS

RESOURCE PAGES

VIDEO AND AUDIO CONTENT

- Tutorial—5 Sound Rules to Live By
- Preview—Filmmaker Interviews
- Trailer—Instructional DVD Series
- Podcast—Learning the Process of Filmmaking

This Ain't Your Mama's Film Book

This is not a book for people who want to study documentary filmmaking. This is a book for people who want to *make* documentary films. There are many good books that you should read that cover the history, philosophy, and theories of documentary filmmaking in great depth. But this ain't one of those books. This book is for people who are done *talking* about the films they want to make and who are ready to shut up and shoot.

It's an ultra-user-friendly reference guide to basic documentary production from the technical specifics of camerawork, lighting, and sound to the practical intangibles of hustling up a crew, conducting interviews, and stealth shooting. While it's documentary specific, most of the advice and techniques in this book can be applied equally to narrative projects or event video. It's written casually with healthy doses of humor, lots of pictures, and all in plain English (with a little slang thrown in just for fun). In other words, this ain't ya mama's film book.

Why I Wrote This Book and Who I Wrote It For

As a young, broke film student I often found myself combing through thick and overwhelming film books with illustrations and terminology so advanced that it sometimes seemed like they were actually *trying* to confuse me. The equipment they showed was often beyond the reach and level of a novice. (That's a nice Ultra Max 5000 Crane—now could you teach me about something that costs *less* than half a million dollars that I might actually use on my film?!) Even more aggravating, the information that was most relevant to me was always scattered between a bunch of unnecessarily long words, technical terms, and crazy scientific diagrams that were completely over my head and mostly useless to me at that early stage.

I'd sometimes read the same paragraph three times over and *still* not get the concept or why it was important. (Granted, I wasn't the brightest kid in the class, but I wasn't the slowest either, so I know I was not alone.) On the flip side, the less formal film books I bought were just too general and short on specifics to be of much use. Ultimately, I'd get frustrated and end up learning many concepts through the more painful process of trial and error for lack of a simple explanation that would help me get started.

I knew that there was a whole science and intricate technology behind everything and that I would eventually have to learn about terms such as "footcandles," "decibels," and the aptly named "circle of confusion," but I just didn't *care* in the beginning. It was a simple case of information overload. Starting out, I just wanted basic information to help me turn my ideas into films. I wanted straight, easy-to-find answers about the *core* things I needed to know to make my films look and sound more professional. I rarely found those answers and hardly ever in a single book. It didn't stop me from learning filmmaking in the end. It just forced me to learn many things the hard way.

Years later as a filmmaking instructor and production consultant, I began to train many students who were just as intimidated and confused as I was then. These novice filmmakers were making all the same mistakes I had once made, and they were suffering through all the same pains and frustrations that I had felt. They didn't lack intelligence or ability. What they lacked most was *simple, practical, beginner instruction* to give them a foundation (and sincere interest) in the more complex nuances of cinematography, storytelling, and filmmaking science. They were trying to cram the whole technical, historic, and philosophical aspects of filmmaking into their head all at once before they even shot a single frame of film or video. While some teachers still favor this approach, they fail to recognize that it just doesn't work for many students. And if it doesn't work for the *students* . . . it doesn't work.

So after years of talking about it, I finally shut up and wrote a book that I hope will break the complex process of filmmaking down into manageable, bite-sized chunks of practical instruction and advice for filmmakers of all budget levels who just want the specific basics to get them started. As best as I could, I've tried to illustrate everything, give step-by-step procedures, and offer all the practical advice and wisdom that I wish I had had at the start of my own filmmaking career. Peppered throughout this book you will also find the candid advice of other notable and up-and-coming documentary filmmakers that have "been there and done that," so that you might learn from even more people who have blazed the same trail.

The end goal of this book is to cut through the clutter to save you hours of heartache and countless dollars, and to enable you to successfully overcome the obstacles of filmmaking whether you are an aspiring film student looking to shoot your first project or a veteran filmmaker looking for a quick reference guide to some of the areas with which you're not as familiar. In short, this is an illustrated jump start for filmmakers who are ready to *execute* their vision now and don't have a lot of time to read between the lines.

This book provides simple practical beginner instruction in plain language and illustrations.

The Down and Dirty DV Filmmaking Approach

What is "Down and Dirty DV" filmmaking? In the simplest terms, it's a savvy new age of digital guerrilla filmmaking. It's a modern filmmaking mindset that bucks the tradition of raising production value through bigger budgets and more expensive resources. If you've got the money, you can get more professional equipment and crew, but if you've got a Down and Dirty mindset, you can get more professional results from *any* equipment or crew.

Down and Dirty DV is about maximizing your resources by teaching you how to enhance and get the best use out of the things you *do* have and *can* afford, and how to substitute or workaround the resources you don't have. It's about focusing all of your filmmaking efforts on improving the final result onscreen, rather than the tools used to achieve it. It boils down to the fine art of doing more with less. Let me break it down in pictures:

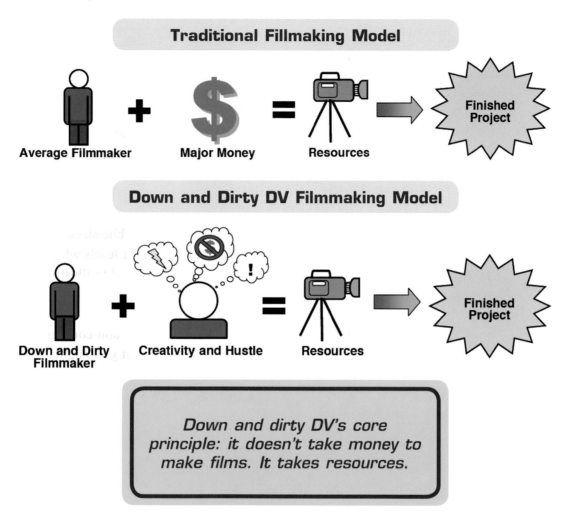

Down and dirty DV's core principle: it doesn't take money to make films. It takes resources.

The Down and Dirty DV Project

Much more than just this book, *Down and Dirty DV* is my personal labor of love. Everyone learns differently, and at the end of the day, filmmaking is a visual and hands-on process, so I'm busy designing an *entire family* of concise and easy-to-use instructional filmmaking resources that are both educational and entertaining. Me and the Down and Dirty DV team of coconspirators are already hard at work on future titles that will cover narrative filmmaking, working your way up in the industry, commercials, and more. So stay tuned. More practical filmmaking instruction is on the way.

I've been assembling this project for over two and a half years in my "spare" time. (Which is pretty much a joke since I have a full-time job, a wife, an energetic 3 year-old, and spend at least two hours commuting each day!) In the end, I had to write this book the same way I shoot video—by being practical and maximizing my limited time and resources for all they're worth. More than half of this book was written guerrilla-style and underground (literally) on the subways of New York City during my daily commute. I sincerely hope you enjoy and learn from the effort. I've done my best to give you a jump start in the film game and help you avoid the most common mistakes that trip people up.

That's it. The back door to film school is now open. I hope you will enjoy *The Shut Up and Shoot Documentary Guide*. I've done my best to keep it real, practical, and helpful. It's my fondest wish that each and every person who reads this book will be empowered to overcome the intimidation and obstacles to filmmaking (real and imagined) and successfully execute their vision. Remember, the only thing that really matters is what's in your heart and what's on the monitor. Everything else is static. Happy guerrilla filmmaking!

Peace, Love, and Video,
Anthony Q. Artis
Down and Dirty Filmmaker

8:40 a.m. Friday, April 12, 2007
Manhattan-bound F-Train, New York City

Learn DV Filmmaking.
How You Want and When You Want.
Straight Up. Guerrilla.

Web site

Blog

Video Podcasts

THE COMPLETE SERIES

Workshops

DVDs

Books

The first documentary I ever remember seeing was *Scared Straight* by Arnold Shapiro. It was about a program for juvenile delinquents that took groups of law-breaking teenagers into a state prison for a day to be "mentored" by a group of hardcore convicts serving minimum life sentences or longer. (I should point out here that prison mentoring is *a whole lot* different than regular old mentoring.)

I was about 9 or 10 years old and it was billed as a major TV event. They told parents to watch it with their kids. It was shown uncut and uncensored on primetime TV with a bunch of warnings about the language and subject matter. And it scared the living hell out of me! From that day to this, I largely credit that documentary for keeping me out of trouble with the law. It was the first of many docs that changed the way I came to look at the world around me. (Coincidentally, I ended up working for Arnold Shapiro two decades later, but I never got to go on a prison shoot. Bummer.)

I've always found documentary content to be more compelling than the fantasy narrative films that were offered up to me as a young person. You simply can't make up a narrative story that is as fascinating as films like *Scared Straight*, *Streetwise*, or *The Devil's Playground*. And it's pretty hard to come up with characters that are as quirky and interesting as those in *The Cruise* and *American Movie*. And I think all the great screenwriters in the world would be hard-pressed to invent fiction that would move people and elicit as much emotion as films like *Lalee's Kin*, *When the Levee's Broke*, or *TV Junkie*.

At the end of the day you can always dismiss powerful fiction as the work of someone's imagination or an exaggeration of the real events. Powerful *documentaries* on the other hand, grab you by the collar and force you to seriously contemplate societies, ideas, and human realities that you might otherwise never acknowledge or think twice about. (How would you know that right along side the gang culture of L.A. is a whole other underground culture of make-up-clad, clown dance groups who "battle" each other with hyperkinetic dance moves unless you saw the documentary *Rize*? . . . You wouldn't.)

In the best case scenarios, I truly believe this medium has the power to change the world—sometimes in big ways, but usually one person at a time, in a thousand little ways, from helping people confront their own serious illnesses (*A Healthy Baby Girl*), teaching them what they can do to slow down the destruction of our environment (*An Inconvenient Truth*), or just giving them the courage and inspiration to pursue their dreams and goals (*Hoop Dreams*). And to me, that's about as good as filmmaking gets. There's a big world out there in desperate need of understanding, change, and inspiration and documentary gives us the power to help make it happen. If not us, then who? . . . We're *it*, baby! Time to shut up and shoot.

DownAndDirtyDV.com
Any Budget. Any Camera. Any Time.

CHAPTER 1
PREPRODUCTION

Plenty of people have bright ideas. Plenty of people are geniuses, but will never know it, because they don't <u>execute</u>.

—Fat Joe
from the documentary **Paper Chasers**

Shut up and shoot.

—Anthony Q. Artis

Know this: Filmmaking is not magic or rocket science. All the crafts and practices of filmmaking can be learned. Pretty much anyone can be a filmmaker (or even a rocket scientist for that matter). All you've gotta do is *study and learn* what the task involves, then methodically do it, step-by-step, and at the end of the day you will have a film (or a rocket). Whether or not your first efforts take off is another story, but you will be well on your way to success if you study, practice, and—above all else—persist.

Filmmaking, especially DV filmmaking, is constantly evolving. The tools, practices, and industry are all constantly changing and you need to stay up to be Down and Dirty. If you weren't in film school, once upon a time, it would've really sucked to be you, but in this new digital age you have many options outside of film school to learn and hone the craft. Use them all.

Film Books

You're already off to a great start with this book, but you need more. In my personal filmmaking journey, books have been invaluable to expanding my knowledge as a filmmaker. Film books come in many flavors and styles. Some are simply collections of inspirational filmmaking anecdotes, some are technical blueprints, some are more academic and philosophical, and others are in-depth case studies. I have found they all have something to offer. Ask fellow filmmakers what they recommend. (At DownAndDirtyDV.com you can find a collection of specific film books I recommend.)

Film Books

DVD Extras

DVD extras are probably the best thing to happen to film education in a long time. Whenever possible, try to rent or purchase DVD versions of your favorite movies that include director commentary and other extras that detail the filmmaking process. Apart from telling you specifics about how certain scenes were pulled off, you can learn a lot about how a real crew functions and how the film actually came together from idea to distribution. Mini-documentaries that show the behind-the-scenes struggle to make a film are also becoming quite prevalent. Moreover, many of these DVDs also contain storyboards, set and costume sketches, director's early works,

DVD Extras

research material, scripts, crew interviews, deleted scenes, and other previously unseen elements of the filmmaking process. Try watching a movie once, then look at the making-of documentary (doc) and all the extras, then watch it again with the director/crew commentary. After that, you'll never look at that film the same way again. Every time you look at it, it will be like taking a mini-film studies course.

Podcasts

Podcasts

The newest entry to filmmaking instruction is podcasting. If you're not down with podcasting yet, you really need to get down, because you're sleeping on some amazing free resources. In short, podcasts are audio and high-quality video clips that can be downloaded, saved, and played on your computer or your iPod or other portable media player. There is of course the pimped-out superfly Down and Dirty DV Podcast, which I highly recommend. And there are also many other great audio and video shows out there that can help you understand the filmmaking process, if not teach you in outright step-by-step lessons. The filmmaking podcasts out there include feature interviews, tutorials, call-in Q&As, news, Web links, interviews, product reviews, trailers, shorts, and even feature-length films. See the Resources section of this book for a list of filmmaking-related podcasts.

Workshops

Workshops

In major cities all over the country there are filmmaking workshops, panels, and classes that will help you learn the craft of filmmaking. These range from scriptwriting classes to hands-on workshops to Q&A panels about industry issues. Time and price also vary from one hour to one year or free to thousands of dollars. There is something out there for everyone from kids to old-school video veterans. Filmmaking organizations typically sponsor panels and workshops, but there are also commercial and college workshops to help every level of filmmaker expand their skills and knowledge. Down and Dirty DV offers short guerrilla filmmaking workshops, but there are plenty of other workshops out there with different focuses. Poke around on the net, ask fellow filmmakers, and comb your local college course listings.

Cable TV

There are always a handful of cable TV shows about filmmaking. IFC and The Sundance Channel have programming entirely dedicated to indie films and filmmaking. Among my past and present favorites are *Project Greenlight* (Bravo), *MTV's Making the Video* (MTV), *Iconoclasts* (Sundance Channel), *Film School* (IFC), *Inside the Actor's Studio* (Bravo), *On the Lot* (Fox), *Anatomy of a Scene* (IFC), and *E! True Hollywood Story* (E!). All of these shows feature filmmakers discussing the craft and in many cases cameras are rolling behind the scenes to show you the filmmaking process unfolding up close and personal with all the ugly seams showing.

Cable TV

Instructional DVDs

Books are cool, but ultimately filmmaking is a visual process that's easiest explained in pictures. There are a number of DVDs out there (seemingly all with the subtitle "film school in a box") that will help walk you through the technical aspects of the filmmaking process step-by-step. From lighting tutorials to camerawork to non-linear editing, there's probably a DVD product out there to teach almost every aspect of DV filmmaking. If guerrilla is your style, check out the Down and Dirty DV DVD Series at www.DownAndDirtyDV.com.

Instructional DVDs

Web Sites

There are endless filmmaking blogs and Web sites online. You can look up do it yourself (DIY) projects, case studies, articles, tutorials, get your filmmaking questions answered, join an online filmmaking community, research equipment and prices, and on and on. Some such as FilmSchoolOnline.com or CyberCollege.com offer free and low-cost filmmaking instruction in the form of online tutorials and instruction. See the Resources List in the back of the book for more film-related Web sites.

Web sites

Magazines

Magazines are a great way to stay down with the latest trends and practices of the industry: in-depth case studies, equipment reviews, tutorials, and interviews with today's filmmaking movers and shakers. Some mags, such as *StudentFilmmakers* and *DV*, are offered free to qualified people in the industry. As far as I can tell, qualifying usually involves giving up your e-mail address and filling out a brief survey once or twice a year. It's a fair trade-off and beats the cover price.

Magazines

Crewing

Any place where people are making films and videos is a great place to learn the process up close and personal. If you are willing to work for free, there are infinite opportunities to work on film and video crews. (I call this OPM Learning, because the only thing better than learning from your own mistakes is learning from **O**ther **P**eople's **M**istakes on **O**ther **P**eople's **M**oney.) Crewing is cheaper and less stressful and painful with many of the same first-hand learning benefits of working on your own film. More important, you will have informal teachers and you will meet

Crewing

and feel out people who you can later recruit to work on your own projects. I've worked for no money a hundred times over, but I've never worked on a project "for free" in my life. The knowledge, skills, and contacts I've acquired while helping fellow filmmakers with their efforts have been invaluable to me. Never think of it as *working* for free, but *learning* for free. In the best case scenarios where there is a real budget for crew and you have some experience under your belt, you will actually be getting *paid* to learn. Production Assistant, Craft Services, and boom operator are all excellent positions for observation. Check your local film organizations, college bulletin boards, and Web sites like Mandy.com or Craig's List for film crew announcements.

Doing

It doesn't matter whether you study all or none of the previous resources first, at some point you are going to have to actually make like Nike and *just do it*. This is the hands-down most effective way to learn. Don't worry that you don't know everything (you never will). Don't worry that you're not as good as that other kid (you will be later). Don't wait until you can afford a better camera (it's just a tool). Don't worry that it's gonna suck (it probably will).

Doing

Stop BS-ing yourself and everyone around you and just shut up and do it! The real learning process begins the moment you commit to a project and hit the record button. I've had one simple goal on every project I've shot, and that is to make it suck *less* than the last project. When you take this approach a magic thing happens over time . . . you go from sucky to mediocre to good and maybe, just maybe, if you eat your guerrilla vitamins and say your prayers, someone will call your work "great." But you'll never know if you don't actually start doing it, screwing it up, and getting better at it. No professor, course, book, or DVD can teach you nearly as much as actually hitting the streets with a camera and doing it. Straight up. Guerrilla.

WHY MAKE A DOCUMENTARY?

ALBERT MAYSLES, DIRECTOR/DP
(Grey Gardens, Gimme Shelter, Salesman, Lalee's Kin, etc.)

Photo Credit: Kendall Messick

Very simply put one of the great needs—maybe certainly one of the greatest needs in our world—is for us to know one another, to know what's really going on in the world around us and to feel a commonality of need and purpose with other people. People of different walks of life, other nations, other ethnic backgrounds, economic statuses, different philosophies, and religions . . . We need to find a common bond with the rest of humanity and the documentary allows us to do that. I think it's the most effective way of connecting with another person's life. You film somebody in a particular situation that is the same or different from that of the viewer, and that viewer feels a connection with that person and that person's experience—an engagement with the life around that person, who is the viewer. And it's what we need. As I think of it, it's a documentary filmmaker's way of making a better world.

If you go into documentary filmmaking, you are making a connection with life itself. And you have an opportunity to inform people in such a connective fashion. You know the word "entertainment" is an interesting one. A documentary is an entertainment, but not as a diversion, which is the first definition in entertainment, but in engaging. You're engaging that person by making a good documentary and that's a wonderful form of entertainment.

I've always had a great deal of confidence in the value and even in the eventual popularity of documentary as a form of filmmaking . . . Also, I've felt that eventually just as we say, "the truth will out," so there will be a very strong trend toward nonfiction, away from fiction, because the nonfiction has already within it a source of truth that is difficult for fiction to match. And so, that's what's happening now. There was a movement in the direction of documentary. I just hope that that movement flourishes and becomes stronger and stronger as people make good documentaries and we don't rely on so-called "reality television" and that way of recording reality in a way that's really kind of documentary, but not really.

Basic Steps of Documentary Preproduction

1. Brainstorm ideas and develop goal(s)
2. Research story
3. Choose interview subjects
4. Choose equipment package
5. Make budget
6. Write production plan
7. Hire crew

Introduction

A good shoot begins long before production with extensive preparation, otherwise known as **preproduction**. Carefully planning out what you will do and double-checking your equipment will help ensure that you get it right the first and perhaps *only* time. Proper preparation will also greatly boost your confidence when it's time to shoot, particularly if you're new to filmmaking. Just say the tongue-twister to the right three times and never forget it.

✔ *Proper preparation prevents a poor performance.*

Documentary Goal

Regardless of whether you're making a documentary feature, short, news story, reality show, or even shooting a wedding, you should always start with the same basic questions: What's the focus? Why are you making this project? What story do you want to tell? What topics will be explored? What information do you hope to convey to your viewers? What aspects of your topic are most compelling? Are there new angles to explore on your topic? In short, ask yourself what story do you want to tell and why? You should to be able to make a statement such as:

- I want to make a documentary about the birth of modern video games, because most people don't know the fascinating story behind the people who started it all.
- I am making a video project about the history of my church to inform new members and preserve the story of the founders for future generations.
- I am documenting the underground culture of squirrel fighting to expose the exploitation of rodents to a prime time news audience.

✔ *Determine the goal of your doc first in order to focus your preproduction in the right direction.*

The primary purpose is for you to get a clear grasp of what it is you want to do, then gear everything else toward that goal. These are some of the first questions you should ask yourself, because your ultimate goal will affect many of your decisions during preproduction.

BRAINSTORMING YOUR IDEA

Use the Internet, personal contacts, trade organizations, books, magazines, and newspapers to begin researching your topic, then track down potential interview subjects. If you don't spend a lot of time on the Web, you need to start. There simply is no single greater, cheaper, or more convenient source of *starting point* information for documentaries than the Internet.

Once you pick a topic, you can begin looking up information on that topic by using search engines such as Google, Yahoo, or Dogpile. If you haven't already determined your goal or the focus of your documentary, this process will help you brainstorm and clarify exactly what aspect(s) of the broader topic you want to examine. The chart below illustrates just some of the information you could easily find on three diverse topics depending on where you decide to look.

	SKATEBOARDING	POLITICS	DEATH PENALTY
News Web Sites	■ Products ■ Recent events ■ Photos/video ■ Major skaters	■ Recent events ■ Major figures ■ Photos/video ■ Upcoming events	■ Statistics ■ Upcoming executions ■ Photos/video
Personal Web Sites	■ Tricks and tips ■ Most popular skaters ■ Fan perspective	■ Public opinion ■ Activist movements ■ Upcoming events	■ Pro/con activists ■ Protests ■ Essays
Blogs and Podcasts	■ Fan perspective ■ Tricks and tips ■ Popular products	■ Latest rumors ■ Insider info ■ Public opinion	■ Public opinions ■ Inmate POVs ■ Advocate POVs
Trade/Professional Organizations	■ Upcoming events ■ New developments ■ Pro skater perspective	■ Organizations' political stance ■ Upcoming events ■ New initiatives	■ Law enforcement opinion ■ Statistics

Also check a *major* public library and sites like Amazon.com or Netflix.com to see what films and books already exist on the topic and what approaches have been taken to the material in the past. Try to gauge what was successful and why. Did these previous works exhaust the subject or are there still new angles, stories, and approaches to be mined?

> ✔ **Use the Internet to help you identify potential themes, characters, and stories to pursue.**

THE IMPORTANCE OF RESEARCH

It's important that you try to keep an open mind during this phase of preproduction. You want to gather all the potential directions you could take before settling on an approach. Once you've done your preliminary "brainstorming" and research you'll be ready to further define exactly what your documentary should and should not cover.

By mentally separating the normal from the extraordinary in your observations, you will know what's interesting and worth shooting and what's routine and boring. Potential characters, themes, and, most important, *stories* will begin to emerge. Think about how these will play onscreen. Has the general public seen these stories and people before? From what angle were they presented? Is there enough compelling material to hold an audience's interest? What *new* ideas or questions will you examine in your doc?

Research is simply forming the answer to these questions *before* you dive in. If you skip this vital step, you may easily find yourself wasting countless hours and budget dollars pursuing people, themes, and events that will never see the light of day. The better you know your story ahead of time, the more focused and successful your efforts will be.

I know fellow filmmakers who have spent months shooting hours of video of some subject only to discover in the end that the material has no useful or coherent narrative thread. There is no focus, no compelling new info, no real characters . . . no story. All they have is some bits and pieces of interesting footage that don't add up to Jack. (And you know his last name!)

✔ *Research and study your topic beforehand to determine which aspects are most worth shooting.*

RESEARCH AND FACT CHECKING

SAFIYA MCCLINTON, PRODUCER

(Diamonds: The Price of Ice) and Assoc. Prod. (Brown vs. Board of Ed.)

The main thing with researching documentary is to not approach it like you did your senior English paper. Don't just stay on the Internet and think that those are sources that are reliable, because many times they're not . . . How do you present something and say, "This is official. This is true?" Now you might have one professor at the university of such and such in Iowa and he says this is the case and this is how it went down. You can't stay with that one man's approach to it. You can present it, but you definitely have to show a balanced picture.

The best way to do research is to just take a camcorder and go to as many people as you have access to and really just interview them. First person primary sources are the best way to make sure that your information is valid and is truly coming from the horse's mouth.

In addition to that, just make sure if they [offer] statistics you can back up those statistics. If someone says, "35% of the people . . . blah, blah, blah," you can go and dig up that information in journals, in newspapers . . . If they're saying that 35% of women who have this problem are XYZ, then go find that, because many times people know that their authority and their expertise will make it so they can say anything and you're not going to research it. So you really just have to follow up with reliable sources.

You just have to look at the standards in particular periodicals or any type of media, any type of additional media . . . you really have to look at their standards for journalistic excellence or fact finding. People can be very convincing in their accounts . . . and you're listening to this story thinking, "Man, this is amazing! This is gold!" And you just have to make sure that the gold that you have is not *fool's* gold.

The people you select to appear onscreen will ultimately make or break your documentary. Choosing interview subjects is to documentary productions what casting is to **narrative filmmaking**. The only difference is that docs have *real* characters instead of character actors.

A compelling character can really make a project. In fact, many of the most successful documentaries are **character studies**. *American Movie* (about a filmmaker), *Crumb* (about a comic strip artist), and *The Cruise* (about a NYC tour guide/poet) are all notable documentary character studies. All of these docs are built around the unique perspective of a compelling central character. These docs would be entirely different creations without these colorful individuals. You can't separate the two and still have the same film, if you'd even have a film left at all.

Don't get it twisted. You can't just point your camera at someone interesting and make a good character study doc. You still need to manage structure, pacing, story development, and approach the same as you would for any other doc, but the most important core element will always be the character(s) at the center of it all.

While your project may not be a character study, the people you ultimately choose to speak on your topic are still equally crucial to the success of your doc. The better your subjects communicate and express themselves verbally, the more articulate and interesting your piece will be. So what else makes for a good interview subject?

The Ideal Character/Interview Subject
- ❏ Candid and forthcoming
- ❏ Able to speak coherently about topic
- ❏ Unique perspective
- ❏ Knowledgeable about topic
- ❏ Passionate about topic
- ❏ A recognized expert
- ❏ Clear viewpoint

If you can check off three or more of the above, you've probably got a decent candidate on your hands. If you crap out and choose a poor character, it only means you've wasted your tape, time, and resources and you'll have to find another subject or cut that segment from your finished piece. You may have plenty of videotape, but time and resources are always limited. Research and choose wisely.

✔ *Choose interview subjects who are compelling and knowledgeable about your topic.*

The one thing that separates documentaries from each other, especially those dealing with the same subject matter, is **approach**. Approach is just a general term that refers to how you choose to tell the story on screen. What tone, storytelling techniques, and elements will you use? For example, will the subject of your documentary read narration or will you hire an actor? Or will you forego narration entirely and use **screen captions** to tie elements of your story together? Or will you just let the action speak for itself without any embellishment?

Will you be an onscreen character in the documentary like Michael Moore (*Fahrenheit 9/11*) or Morgan Spurlock (*Supersize Me*)? Will there be re-enactments in your piece? If so, how will they be stylized to distinguish them from the rest of your footage? Are you going to include an animated segment? Will your doc be shot "naturally" with no artificial lighting? The answers to all of these questions will form your doc's *approach*.

Think it out. Experiment. Look at other documentaries and analyze how different filmmakers approached their subject. The possibilities are as endless as your imagination. Even though there have been countless documentaries on Tupac or teen pregnancy or corporate pollution (often using much of the same source material), yours can be made compelling and unique with a new *approach*. The story may have been told before, but you have your own perspective, focus, and a unique voice that the world has never heard before. Your storytelling style *is* your approach. It may include any of the following or more. Mix and match, research, and invent new ways to tell your story.

> ✔ Decide on an approach and storytelling techniques that are most effective for your material and style.

What's Your Approach?

- ❑ **Narration** (*Fahrenheit 911*)
- ❑ **Reenactments/recreations** (*The Civil War*)
- ❑ **Animation** (*Bowling for Columbine*)
- ❑ **Direct or natural cinema** (*Grey Gardens*)
- ❑ **Filmmaker as part of story** (*Paper Chasers*)
- ❑ **Interviews** (*The Fog of War*)
- ❑ **Confessionals to camera** (*Blue Vinyl*)
- ❑ **Archival footage** (*Eyes on the Prize*)
- ❑ **Archival photos** (*4 Little Girls*)

CONCEPT AND STORYTELLING

SAM POLLARD, PRODUCER/EDITOR

(4 Little Girls, Jim Brown All-American, Eyes on the Prize II, When the Levees Broke, etc.)

As a producer, part of my job is to figure out what the material is, which is all in my head. So, now I have to translate all these ideas from my head to communicate to a cameraperson and a sound person to shoot that stuff . . . Really, the ideas, the concepts are all in my brain, as a producer, and I have to make them become real when someone goes out to shoot the material . . .

The key thing as a documentary producer is to develop the concept. To find the subject is number one. Then after you find the subject, what's the concept? What's the theme that this subject is going to help you tell? The third thing is, how to tell the story. What is the story and how to tell it?

So, for example, I'm leaving on Tuesday to go to Minnesota to shoot on a pig farm, with a lady and her husband. The lady's a singer and the husband's a farmer. So, I have to figure out what the story is. The story is how they met, their lives on the farm, the pros and cons of her singing career, and being married to this farmer who has this very big farm. So, that's the story I'm gonna tell. I have to figure out what to visualize to help tell that story. Okay, so I'm gonna go out and shoot the pig farmer early in the morning feeding the pigs, sunrise, the waving fields, planting corn, planting soybeans. Then parallel, back at the house, the wife is rehearsing, practicing her singing, playing the piano, and warbling to the mirror.

Then, maybe there's a scene with the husband and the wife together out in the fields; then, an interview with both of them in the house; then, single interviews with each individual so I can get their own particular, personal backstories. It's good to shoot stills, if they have scrapbooks, pictures of them together and them separately . . . , so I'm thinking about the story and how to visualize it.

Once you determine the goal and approach of your piece, you can begin to put together a **production plan**, which includes all of the specific elements you will need to realize your documentary. The production plan simply answers the overall question: "How can I make this happen?" To answer this big question, start with your goal then ask yourself a series of smaller questions such as:

1. What specific aspects of the topic should be covered?
This will determine your sources and depth of **research**.

2. Who is most qualified to speak on this topic?
This will determine your choice of **interview subjects**.

3. Where does the action of this topic take place?
This will affect your choice of **locations**.

4. How will I tell this story? Style? Structure?
This will determine your **approach**.

5. Where will this documentary end up? Theaters? TV? DVD?
This will help determine your **equipment package**.

6. Who will I need to help me make it?
This will dictate the size of your **crew**.

. . . and all of these questions will affect your **budget**. So when all is said and done, your production plan should contain specifics on:

- ❏ **Research**
- ❏ **Interview subjects**
- ❏ **Locations**
- ❏ **Approach/style**
- ❏ **Budget**
- ❏ **Crew**
- ❏ **Equipment package**

Armed with this information, you will have a clear blueprint for producing your documentary and formulating a budget. Now you are ready to begin to make it happen.

> ✔ *Prepare a production plan that spells out all the elements needed to make your doc happen.*

How to Raise Money
Hints for Embarking on the Fundraising Journey
by Michelle Coe

The following was originally published in **The Independent Film and Video Monthly,** *a publication of AIVF.*

Probably the most common can-of-worms question pressing the emerging filmmaker is: How do I find money for my film? It's never a simple question to answer, since film/video funding and financing involves a lot of time, research, skill, and perseverance. Today's funding climate is extremely competitive. Government funds have just about dried up. The stock market is squeezing private investors. And both commercial and nonprofit companies are trimming their budgets. There is still money out there, but this is a time to think creatively on where to find it and how to ask for it. There are two basic streams to go down to raise money for a media project—fundraising and financing. Fundraising involves grants and contributors who do not expect any financial return. This is mostly for noncommercial projects, such as social-issue documentaries, short films, and experimental projects. Financing involves investors who expect a return on their investment and is generally the direction pursued by commercial projects such as feature films. Both these categories are fluid. Some fiction films do receive funding from nonprofits, and there are documentaries that may be enticing to investors. Whatever source you pursue, creative thinking and detailed preparation are your most important tasks.

Fundraising

Asking a foundation for money may seem more overwhelming than actually making a film. First you must find a good match for your subject, and then there are endless forms and proposals to hand in. The thing to remember is that it is a foundation's job to give away money. It is your job to convince them to give it to you.

FUNDING RESOURCES

Packaging Your Project
Whether you apply for grants or approach investors, the better "packaged" your project is the greater the likelihood you'll end up with a check. Well packaged means presenting your project as creatively and professionally as possible. Your packet should include:

- The script
- A thorough synopsis of the project
- Resumes of key personnel
- The project's budget
- A fundraising plan
- A distribution plan
- Letters of intent from funding entities, cast, or advisors
- A sample reel of past work and/or footage of the project

It is very important, even in this early stage, to consider where your project will ultimately end up. While theatrical release, broadcast, and/or cable distribution may be your goal, the truth is many projects are never

How to Approach Foundations

Do your research carefully. It's important to know who would truly be interested in your project. Most foundations do not have specific media funding programs, but they do have mission statements. Your job is to study the foundation, their guidelines, annual report, anything that will help you evaluate how your project advances their mission. Once you're confident that you have found a foundation that meshes with your topic, call their offices. If they do not fund media projects directly, explain that while you are aware that they do not traditionally fund media, the subject of your film/video directly fits into their funding goals. Never write a generic proposal and send it out randomly. Proposals must be tailor-made to fit your project with the funder's mission.

The Application Process

Funds from foundations, the government, and corporate giving programs require an application process. Here begins the intensive phase of grant writing. If your writing skills are not solid, never fear; there are grant writers who fundraise for a living, and producers who have honed their grant writing skills, who you might bring on as a consultant or coproducer. Your local media arts center will have a membership directory or résumé bank to help you find these people. Bringing on a producer with a track record may also improve your chance of actually getting the grant, because some funders hesitate to fund lesser-known media makers. A producer with a longer résumé helps assure that the project will be completed and look professional. Even if you don't need help with grant writing, consider developing a board of advisors to assist you on some level. Having a person of stature onboard can make all the difference. It's also important to mention other grants or contributions already received. Commitments from other entities or individuals are always reassuring to a prospective contributor. Read the application carefully. Yours is one of hundreds of requests for money; a weak or incomplete applica-

picked up for distribution by these outlets. Don't limit your project's life by not addressing how you will reach your audience if the project is not bought by a distributor. The people investing in your project—whether they represent a foundation or are an investor—will want to know this, and being prepared will only make you a more attractive prospect.

Funding and Financing Sources

- The government (the NEA, the NEH, State Arts Commissions and Humanities Councils)
- Private foundations
- Corporate giving programs
- Individuals (donors and in-kind goods/services)
- Production companies and studios
- Investors
- Coproductions

About Fiscal Sponsorship

Most foundations require applicants to have nonprofit status, and many do not offer grants directly to individuals but to organizations for an individual's project. Plus individuals can only make a tax-deductible

tion can be the deciding factor of who gets set aside and who gets a check. Remember, the grant proposal isn't just about procedure and jumping through hoops; this is your vehicle to present yourself as a professional, and your project as worthy of funding.

The most common application mistakes:

- Not reading the guidelines
- Not filling in all the blanks or providing enough information
- Not fully comprehending the foundation's mission (i.e., your project is not a good fit)
- Inflating or low-balling the budget (not paying yourself is an immediate red flag!)

Where to Find Them

The Foundation Center (fdncenter.org) is a comprehensive resource of grants and funding entities online, in print, and in person through facilities (New York; Washington, DC; Cleveland; San Francisco) and Cooperating Collections Networks in other American cities.

Foundations Online (foundations.org) links to foundations and corporate giving programs.

Film Arts Foundation in San Francisco (filmarts. org) lists your local media arts center. They often post deadlines for grants, both local and national. They may also offer equipment/ services grants. Also, if you're shooting your film in another city, out-of-town productions may be eligible for local grants, provided you use local crew and resources.

Read the Fine Print

Once you've gotten a contribution or grant, be sure you know what is expected of you in return. Fundraising guru Morrie Warshawski advises clear communication with donors, and reading the fine print. "[While a granting agency] may not expect financial return, they may have other expectations for other types of things (i.e., free tapes, a mention in the

contribution to your project if you have nonprofit status. This is where a fiscal agent comes in. A fiscal agent, sometimes referred to as a sponsor, is a nonprofit 501(c) (3) organization, which takes legal and fiduciary responsibility for a project and can, in return, receive and administer grants and donations made in the name of the producer's project. The production basically borrows the organization's nonprofit status. The fiscal sponsor often takes a percentage fee for administration of the project, averaging five to ten percent. Any nonprofit 501(c) (3) is qualified to be a fiscal agent. Just be sure its mission matches yours, and think of ways in which you can work together: Are you creating a film on a topic they care about? Can they assist with resources other than funding, such as interview subjects, perhaps promotional help in their newsletter, or provide a venue for meetings or events?

Production companies can apply for nonprofit status, but it's a

credits, etc.).” He notes that the lines between financing and fundraising are beginning to blur: “Some donors, like the NEH, ask that you pay back that grant if you see a profit; others, like ITVS, are not grants at all but have an application process similar to that of a grant.”

Financing

Most first features and usually all short films are paid for at least partly through contributions of friends and family. Most often these are gifts, not investments. But at some point you may want to pitch your project to private investors or possibly a studio or independent production company that is open to working with new directors. You’ll need to do the same type of research to target for-profit companies that you would for nonprofits.

About Investor Financing

An investor will make a contribution or buy a share of the film’s equity. To get investors involved, you need to know who is interested in your film’s subject or theme, and who has money to give. An investor may also contribute because of her support of you. People support people, not just projects. Know who believes in you, and start from there.

No filmmaker should approach investor financing without a good lawyer. Your attorney (one who specializes in entertainment law) can help you determine what kind of legal entity to set up (S-corporation, limited liability corporation, limited partnership, sole proprietorship, etc.) and can draw up the necessary contracts. Contact your local media arts organization (or AIVF) for referrals.

How to Approach Financiers

Never randomly send out your script! Always make contact ahead of time. Most production companies won’t accept unsolicited scripts. Usually, they require that an agent or lawyer send it in. Others ask for a one-page query letter detailing your project, including a brief synopsis and a description of any attached

complicated process that’s generally not worth it unless the company will be producing noncommercial work for a number of years. Many media arts organizations often have official fiscal sponsorship programs offering advice and assistance throughout the production process. Film/Video Arts (F/VA) in New York is one. F/VA director Eileen Newman advises, “Be sure the organization has worked with film projects before and knows how to be a fiscal sponsor, meaning they have adequate staff and systems in place.”

Newman recommends knowing what you want from your sponsor ahead of time. “Both parties should be clear on what kind of relationship they will have, how much interaction and support will be given, and how much paperwork is needed.”

elements, such as financing, cast, and key personnel. If they do invite you to send your script, expect a response in no sooner than six weeks. Your script will most likely be read by a reader (entry-level staff or intern) who will recommend it or not. Try not to be discouraged if they pass. Companies are often looking for a certain type of film. It's a little like casting your film—the most amazing actress in the world might not be right for the part. This is why it's important to research the company first.

Where to Find Them

Again it's all about research. Browse industry trades (*Variety*, *Hollywood Reporter*, *indieWIRE*) to find out what types of projects companies are producing. Visit the companies' Web sites. Rent their films. Pay special attention to the credits. What production companies have their name on films like yours?

Internet Movie Database (www.imdb.com and www.imdbpro.com) lists films and key personnel. Like what one producer did with a particular film? Look them up on IMDB to see what else they've done.

The Hollywood Creative Directory (www.hcdonline.com) lists production and financing companies, including names of development executives. Published three to four times per year, online and in print.

The Blu Book (www.hollywoodreporter.com/hollywoodreporter/thrblu/letter.jsp), published by the *Hollywood Reporter*, lists industry companies.

The Independent. Check out Funder FAQ.

Many producers don't use business plans; the script sells the film. But this is when pitching to film financiers, who understand the business, its probabilities, and risks. In these cases, predicting anticipated returns (i.e., comparing your film to *The Blair Witch Project*, and predicting similar box office receipts) can make you seem unprofessional and unreliable. Know who you're talking to. If you're appealing to professional investors such as venture capitalists who don't know the entertainment business and who need facts and figures, then a prospectus is needed.

Creative Fundraising

Raising money is an unpredictable process. Even if you've gained the support of a foundation's program officer, or you're a favorite of Wealthy Relative #3, there's no guarantee. Try not to take rejection personally. Funders and financiers have missions to fulfill and limited resources. They may well like your project but not have the means to support it. Think creatively about how you can raise money, such as putting on special events and parties, and inviting people you know are interested in your film's subject or theme (see page 24). Also, donations don't only come in the form of cash. You can save a lot on your bottom line if you can acquire goods and services. Filmmaking is a group effort; engage community support. Take a look at where you're shooting and form relationships with businesses nearby: a neighborhood restaurant can donate lunch for one day, a few discounted hours in an edit facility can get a trailer cut, some free copies from the local copy shop can provide new script pages for the cast. This not only helps with immediate resources, but connects people to your film and develops its future audience.

Recommended Reading

Achieving Excellence in Fund Raising: A Comprehensive Guide to Principles, Strategies, and Methods, Henry A. Rosso

The Art of Winning Corporate Grants, Howard Hillman

Film Finance & Distribution: A Dictionary of Terms, John Cones

Film & Video Financing, Michael Wiese

Filmmakers and Financing, Louise Levison

Fiscal Sponsorship: 6 Ways to Do It Right, Gregory Colvin

43 Ways to Finance Your Film, John Cones

The Foundation Center's Guide to Proposal Writing, Jane C. Geever

The Fundraising House Party: How to Get Charitable Donations from Individuals in a Houseparty Setting, Morrie Warshawski

The Grassroots Fundraising Book: How to Raise Money in Your Community, Joan Flanagan

Shaking the Money Tree: How to Get Grants and Donations for Film and Video Projects, Morrie Warshawski (out of print; order online at www.warshawski. com, site also has extensive bibliography for grant writing)

Michelle Coe has worked in various capacities for a number of film/video festivals and media arts organizations.

Budget Forms

One of the easiest ways to start a budget is by simply filling in the blanks on a pre-made film/video budget form (like the one included on the DVD in the back of this book). There are also a few film/video budgeting software programs available online as freeware or reasonably priced shareware.

Budgeting Software

Filmmakers have been budgeting movies without software for decades with no problem, but today's budgeting software gives you much greater flexibility to make quick changes, share, and examine different budget scenarios. However, it doesn't really matter whether you use comprehensive budget software like **Movie Magic Budgeting** or **Gorilla Scheduling and Budgeting** or just fill in the blanks of a previously existing budget that was used on another project—the important thing is that your budget form includes *every possible expense* that may occur in making your project. Use whatever works best for you. Just make sure you include everything.

Estimating Costs

Once you have your production plan in place you will be able to break down your shoot into production elements such as locations, travel, equipment, etc. You can *estimate* a good chunk of your budget just by researching on the Internet. Bookmark, print out, and save the **rate cards** and contact info you find online so you can easily find them again when needed. The rest will require a few phone calls and e-mails to get specific vendor quotes. Anyone selling or renting equipment will be more than happy to fax or e-mail you a price list. Contact vendors directly and ask if you can't find it online.

Costs for equipment can vary widely depending on the source and region of the country. Shop around to get the best prices. Rate cards are not carved in stone. Almost always, you can negotiate better rates for longer rentals or rentals during off times such as the dead of winter or holiday weekends. Keep in mind, as with anything else, *price alone does not tell the whole story*. If you're dealing with rental houses you should take customer service, equipment condition, availability of latest equipment, convenience, and reputation all into consideration as well. Carefully scrutinize and ask questions about any price that seems too good to be true—it almost always is. The best source for rental house info is always other filmmakers.

> ✔ Make sure your budget form includes all expenses. You can estimate many items by researching online.

HOT TIP

When it comes right down to it, budgeting is an exercise in guesswork. But there is a difference between blind guessing, as in the lottery, and educated guessing, as in the stock market. Nobody knows what lottery ball will pop up, but with stocks you can see certain things coming if you know what to look for. It's the same with guerrilla filmmaking. Here are some things to look out for when trying to balance your budget:

4 COMMON BUDGETING MISTAKES

1 EXCLUDING OR DISCOUNTING ITEMS YOU *HOPE* TO SECURE

Your roommate's boyfriend is a camera operator for a production house and while you're out for drinks he says he can get you a free HD Varicam for a weekend, but a week before production, he has no idea what you're talking about and says he can't do it . . . The principal of the elementary school said you can shoot there for free, but the day before the shoot the school board president calls you demanding a $500/day location fee . . .

These are what I call "phantom freebies" and they can easily send your production into a panicked tailspin. The bottom line is unless you are extremely positive that this is a sure thing, done deal, rock-solid agreement, you should leave that item in your budget at full price. Whenever possible, try to get things on paper or save a trail of e-mail conversations so there's no confusion about what you're getting, when you're getting it, and how much it will cost you. The closer you get to production without these great deals and favors fully secured, the harder it will be to change course and get another camera or school or whatever it was you planned on getting for free or at a discount. Don't let your budget be led astray by the siren call of "free" or "cheap" unless you're confident. Once it's secure, *then* you can move that money elsewhere in the budget.

2 NOT INCLUDING ENOUGH CONTINGENCY MONEY

Your contingency is your "what if" money. It's your all-purpose slush fund for unexpected things that happen during production or items that run over their estimated budget. Unexpected things will ALWAYS happen in filmmaking and it's a pretty sure bet that at least one category of your budget WILL run over. I can't overemphasize how important it is to keep some contingency money in the budget on standby. Don't make the amateur mistake of eliminating your contingency as a line item to balance your final budget. If you're truly desperate and the numbers still don't add up, you can cut that 15% figure down to as little as 10%, but anything less than that is opening the door to hasty compromises and a potential production shut down.

3 NOT CREATING ALTERNATE BUDGETS

Films rarely have one budget. There's the 35 mm film budget, the HD video budget, the mini-DV budget, the budget with name actors, the budget with unknown actors, etc. Each of these budgets represents an alternate production scenario based on unfolding events and access to money and resources. Once you write out your initial budget, you should then save alternate versions with different sets of line items based on all the likely scenarios. The only thing these budgets need to have in common is the grand total. Making alternate budgets further forces you to consider the true production value of each resource. They are also invaluable to your decision making if you do suddenly have to change your production plan.

4 OVERLOOKING A HUNDRED "LITTLE THINGS"

Remember, the budgeting process is essentially brainstorming *every* cost you're going to incur to make your shoot happen. Every cost includes all those "little things" that new filmmakers often overlook, such as the cost of taxes, permits, cab fare, photocopies, cell phone charges, insurance, overtime meals, and on and on. All  these "little things" can add up quickly and eat away at your precious contingency if they're not in the original budget. Just because it seems insignificant or you don't write it down, doesn't mean you don't have to pay for it. Estimate what it will cost and put it in there.

RAISING THE M·O·N·E·Y

ROSE ROSENBLATT & MARION LIPSCHUTZ PRODUCERS/ DIRECTORS

(The Education of Shelby Knox, The Abortion Pill)

Both: M-O-N-E-Y . . . That's by far the hardest thing.

Rose: Everything else is a piece of cake.

Marion: The only positive thing I can say about raising the money is that by the time you're making the film, it's been put through a real vetting process because somebody's decided to give you the money, usually a couple of people, and you've had to really prove that it's a good enough idea and planned it out, but . . . We'll launch things with a grant, or a couple of grants because everybody needs to see footage these days, like commercial [media outlets], and by that I mean cable or HBO or any of those places. They usually want to see footage before they'll commit money. And the trick is how do you get footage? And footage means, unless it's an amazingly compelling character or you've got great access, they want to see that *story*. So it's a tough thing to raise enough money to get the story far enough along to show it to people . . . 'Cause it's such an old Hollywood joke. How do you raise the money? Uh . . . persistence. That you know, that's one of the most critical things. It's practice, practice, practice. Persistence really is such a key ingredient. Also knowing when to give up, knowing when, "I've persisted with this idea, I've gone to every place I can think of, um, I've embedded myself in the network of people who care about this." That's very important because, certainly if you're raising money from foundations the people who are gonna give you money aren't filmmakers, but they're expert in the subject you're making your film on.

Rose: And I learned this, and I don't know if there's a short cut, but it's this idea of appropriateness. You think you have a great idea and you go to a person who couldn't possibly fund that because that's not what they're supposed to be funding. And you think, "It's such a great idea and it's a great movie, and you fund movies, you should fund this!" You take this rejection so to heart. But you have to really know who you're going to and what they're about and there's this thing called a mandate, which [means] they're supposed to fund films on this topic. Don't bring them films on another topic: mentally retarded if they're funding the environment. There's no way they're gonna fund you. You gotta do your homework.

10 WAYS TO LOWER YOUR BUDGET

1 GET FREE OR INEXPENSIVE EQUIPMENT

One of the easiest things you can do to shave some dollars off the bottom line is to beg, borrow, or maneuver your way into the equipment you need for your project.

Free or inexpensive equipment is all around you. You just have to sniff it out. If you find a DP, crew member, or friend with their own equipment or access to equipment, you can: (a) convince them to work for free, (b) barter for their services, (c) borrow or offer to rent their equipment, or (d) negotiate a good rate for them *and* their equipment. The other route is to *maneuver* your way into a free equipment situation. Hands-on filmmaking workshops are one way, but there are also multiple jobs at TV stations, film/video rental houses, colleges, production companies, and in corporate video departments where you (or a very close friend) may borrow equipment as a standard perk. Imagine that. You can actually get paid to borrow the equipment you need for your project. Now *that*'s resourceful filmmaking! (Also see "Hot Tip: Educational Equipment Access" on page 41.)

2 GET FREE OR INEXPENSIVE CREW

Free or low-cost crews are pretty standard for tight budgets. Look for people who are serious and take a professional approach to their job, even if they are less experienced. Seek out the hungry boom operators looking to move up to sound mixer. Look for the 2nd Unit DP or Asst. Camera with a gleam in her eye, who's ready to be a DP. If you have production skills, you may also barter your services for those of a colleague. It's a fairly standard practice for small groups of indie filmmakers to just take turns cooperatively working on one another's films for free. (Just make sure this is mutually understood before you give up half your summer for your friend's film only to find out that he'll be vacationing in Cancun during *your* shoot.) If you enroll in a film school or workshop, there's a good chance you'll get a free crew. If you pay any of your crew (and you really should if you can), start with the DP, Sound Person, and/or Editor as these are your make-or-break positions. (Also see "Assembling a Crew" on page 48.)

3 GET FREE OR INEXPENSIVE FOOD

Feeding your crew good food can get expensive, especially with larger crews and longer shoots. As any hungry college student knows, free or cheap food isn't too hard to come by if you know where to look and who to ask. (For specific food tips see "Hot Tip: 5 Down and Dirty Food Ideas" on page 52.)

4 USE CARS INSTEAD OF PRODUCTION TRUCKS

I don't know about where you live, but here in New York City cargo van rentals start at about $100.00/day and Cube Trucks rent for almost double that. Add in the price of gas and insurance and you're talking about a good amount of change. Since most DV equipment is fairly small and portable, a cheaper alternative is to just use cars for transporting crew and gear whenever possible. If you empty out the trunk first, you should be able to easily accommodate a DV camera, sound gear, light kit, and accessories. Even if you don't own or have access to a car, renting a car is always cheaper and more fuel-efficient than renting a van or truck.

5 SHOOT AND TRAVEL OVER LESS DAYS WITH LESS PEOPLE

This is simple mathematics. The more you shoot and the longer you travel, the more your film will cost. With unfolding subject matter, knowing when to stop shooting and start editing is often difficult, but many projects such as historical docs or reality shows can be scheduled and planned ahead of time. Do the math for each shooting day and look for shoots that can be eliminated or combined. Travel is a necessary part of following a story, but you want to make sure your travel is cost-effective and adds value to your project. Traveling for 6 hours and feeding and putting up a 5-person crew in a hotel just to shoot some B-roll for a montage of your subject's hometown is not a wise investment of your resources. Instead, you could just shoot it with your DP only. You could also make the most of the trip by interviewing your subject's family members and friends while there. Maybe instead of video of their hometown, a montage of still pictures will suffice . . . Make travel count. Just take a few people and stay only as long as necessary.

6 GET CORPORATE/AGENCY SPONSORSHIPS OR PRODUCT PLACEMENT DEALS

Making a documentary about the history of video gaming? Why not see if the good people at Atari or Activision will support your project with grants or donations? Want to highlight the plight of teen mothers? Why not seek funding from a national charity that shares the same mission? Look for natural allies in your mission who have deeper pockets than you. While not appropriate for many docs, some subject matter or doc genres may seek a product placement deal to show a sponsor's product onscreen in exchange for value. Trying to line up product placement deals for the documentary, *Paper Chasers*, which is about hip-hop entrepreneurs, we did not get any cash (typical for indies). But we did convince sponsors to supply specific budget items such as food, drinks, wardrobe, and discounted hotel, car, and RV rentals, which freed up precious dollars in our micro-budget.

7 USE ORIGINAL MUSIC

Why pay an expensive fee to use a popular song or stock music from a library when there are thousands of independent musicians looking for exposure? Most of these fellow indie artists will gladly give you prerecorded tracks. Better yet, you can easily find talented musicians and composers who will even create original music for your project for free or a fraction of the cost of the average music license. Original music tailored to your project can be an inexpensive, but powerful storytelling aid.

8 USE PUBLIC DOMAIN FOOTAGE

Did you know that there are hundreds of hours of footage and thousands of historical photos and musical recordings available for anyone to use free of charge? This is mostly historical material on which the copyright has expired. In other words, it is in the *public domain*. Try a Google search for public domain photos, footage, or music. You'll nevertheless have to pay to have material transferred or copied, but it's still a great bargain. In the same vein, you can investigate whether your interview subjects have old photos, videos or home movies they'd be willing to let you use for free.

9 USE NATURAL LIGHT AND CHINA LANTERNS

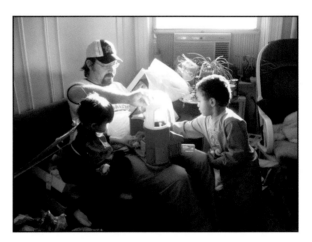

You can avoid the cost of rentals and the hassle and setup time needed for professional lighting instruments by using available lighting instead. Position your subject strategically to use the natural light on location. As illustrated in the lighting section of this book, you can get some beautiful lighting with a simple house lamp, inexpensive china lantern, or sunlit window and a reflector. Staging your shooting and interviews outdoors is also a common way to get around professional lighting.

Position subjects and compose shots to take advantage of natural light.

10 LOG AND TRANSCRIBE YOUR OWN FOOTAGE

Transcripts and logs are a doc necessity. However, professional video transcription is costly even on the *low end*. If you have 20 or so tapes to log and transcribe it could break your budget. Enlist an intern, a good friend, or just do it yourself. You'll be much more familiar with your footage, plus you'll save hundreds or even thousands of dollars to boot!

Producing guides such as "L.A. 411" and "N.Y. 411" are great for film vendor listings, but they often omit smaller vendors and only cover major cities. Here's some other sources to check for prices:

LINE ITEM	WHERE TO LOOK
Equipment Rental	■ Rental House Rate Cards ■ Film Cooperatives Rental Rate Cards ■ Craig's List Ads
Equipment Purchase	■ Froogle.com or Pricegrabber.com ■ B&H Photo and Video Catalog ■ Manufacturer Web Sites
Crew	■ Rate Quotes from Potential Crew Members ■ Consult Other Filmmakers with Similar Projects ■ Filmmaking Job Boards for Going Rates ■ Union Rate Cards (SAG/Aftra, ASC, etc.) ■ Crew for Hire Services
Transportation and Lodging	■ Car/Van/RV Rental Company Web Sites ■ Airline Web Sites ■ Hotel Web Sites ■ Travel Web Sites (i.e., Expedia, Travelocity)
Location	■ Offers/Quotes from Potential Locations ■ Local Film Commission Location Books ■ Consult Other Filmmakers who have shot at Similar Locations
Post-production	■ Post House Quotes and Rate Cards ■ Transcription Company Web Sites ■ Published Film Budgets
Music and Sound Licenses and Rights	■ Quotes from Musicians/Performers ■ Music and Sound Effects Library Sites ■ Music Supervisor/Sound Designer Quotes
Meals and Craft Services	■ Caterer Web Sites ■ Local Restaurant Menus

(See the Internet Resources section on the DVD for specific Web sites.)

BUDGETING—A FINAL WORD

Budgeting is truly an art form that improves with experience. The less experienced you are, the greater the contingency you should have. It's much better to err on the side of having an overinflated budget that takes into account all the possibilities, rather than an overly optimistic (i.e., unrealistic) budget that relies on unsecured contributions to the production and a perfectly smooth shoot. Like many other steps in preproduction, budgeting forces you to really examine and think through your production decisions.

Do you really need to shoot that scene with a SteadiCam for an extra $1200.00? Or is it better to go handheld for no money and use that $1200.00 to license some more stock footage or music? Should you rent a high-end camera package? Or are you better off renting a less expensive camera package and using the money you saved to hire an experienced documentary editor?

There isn't necessarily a right or wrong answer to these issues, just a long list of choices that will impact your final film and budget. Your job is to figure out what that impact will be and decide what *value* it brings to your finished film. Remember, every dollar you spend here is a dollar you can't spend there. Think through your budgetary decisions and try to get as many dollars on the screen as you can.

Your choice of equipment is largely going to be determined by the budget and resources you have readily available. However, other factors such as approach, subject matter, crew size, and intended distribution will all affect this decision as well.

For example, if I wanted to shoot a segment on gang activity in the inner city, I probably wouldn't show up with a high-end HD camera and the full crew that goes with it. By the same measure, if I was going to shoot a doc on active volcanoes of the South Pacific that is going to appear in IMAX movie theaters, I wouldn't shoot it with a mini-DV "prosumer" camcorder. You want to make sure you get the right set of tools to do the job at hand. Any less than that and you are screwing yourself out of the crucial resources you need to fully execute your vision. Any more than that and you're screwing yourself out of money that would otherwise go toward important production resources, such as pay for a more experienced crew or an extra few days of shooting. Think it through thoroughly.

I think it's generally best to travel light when shooting documentaries. Documentary filmmakers are like the Special Forces of the filmmaking army. They must be mobile, flexible, and prepared to deal with a variety of dynamic situations quickly and efficiently. The more equipment you have, the more crew and time it's going to take to prep, transport, and set it all up. Moreover, you will be a much more conspicuous presence with a lot of gear. Peep out the "Doc Equipment Packages" chart on page 42 for an overview of the basics required on just about any sized down and dirty doc shoot.

✔ *Choose an equipment package that is appropriate for your documentary content and intended distribution.*

USING AND LEARNING THE TOOLS OF THE TRADE

SUSAN BUICE AND ARIN CRUMLEY, CO-DIRECTORS/PRODUCERS

(Four-Eyed Monsters Feature Film and Video Podcast)

Arin: So, I've always studied up on as much technical stuff as I can, some creative techniques, but mainly I've figured that stuff out through experimentation. Just doing something for an audience of nobody half the time, just for myself, like making something extremely experimental, some kind of visual, then something else totally documentary-based, some music videos . . . just experimenting with all these different mediums and building my own tool belt rather than being taught the tool belt from the film school. And that way, I feel like when I need the tool belt, it's going to be a more unique thing because it's inherently a unique tool belt that I designed, just in experimentation.

I'm kinda the Swiss army knife guy. When you need a Web site jump on Word-Press. When you need posters jump on Photoshop. When you need audio mix jump on Sound Track Pro. Basically, with Final Cut, DVD Studio Pro . . . I'm an enthusiast about that kind of stuff. As things would come out, I've always been tracking whatever's right around the next turn, like DVDs on an Apple computer—I bought the first G4. Actually, I made somebody else buy it! But, I made sure I got DVD Studio Pro because that seemed incredibly powerful to be able to do that.

So, for me, it just seemed kinda natural. Like when the Panasonic DVX-100 came out—absolutely, gotta get that! We got it right away, within a couple of months after it being out we started working with it right away. And with video podcasting, the same thing. That's a really powerful tool. I want to be right there doing stuff with it. So, coincidentally, the way that we want to express ourselves uses all these things. It's not just for the technical, "Oh it's cool, it can do cool things." It's always because I'm gonna *use* this tool.

All video formats are not created equally. Similar to the term "documentary," "video" is a general word that describes a wide variety of formats and spans a vast range of picture qualities. This is one of the first production decisions you will need to make, because the difference between the cost and complexity of shooting and editing on various formats can completely alter your budget, schedule, and crew decisions.

This book focuses mostly on the HDV and mini-DV formats, because they are the most common cameras used by students, guerrillas, and the like. However, there are other formats to consider when you're ready to step up to the next budget level. Here's a short overview:

FORMAT	RESOLUTION	DATA RATE
Film	4000 + lines	1 GB/sec
Red Code Raw 4K	4520	27.5 MB/sec
Viper	1080	2.9 GB/sec
D-5	1080	235 MB/sec
HD-CAM	1080	140 MB/sec
DVCPRO-HD	720	100 MB/sec
D-1	525	166 MB/sec
DigiBeta	525	90 MB/sec
DVCPRO-50	525	50 MB/sec
DVCPRO	525	25 MB/sec
Mini-DV	525	25 MB/sec

What's Up with High Def?

High definition video can be a confusing world with a barrage of specs, similar-sounding terms, and numbers that may as well be Chinese algebra for most people. (Okay, I'm really talking about myself here, but I don't think I'm alone in this sentiment.) We know these formats are better quality, but what exactly does "high definition" mean? Here's the basic lowdown:

To be considered HD, a camera must have some basic characteristics:

1. 16 : 9 Aspect Ratio. The image must have a rectangular widescreen format that is 16 units wide by 9 units high. (See "Aspect Ratios" on page 154.)

2. Record at varying frame rates.

3. Horizontal resolutions of 1080 or 720 lines.

What Are Pixels?

Pixels are the little dots of light that form a picture on video screen displays. The more pixels on a screen, the better the picture quality.

What Is Resolution?

The term resolution refers to the size of a video image in pixels, the little electronic dots that make up screen displays. If a video has a resolution of 1280 × 720 that means it is 1280 pixels wide by 720 pixels high.

Progressive vs. Interlaced

There are two different ways that video cameras create images: interlaced and progressive. Interlaced images are formed by combining two different fields, each representing half of the image, to make one video frame. Interlaced video has some distinct drawbacks; namely, when you freeze-frame or slow down interlaced video, you will often see jagged lines in the image as a result of this electronic combining of two different fields.

Interlaced Video

Video Field 1   Video Field 2   1 Video Frame

A progressive video image, on the other hand, is formed more like film in that each frame is formed by a single image. This is why 24P (P is for progressive) cameras more resemble the look and feel of film, which is shot at 24 fps (frames per second). Progressive camera modes are better. (Similarly, the European standard PAL video is recorded at 25 fps.) This is why 24P is often preferred by narrative filmmakers over standard NTSC video, which is recorded at 30 fps. Believe it or not, subtracting those six little frames of video per second helps make the difference between the more natural look of film and the more artificial look of video.

HDV Image Size and Resolution

There are almost always exceptions and anomalies to the rules when it comes to DV formats, but HDV can basically be put into two distinct categories based on resolution:

1920 × 1080 or 1280 × 720.

WHAT TO LOOK FOR IN A CAMERA

A primary consideration when choosing a camera is how your completed project will be shown. Only on DVD? Broadcast on TV? Projected for an audience? Blown up to 35 mm film? Make sure your camera has all the features you need to properly do the job. Here's my general advice:

1 3 CCD IMAGING CHIPS

Imaging chips are the actual electronic gizmos that capture an image to video. Consumer cameras have 1 CCD imaging chip. Pro cameras have 3 CCD imaging chips. The only thing better than having 3 chips is 3 bigger chips. Think of chip size like negative size in film. The bigger the chip, the better the image. HDV and Mini-DV chips are typically 1/4" or 1/3".

2 MANUAL CONTROLS

Fully automatic video cameras are generally for amateurs. It's absolutely essential that a camera intended to be used for serious filmmaking allows you to manually control vital functions such as focus, exposure, white balance, audio levels, etc.

3 ABILITY TO SHOOT IN LOW LIGHT

Doc work almost always involves some shooting in low-light situations. Check the cameras "lux rating" to see how the camera performs in low light. Manufacturers fudge these a lot, so check camera reviews and consult with other filmmakers as well.

4 XLR AUDIO INPUTS

Most professional filmmaking microphones and sound gear have XLR connectors. If you want the best quality audio (and you *do*), you need to roll like the big boys. If your camera only has a mini-stereo mic input, you can get an XLR adapter box, but built-in XLR ports are always preferable.

5 WIDESCREEN CAPABILITY

Standard 4 : 3 video is still cool, but it's rapidly becoming a widescreen world out there. If you want to look to the future or just shoot more cinematic images, go for a camera that has a 16 : 9 native imaging chip or the next best thing, an electronic 16 : 9 widescreen mode.

There are a mind-boggling number of choices and even more specs to consider when picking a camera today. I have kept the focus on the more affordable prosumer cameras that are out there since they are the staple of most guerrilla efforts. The next few pages represent my best attempt at compiling all of this prosumer camera information in one convenient place.

Some of the real specs were more elusive than others depending on who was presenting the math. I tried to research and sort out confusing or fuzzy manufacturer's information and name prevailing prices as found at major camera dealers. Inevitably, most prices will lower and a new crop of cameras will come out in the not too distant future.

In the meantime, the next few pages chart my personal picks and commentary on some of the best prosumer cameras on the market today from entry-level starter cams to those loaded with professional features. (You can sign up to the free Down and Dirty DV Nation mailing list at DownAndDirtyDV.com to receive the most up-to-date camera guides throughout the year.)

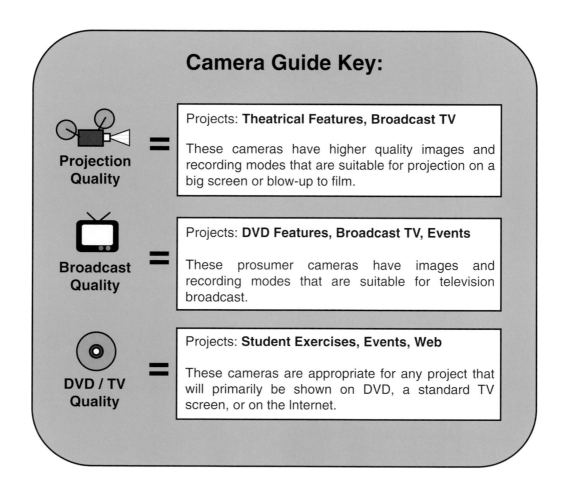

Camera Guide Key:

Projection Quality =

Projects: **Theatrical Features, Broadcast TV**

These cameras have higher quality images and recording modes that are suitable for projection on a big screen or blow-up to film.

Broadcast Quality =

Projects: **DVD Features, Broadcast TV, Events**

These prosumer cameras have images and recording modes that are suitable for television broadcast.

DVD / TV Quality =

Projects: **Student Exercises, Events, Web**

These cameras are appropriate for any project that will primarily be shown on DVD, a standard TV screen, or on the Internet.

CAMERA GUIDE KEY

CANON 3-CHIP MINI-DV CAMERA GUIDE

MODEL	IMAGE SPECS	IMAGING CHIPS	BEST USE	NOTES
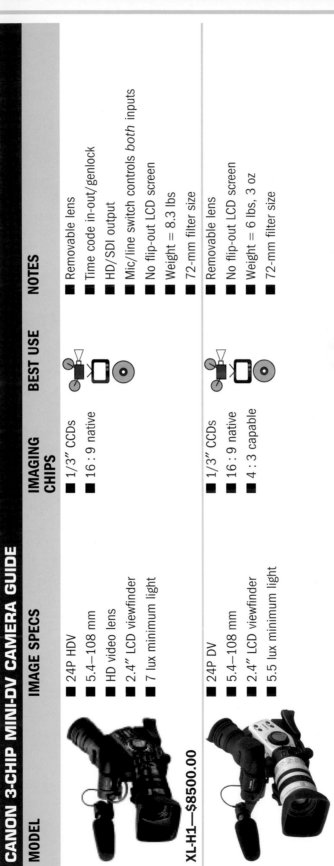 XL-H1—$8500.00	■ 24P HDV ■ 5.4–108 mm ■ HD video lens ■ 2.4" LCD viewfinder ■ 7 lux minimum light	■ 1/3" CCDs ■ 16 : 9 native	■ Removable lens ■ Time code in-out/genlock ■ HD/SDI output ■ Mic/line switch controls *both* inputs ■ No flip-out LCD screen ■ Weight = 8.3 lbs ■ 72-mm filter size
 XL-2–$3400.00	■ 24P DV ■ 5.4–108 mm ■ 2.4" LCD viewfinder ■ 5.5 lux minimum light	■ 1/3" CCDs ■ 16 : 9 native ■ 4 : 3 capable	■ Removable lens ■ No flip-out LCD screen ■ Weight = 6 lbs, 3 oz ■ 72-mm filter size

CANON 3-CHIP MINI-DV CAMERA GUIDE—CONT'D

MODEL	IMAGE SPECS	IMAGING CHIPS	BEST USE	NOTES
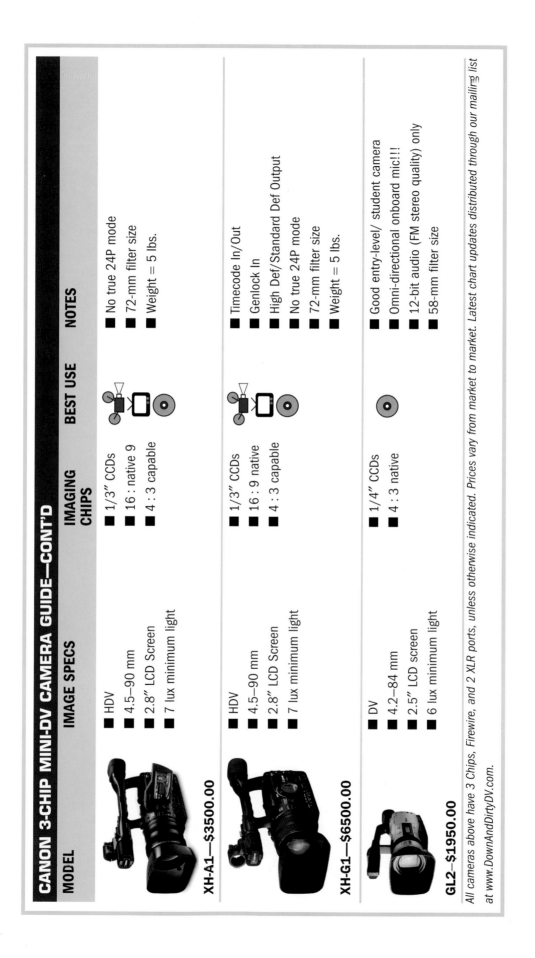XH-A1—$3500.00	■ HDV ■ 4.5–90 mm ■ 2.8" LCD Screen ■ 7 lux minimum light	■ 1/3" CCDs ■ 16 : native 9 ■ 4 : 3 capable		■ No true 24P mode ■ 72-mm filter size ■ Weight = 5 lbs.
XH-G1—$6500.00	■ HDV ■ 4.5–90 mm ■ 2.8" LCD Screen ■ 7 lux minimum light	■ 1/3" CCDs ■ 16 : 9 native ■ 4 : 3 capable		■ Timecode In/Out ■ Genlock In ■ High Def/Standard Def Output ■ No true 24P mode ■ 72-mm filter size ■ Weight = 5 lbs.
GL2—$1950.00	■ DV ■ 4.2–84 mm ■ 2.5" LCD screen ■ 6 lux minimum light	■ 1/4" CCDs ■ 4 : 3 native		■ Good entry-level/ student camera ■ Omni-directional onboard mic!!! ■ 12-bit audio (FM stereo quality) only ■ 58-mm filter size

All cameras above have 3 Chips, Firewire, and 2 XLR ports, unless otherwise indicated. Prices vary from market to market. Latest chart updates distributed through our mailing list at www.DownAndDirtyDV.com.

JVC AND PANASONIC 3-CHIP MINI-DV CAMERA GUIDE

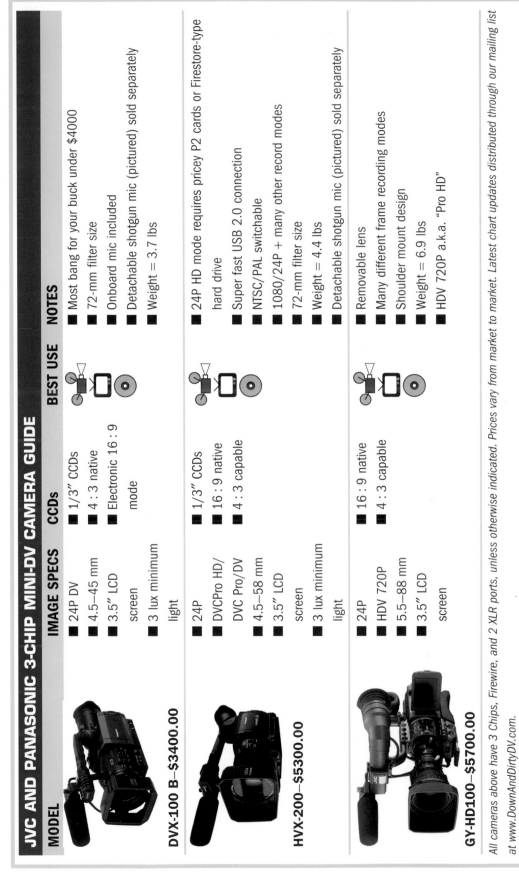

MODEL	IMAGE SPECS	CCDs	BEST USE	NOTES
DVX-100 B—$3400.00	■ 24P DV ■ 4.5–45 mm ■ 3.5" LCD screen ■ 3 lux minimum light	■ 1/3" CCDs ■ 4 : 3 native ■ Electronic 16 : 9 mode		■ Most bang for your buck under $4000 ■ 72-mm filter size ■ Onboard mic included ■ Detachable shotgun mic (pictured) sold separately ■ Weight = 3.7 lbs
HVX-200—$5300.00	■ 24P ■ DVCPro HD/ DVC Pro/DV ■ 4.5–58 mm ■ 3.5" LCD screen ■ 3 lux minimum light	■ 1/3" CCDs ■ 16 : 9 native ■ 4 : 3 capable		■ 24P HD mode requires pricey P2 cards or Firestore-type hard drive ■ Super fast USB 2.0 connection ■ NTSC/PAL switchable ■ 1080/24P + many other record modes ■ 72-mm filter size ■ Weight = 4.4 lbs ■ Detachable shotgun mic (pictured) sold separately
GY-HD100—$5700.00	■ 24P ■ HDV 720P ■ 5.5–88 mm ■ 3.5" LCD screen	■ 16 : 9 native ■ 4 : 3 capable		■ Removable lens ■ Many different frame recording modes ■ Shoulder mount design ■ Weight = 6.9 lbs ■ HDV 720P a.k.a. "Pro HD"

All cameras above have 3 Chips, Firewire, and 2 XLR ports, unless otherwise indicated. Prices vary from market to market. Latest chart updates distributed through our mailing list at www.DownAndDirtyDV.com.

SONY 3-CHIP MINI-DV CAMERA GUIDE

MODEL	IMAGE SPECS	CCDs	BEST USE	NOTES
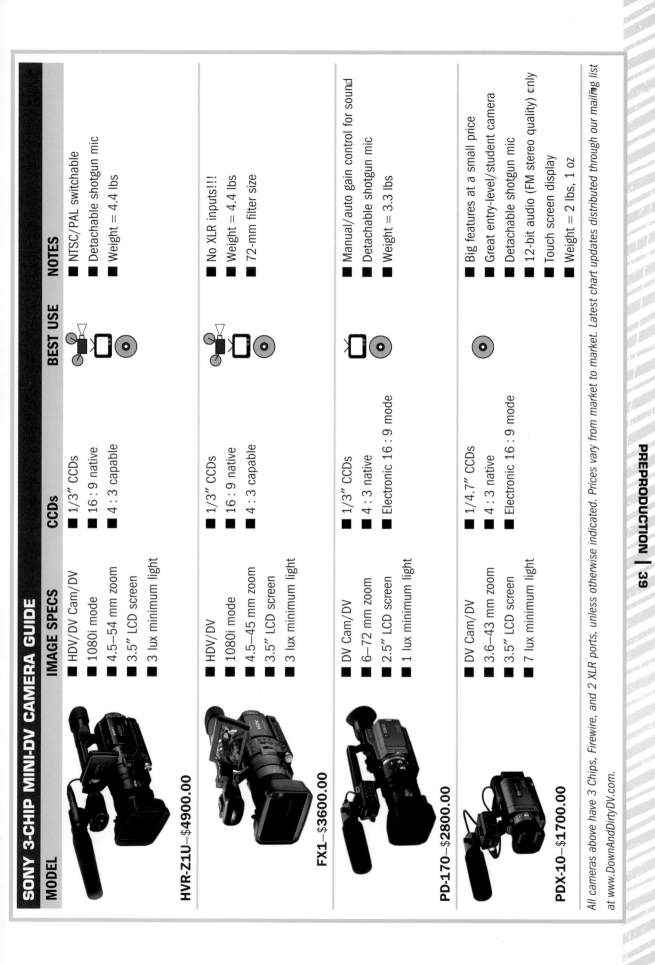 **HVR-Z1U—$4900.00**	■ HDV/DV Cam/DV ■ 1080i mode ■ 4.5–54 mm zoom ■ 3.5" LCD screen ■ 3 lux minimum light	■ 1/3" CCDs ■ 16 : 9 native ■ 4 : 3 capable		■ NTSC/PAL switchable ■ Detachable shotgun mic ■ Weight = 4.4 lbs
FX1—$3600.00	■ HDV/DV ■ 1080i mode ■ 4.5–45 mm zoom ■ 3.5" LCD screen ■ 3 lux minimum light	■ 1/3" CCDs ■ 16 : 9 native ■ 4 : 3 capable		■ No XLR inputs!!! ■ Weight = 4.4 lbs ■ 72-mm filter size
PD-170—$2800.00	■ DV Cam/DV ■ 6–72 mm zoom ■ 2.5" LCD screen ■ 1 lux minimum light	■ 1/3" CCDs ■ 4 : 3 native ■ Electronic 16 : 9 mode		■ Manual/auto gain control for sound ■ Detachable shotgun mic ■ Weight = 3.3 lbs
PDX-10—$1700.00	■ DV Cam/DV ■ 3.6–43 mm zoom ■ 3.5" LCD screen ■ 7 lux minimum light	■ 1/4.7" CCDs ■ 4 : 3 native ■ Electronic 16 : 9 mode		■ Big features at a small price ■ Great entry-level/student camera ■ Detachable shotgun mic ■ 12-bit audio (FM stereo quality) only ■ Touch screen display ■ Weight = 2 lbs, 1 oz

All cameras above have 3 Chips, Firewire, and 2 XLR ports, unless otherwise indicated. Prices vary from market to market. Latest chart updates distributed through our mailing list at www.DownAndDirtyDV.com.

BUYING VS. RENTING

A Quick Comparison

As digital technology improves and prices come down, it's becoming more popular for filmmakers to buy some or all of their own equipment. In fact, you could set yourself up with a complete mini-DV production package for about $10,000. On the flip side, you could rent a high-end production package for three weeks for almost the same price and get much greater production value and variety of equipment for your dollar:

BUYING EQUIPMENT	VS.	RENTING EQUIPMENT	
High-end MAC or Power PC Computer	$1300	Panasonic AJ-HDC27 VariCam DVCPro HD	$7500
3 CCD Mini-DV Camera and Tripod	4000	Dolly or Jib (1–3 days)	150
Lowel Light Kit	1000	Lowel Omni Light Kit	540
Shotgun Mic, Boom, Wireless and Accessories	2000	Shotgun Mic, Boom, Mixer, and Accessories	1200
Filters, Gels, and Misc. Accessories	700	Filters, Gels, and Misc. Accessories	450
Non-linear Editing Software	1000	Non-linear Editing Software (*purchase*)	1000
Firewire Hard Drive(s)	250	Firewire Hard Drive (*purchase*)	250
Total =	**$10,250**	**Total =**	**$11,090**

All prices are approximations. Rental and retail prices vary from market to market.

How to Decide

As with everything else in your budget, you will have to do the math for your particular situation. If you only need the equipment for a short time, it probably doesn't make much sense to buy. One advantage of renting is that you can always shoot with the latest and greatest equipment and take advantage of the newest technologies.

However, if you will be shooting over a few months or producing several more projects over the next year, a purchase may be a better choice in the long run. Just be aware that regardless of what camera you buy, you can be sure that some company will put out an even better (and probably less expensive) one within a year's time. Just accept it. It is the blessing and curse of DV equipment. Research and decide what's most practical for you.

> ✔ Purchasing DV equipment is practical for long or multiple projects. However, renting will allow you to shoot on more high-end equipment.

EDUCATIONAL EQUIPMENT ACCESS

Renting and purchasing equipment are the most common and obvious means for filmmakers to shoot. But in the world of Down and Dirty, do-it-yourself, broke-as-a-joke filmmaking, we sometimes have to be more creative. So another practical means of obtaining cheap or reasonably priced access to equipment and editing facilities is to enroll in an independent film workshop, filmmaking cooperative such as Film Video Arts (FVA) in San Francisco or Downtown Community Television (DCTV) in New York, or a filmmaking class at a local college or university. Virtually every major city has several filmmaking workshops/programs that could serve you well.

Many an indie film began (or was entirely completed) as someone's class project. The acclaimed indie film *Raising Victor Vargas* began as director, Peter Sollet's, short class project at NYU. John Singleton developed the script for *Boyz in the Hood* while a student at USC. Not only will these programs give you access to equipment, but they will also give you access to crew members and instructors who can help guide your vision and solve problems as they crop up. I know of several people who signed up for programs simply to get access to equipment.

As a graduate of and, most recently, administrator in a major film school (NYU), I can testify that there are many advantages to this approach, especially for the novice filmmaker. There are also a few distinct drawbacks, particularly for more independent-minded filmmakers. All film schools and workshops are *not* created equal. Some have the latest and greatest equipment, but strict controls on equipment access and the type of projects they support while others have more liberal access, but the equipment is abused by students and poorly kept. More reputable programs offer better instructors and more competent students (i.e., crew members). If you go with this means of getting equipment, you need to take time to research the workshop/school you are considering. Discuss your project with instructors before you enroll. Be honest. See if it's something they will support. Most important, talk to *students* that have actually attended the program. They will usually be brutally honest and tell you if the program or equipment is lacking in any way.

ADVANTAGES	DISADVANTAGES
Access to full equipment package	Equipment may be in poor condition
Access to editing facilities	Project may be limited by assignment
Instruction and feedback	Must attend classes
Access to crew members	Program may end before you're done
Ongoing technical instruction	You may be assigned to a lame crew

DOC EQUIPMENT PACKAGES

	SMALL	MEDIUM	LARGE
Camera	■ 3-chip Mini-DV or ■ HDV	■ 3-chip Mini-DV or ■ HDV or ■ Pro HD	■ DigiBeta or ■ 4K Digital or ■ DVC-Pro or ■ Pro DV-Cam
Camera Extras	■ Tripod ■ Screw-on Filters	■ Tripod ■ Screw-on Filters ■ Field Monitor ■ Wide-angle Adapter	■ Tripod ■ Matte Box with Filters ■ Field Monitor ■ Waveform/Vectorscope ■ Zoom Control
Sound Gear	■ Shotgun Mic ■ Boom Pole ■ Shockmount ■ Windscreen ■ Headphones	■ Shotgun Mic ■ Boom Pole ■ Shockmount ■ Headphones ■ 1 Lav Mic ■ Windscreen or Windjammer ■ Zeppelin ■ Handheld Mic ■ Wireless Unit	■ Shotgun Mic ■ Boom Pole ■ Shockmount ■ Headphones ■ 2+ Lav Mics ■ Zeppelin ■ Windjammer ■ Handheld Mic ■ Wireless Unit ■ Mixer
Lighting Gear	■ 3 Light Kit ■ Reflector ■ Gels and Blackwrap	■ 3 Light Kit ■ Pro-light ■ Reflector ■ China Lantern ■ Small Grip Package ■ Gels and Blackwrap	■ 3 Light Kit ■ Pro-light ■ Reflector ■ China Lantern ■ Kino Flo Lights ■ Chimera ■ Medium Grip Package ■ Gels and Blackwrap
Other Gear	■ Cloth Backdrop	■ Dimmer ■ Cloth Backdrop	■ Dimmer ■ Cloth Backdrop ■ Camera Stabilizer ■ Dolly

See the Glossary for detailed descriptions.

5 TIPS FOR TRAVELING WITH EQUIPMENT

 CARRY ON SENSITIVE EQUIPMENT

If you can at all avoid it, DO NOT check in or put cameras, mics, or other sensitive and valuable equipment in your check-in luggage. Doing so greatly increases the risk of theft or damage from rough luggage handling. A much safer option is to check in your personal luggage and keep all cameras, laptops, mics, and other sensitive equipment with you as carry-on luggage that will never leave your side. (Even if you go to the bathroom, take it in the stall with you!)

 PROTECT YOUR EQUIPMENT

If necessary to minimize baggage, remove the equipment from it's case and wrap carefully in towels, clothing, or other protective material before placing in your check-in luggage.

 TAG AND BE PREPARED TO OPEN ALL CASES

Put your name, phone number, address, and *destination* contact info on separate tags on all equipment and bags. Airport security will likely inspect all equipment. Don't put locks on check-in luggage as these will be cut off by security.

 KEEP A MASTER LIST ON YOU AT ALL TIMES

Before your trip take a few minutes to type up a complete inventory list that includes all items, their exact quantities, and most important, serial numbers for all equipment. This list may be needed in case of loss or theft while traveling.

5 TRAVELING WITH MASTER FOOTAGE

It's always best to keep your master tapes in your carry-on luggage. After a long and successful shoot these are now your most valuable possession. Guard them at all cost. And *never* check them in with your luggage. DV tapes are not affected by airport X-ray machines.

Using a small luggage cart to make carrying gear simple and fast.

Be Practical

You will also have to take some practical matters into consideration when researching documentary subject matter, talent, and locations. In many cases, these practical considerations will present significant barriers to production. When faced with barriers, you must train, think, and plan harder. You must hear *The Eye of the Tiger* in your head . . . "Dunt! Dunt-Dunt-Dunt!" Always think R-O-C-K-Y before shooting . . .

THINK R-O-C-K-Y BEFORE YOU SHOOT

Relevance: If you make it, will anybody care? Is the timing right?

Originality: Are there six other docs on Tupac? How will yours differ?

Commitment: How long/hard will this shoot be? Can you commit to that?

Kash: How much will it cost? Can you afford to travel there or stay? (Author freely admits that using K is a reach here.)

Your Access: Can you gain entry into the world you want to show?

There's no magic formula here, but you should have satisfactory answers to these questions before you start shooting. Think of everything that could possibly stop you. Then think of solutions and workarounds for each. Get creative. Ask yourself *how else* can you tell this story. Your time, money, and energy are all limited resources. Be realistic about what you can and can't do.

> ✔ Be realistic about what You can and can't do. Always think "R-O-C-K-Y" before shooting.

Okay, you've got your equipment package figured out, but who's going to actually use all this stuff? You still need a crew. Generally speaking, documentary crews tend to be smaller than narrative film crews since they don't require as much equipment and usually benefit from being more mobile and low-key. I like to work with as few people as necessary to keep my subjects relaxed and to maintain my focus on the subject matter rather than directing crew. Here's a basic breakdown of typical production duties for three different sized doc crews.

TWO-MAN CREW	MICRO CREW	FULL CREW
Producer/Director	**Producer/Director**	**Producer/Director**
■ Supervise setup	■ Supervise setup	■ Supervise setup
■ Assist with setup	■ Warm up subject	■ Brief subject
■ Warm up subject	■ Brief subject	■ Quality control
■ Brief subject	■ Conduct interview	■ Secure releases
■ Conduct interview	■ Quality control	
■ Quality control	■ Secure releases	**Interviewer**
■ Secure releases		■ Warm up subject
	Camera Operator	■ Conduct interview
Camera/Sound Operator	■ Light scene	
	■ Set up and run camera	**Camera Operator**
■ Light scene		■ Supervise lighting
■ Set up and run camera	**Sound Operator**	■ Set up and run camera
■ Set up and mix sound	■ Set up and mix sound	
	■ Boom (if necessary)	**Gaffer**
		■ Light scene
		Sound Operator
		■ Set up and run sound
		Boom Operator
		■ Boom
		Production Assistants
		■ Assist with all of the above

Introduction

One of the most important tasks of producing any film or video is hiring crew. Your choices of people to work with are more important than just about any other decisions you will make outside of choosing subjects. It's more important than your format, your equipment, or your budget. Apart from your concept, 50% of the success or failure of your project will be directly related to the quality of the crew you hire.

Good Crew Members

Good crew members will take your vision and run with it. They will use their expertise and creativity to add new layers and ideas to your project. They will put their experience and knowledge to work for you, instantly coming up with clever solutions to problems that have kept you awake for nights. They will push you and everyone else to hang in there during the trying times and keep making the project better. They will tactfully help you avoid common mistakes. They will help bring your project in under budget and on time. They will literally give up weeks of their life, completely forgo sleep, and even *bleed* for your project.

Bad Crew Members

On the flip side, bad crew members will take your vision and squash it. They are inflexible. They will whine and complain about the most mundane or obviously uncontrollable things. They will break your concentration at every turn. They will show up on location late and leave early. They will slowly drag down the morale of the entire set. In short, a bad crew member is a life-sucking, paralyzing ball and chain around your ankles that will stifle your every step, criticize

> ✔ *Whether you're paying them or not, choose your crew members wisely. They may make or break your project.*

every decision, and ultimately become your biggest obstacle to a successful production. Here's how to tell if you've got a good or bad potential crew member.

LOOK FOR CREW MEMBERS WHO:	BEWARE CREW MEMBERS WHO:
■ Come recommended from another filmmaker	■ Don't understand the limitations of your budget
■ Are excited about your project	■ Are more concerned about the equipment than the content
■ Have positive "can-do" attitudes	■ Look down on your video format
■ Are eager and hungry	■ Show up late to or miss a meeting
■ Want to get more experience	■ Have unrealistic expectations
■ Have something to gain	■ Seem overly concerned about the pay rate
■ Have access to equipment	■ Are argumentative or negative
■ Will work for free or little pay	

THE PRODUCER—DIRECTOR RELATIONSHIP

CHRISTINA DEHAVEN, PRODUCER

(My Uncle Berns, The Apple Song—Black Eyed Peas, The Cut Man, 761st)

. . . It is a marriage because [these are] literally the "parents" of a film. These are the two people that carry from start to finish the creative aspects and the practical aspects . . . financial, legal, administrative, everything else that you need to power the creative goals of a film or power a project of this size. I've encountered a lot of directors who try to do everything themselves just because they don't quite understand how important it is to have a producer. They say, "Oh, I'll just direct and produce it myself. Maybe I'll shoot it, too."

It's a collaborative process. I can't emphasize that enough. You are not going to be able to . . . Well, you can make a film by yourself. It has been done before. But, it's not going to be as good as it could be with the help of a collaborative team, a collaborative team effort, and at the forefront of that team is a producer.

Everybody has to have a producer and the communication between these two people is the most important thing because they are the central heart of communication for every single major department, both technical and creative, from production design to the editor to the sound mix to everything, these are the people that keep it together.

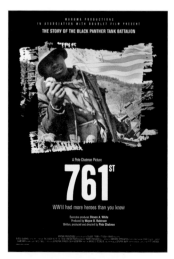

761st—Maroma Productions/Double 7 Film

And people will constantly look to [the producer and director] to be on the same page, to answer questions and to do everything, solve problems when they arise. Keep everyone posted. Keep everyone in the loop. And follow the project along to completion. So, that relationship—I can't emphasis it enough—is probably the most important one on any kind of project.

Okay, so you've developed your idea, you've scraped together the cash, and you're ready to make a movie, but you still need the people who are going to help you make it happen. There are several routes you could go. Some may be more effective for you than others depending on your unique situation and level of experience. Wherever you get your crew, it's important that you understand their expectations, scope of knowledge, and how to best use their talents.

CREW SOURCE	ADVANTAGES	DISADVANTAGES
Film Schools and College Campuses	■ Usually eager to learn and work on a "real" project ■ May bring additional equipment ■ May recruit other crew members ■ Already have some training ■ Open to new approaches ■ More tolerant of low-budget conditions	■ Limited experience ■ May think they know more than they really do ■ May require more supervision ■ May be afraid to admit they don't know something ■ May be preoccupied with their own film projects
Word of Mouth/ Recommendations	■ You already know what you're getting ■ You have advance knowledge of how to get the best from them ■ You can view previous projects	■ There are NO disadvantages to word-of-mouth referrals, they should be taken into account whenever you can get them
Friends and Family	■ Eager and excited ■ More tolerant of low-budget conditions ■ You already know what you're getting	■ Completely inexperienced ■ Must be carefully trained ■ Risky for key crew roles ■ Must be carefully supervised
Film Classified Web Sites	■ Can reach a lot of people at once ■ Brings professionals to you ■ Most ads are free ■ Only people attracted to project and pay rate will apply	■ You really don't know who these people are ■ Must do *extensive* interviews ■ Must sift through many applicants ■ Must plan ahead to meet publishing deadlines

✔ *Word of mouth is best when it comes to hiring crew. Learn how to get the best out of crew members.*

Crew Meeting

The week before any big shoot, you should sit down with your crew and go over everything that will happen during production. This meeting should include the producer, director, camera department, sound department, production coordinator, and anyone else who will have an active role on the shoot. You can do this in a formal office setting or over dinner or drinks—whatever floats your boat. It doesn't matter. What matters is that you clearly communicate your vision, everyone understands their individual roles, and that all logistical issues and crew concerns are worked out *before* your shoot day. Some topics you'll want to cover are listed below.

Crew Meeting Agenda

- ✔ Call Time
- ✔ Plan Changes
- ✔ Topic Briefing
- ✔ Shooting Schedule
- ✔ Equipment Package
- ✔ Transportation and Travel
- ✔ Directions
- ✔ Crew Member Roles
- ✔ Location Logistics and Concerns
- ✔ Handling Talent and Location Owners
- ✔ Shot List/Storyboards
- ✔ Difficult Scenes
- ✔ Estimated Wrap Time

> ✔ *Meet with your crew members beforehand to go over logistics and to get everyone on the same page.*

Meals

Food is one of the great secrets of the pros. It has a tremendous psychological effect on the crew. When the big studios and production companies do a show there is always a "spread" of delicious food and a continuous supply of snacks, drinks, and coffee. Crew members often speak of three things when describing a particular project they've worked on: the quality of the project, the organization of the shoot, and the food. Good food is a *standard* part of the deal for all professional film and TV crews. It is (and should be) expected. I wish I could lean into the ear of every new filmmaker and shout this through a bullhorn:

DO NOT SKIMP ON FOOD FOR YOUR CREW!!!

This is one of those critical "little details" that so many new filmmakers overlook or save as an afterthought. Feeding your crew good food is extremely important, especially if they are working for free. In the long run you will not save a dime by being cheap when it comes to food for your crew. (Oh, you'll save on the food itself, but you will lose immeasurable amounts in crew morale, energy level, pacing, and attitude toward the shoot.) As a general rule, the more hell you put your crew through, the better your meals and snacks should be. The crew is the machine that creates your project. Food is the fuel that runs the machine. The better the food, the better your machine will run, the better your project will turn out. It's that simple.

Food Strategies

Because doc crews tend to be so small, catering usually isn't a practical (or affordable) option. You will mostly be dependent upon local restaurants for meals. It is a vital part of preproduction to scout out and have menus from all the local restaurants. Both Yahoo and Google have excellent tools to search and list local restaurants. All you need is a zip code. You can get restaurant phone numbers, addresses, and maps with a few keystrokes. Also, many restaurants now make their menu available online or would be happy to e-mail or fax it to you. You can let the crew pick from the menu by setting a dollar amount per person. Or, a more simple solution is to just order a variety of different dishes and serve them up buffet style.

If you're feeding a large number of people, make sure you place your order a few hours or a day or two ahead of time and tell them when you need it delivered or will be picking it up. Whenever possible, picking up your order is the best option because delivery will always take longer and it's easier to check and correct the accuracy of the order at the restaurant. Always try to get plates, cups, ice, napkins, and utensils when possible to save a little cash. Also, don't forget to get receipts for your records!

> ✔ Never skimp on food for your crew. The better you feed your crew the better they will perform.

Craft Services

The term **craft services** is just a Hollywood name for the snacks and drinks department. (Yes, craft services is a department.) You should have a craft services table (or box if you're on the road) stocked at all times with a variety of high-energy and sugary foods, spring water, and drinks. Try to find out your crew's favorite snacks ahead of time and have plenty on hand.

I know you may be tempted to save a few bucks, but stay away from generic food items. Name brand snacks and drinks are always better, even if it's only psychological. Instead of giving them "the very best," a table full of *Chumps Ahoy* chocolate chips and *Tropican't* orange juice tells your crew that you care about them enough to get "the absolute cheapest" thing you can get away with, and they may in turn give you the absolute cheapest effort *they* can get away with.

Apart from snacks and cold drinks, it is absolutely essential that you keep a fresh pot of coffee and hot water for tea on hand at all times, morning, noon, and night. If food is the fuel of the filmmaking machine, then caffeine is the lubricant that keeps the parts moving. Keep your filmmaking machine gassed up and lubricated and you will get noticeable results in performance and morale—and a reputation as someone who takes care of their crew people.

If you have a sizeable crew, really try to find a dedicated craft services person. This is a perfect position for those eager friends and relatives that want to help out, but have no filmmaking experience. Their job is simply to keep the food and snacks flowing, help coordinate meals, and help clean up the mess afterward. It's a great position for someone who just wants to be a fly on the wall and observe. If the job's done well, the craft services person is often the most popular person on set.

Taking Care of the Vegetarians

Personally, I'm a carnivore, but these days I have rarely done a shoot that didn't involve at least one vegetarian or vegan (no meat, dairy, or egg products) crew member. Make sure you survey the crew members ahead of time for vegetarians or other special dietary needs, so you'll know how many veggie or special meals you'll need daily. To make life even easier, find out what types of common dishes they like and which local restaurants they prefer.

Vegetarians, and especially vegans, are sometimes treated like second-class citizens when it comes to meal time on a film crew. However, do not ignore these crew members' dietary needs. I can tell you from experience that vegetarians will not want a salad or a simple side dish for *every* meal. It's definitely harder to find menus that accommodate vegetarians, but you've gotta put in the leg work to make it happen or else you will have some miserable souls on your crew and it will be reflected on the shoot. Take care of these people and they'll take care of you.

> ✔ Keep snacks, water, and caffeine flowing at all times. Take care of the vegetarians on set.

5 DOWN AND DIRTY FOOD IDEAS

1 **GET LOCAL RESTAURANTS TO DONATE FREE FOOD**
This is a common practice that many indie filmmakers use to supplement their food budgets. With a little *advance* leg work and salesmanship, any producer should be able to talk at least one or two local restaurants into providing a free or greatly discounted meal or two for the crew, in exchange for a film credit or a shot of their business in the film (as B-Roll or an actual location). Although we know the truth, filmmaking is still sexy to a lot of people who will be glad just to be a part of your project. Find these people and ask them to help you.

2 **HAVE FRIENDS OR RELATIVES COOK FOR THE CREW**
If your mom or friend is a great cook, have them hook up a hot home-cooked meal for the crew. Do not underestimate the power of a good home-cooked meal. For some crew members it will be their first in weeks.

3 **TREAT THE CREW TO A LOCAL DELICACY**
Okay, this isn't really a money-saving suggestion, but if you occasionally arrange for a shrimp cocktail, premium ice cream, or some other little rare or gourmet treat to be on set, it will provide a nice boost to crew morale before you tell them it's going to be another 16-hour day.

4 **BREAK OUT THE GRILL**
Designate a Grill Master and cook up some steaks, burgers, and vegetables and turn it into a cookout. This is a good idea for remote locations. It can be messy, but it's a fun and cheap way to serve hot food cooked to order.

5 **GET ALL THE FREEBIES AND EXTRAS YOU CAN**
Whenever possible, get free extras from the restaurants you order from. Many will offer these standard, but if they don't, make sure you ask. Nothing makes a restaurant manager happier than a large order from a potential repeat customer. So I recommend that you always dangle out the possibility of ordering more meals during your shoot to encourage them to provide any or all of the following items for free: utensils, plates, cups, napkins, ice, condiments, tablecloths, tea bags, sugar, creamer, etc. (I've even been allowed to borrow an industrial coffee maker for the day!) If you work it right, you can get any or all of these items and sometimes even barter for a few free appetizers, drinks, or desserts. The bigger the order the more leverage you have. Remember, every free item is money back in your budget.

CHAPTER 2
LOCATION, LOCATION, LOCATION

Making Arrangements with Your Subjects

Documentary filmmakers often have to be flexible and "on call" as their story develops. Be mindful of the fact that your subject is accommodating you into their personal/professional life and you will often have to shoot *at their convenience*. Try to schedule shooting or interview times that are most convenient for your subject, as this will allow them to be the most relaxed.

Interview Locations

Choose a location with characteristics that help tell your story. Don't just choose a spot at random. Just like all other elements of filmmaking—lighting, camerawork, music, etc.—your choice of location is yet another aspect of your storytelling that helps reveal character and theme.

Scouting a location in advance is always your best bet. For interviews it's preferable to find a controlled environment. The less control you have over an interview environment, the more headaches you will have trying to make it look and sound right. *Sound* should also be a primary consideration when location scouting. (See also "5 Sound Rules to Live By" and "Location Sound Hazards" on pages 142–144 and 146.)

Generally, the best location for interviews will be a room in your subject's home or place of occupation. First off, this is where they will be most comfortable and it's probably the place where the themes and subject of your documentary are most *visual*. For example, you could interview a race car driver in his living room, but in his racing garage or next to his car would be more visually interesting. You could interview a former boxing champion on a bench in a public park, but wouldn't a boxing gym or locker room communicate more about your subject's world? . . . *The correct answer is, "Yes!"*

Another practical consideration is lighting. Is there ample sunlight or indoor lighting in the room? Is there ample electricity if you need to add lights? Is there enough room to shoot? Comfortable temperature? Does the room portray the character of your subject accurately? How long will it take to prep the room? If you are stuck with a barren, ugly, or inappropriate location, some

alternatives are to use a neutral background such as a brick wall or cloth backdrop, shoot outside, or use shallow depth of field to keep the background out of focus. (See also "Hot Tip: Easy Do-It-Yourself Backdrops" and "Hot Tip: Shallow Depth-of-Field" on pages 186 and 175, respectively.)

✔ Choose a location that will help tell your story visually.

LOCATION MANAGEMENT 101

Introduction

Although documentary is a different animal than narrative production, you still must manage your locations with the same (if not more) deft social skills to ensure the complete success of your shoot. Do not make the common mistake of thinking that just because your subject works, frequents, or has access to a location, that you, your crew and camera will be automatically welcomed there. Often that will be the case, but many

times it will not. Even if your subject assures you that everything's cool and you trust them, make sure that they have *asked* the owner and explained the subject and scope of the shoot.

Your subject may be a doctor at General Hospital, but the hospital administration may have very strict policies about cameras in the building. Often subjects will be completely oblivious to such matters. If permission hasn't been secured from the proper people beforehand you may find yourself in a situation where you and your subject are embarrassed or even reprimanded. Worst of all, your big planned interview in that great location will be a total bust.

Corporate-owned locations, franchises, entertainment venues, government offices, military sites, schools, and places housing adult or illegal activity are all locations that must be researched and secured properly before you ever show up with a camera. Many of these institutions will have a public relations (PR) person whose main function is to act as a liaison between the institution and the media. That's you.

If your story will show the institution in a favorable light, help educate people about their business, or serves the political goals of the organization or individuals in charge, you are much more likely to get a "yes." If your story involves a controversial topic, you can almost definitely expect to get a "no." (I'll get into how to combat this later.) Either way, you need to communicate with these institutions as far in advance as possible. The following chart will help you determine who to contact and some of the issues you will likely confront.

> ✔ *Make sure you have permission to shoot from the location owners and not just your subject.*

LOCATION	LIKELY CONTACT(S)	COMMON OBSTACLES
Hospital	■ PR/Media Rep. ■ Administration	■ Policies against shooting ■ Patient privacy ■ Pending legal issues ■ Employee privacy ■ Internal politics
School	■ Principal/VP ■ Superintendent ■ District Spokesperson	■ Student privacy ■ Policies against shooting ■ Internal politics
Government Office (i.e., military, welfare, housing dept.)	■ PR/Media Rep. ■ Agency Head	■ Policies against shooting ■ Touchy political situations ■ Employee privacy ■ Internal politics
Entertainment Venue (i.e., nightclubs, concert halls, arenas)	■ Venue Manager ■ Venue Owner	■ Union rules governing film crews ■ Contractual obligations to talent that restrict shooting ■ Contractual obligations to other media that restrict shooting
Corporate/ Franchise Office (i.e., Microsoft, Subway, Sony)	■ PR Rep. ■ CEOs Office ■ Business Affairs	■ Bureaucratic shooting policies ■ Slow response to requests ■ Internal politics ■ Pending legal issues
*Adult Business (i.e., strip club, massage parlor, bar)	■ Owner ■ Manager	■ Customer privacy ■ Pending legal issues ■ Desire for low profile
*Illegal Location (i.e., gambling house, brothel, crystal meth lab)	■ Organization Leader ■ Operation Manager	■ Fear of arrest ■ Desire for low profile ■ Customer privacy

*Adult and illegal locations always require extra special care, research, and safety precautions. Don't get assaulted, arrested, or shot at for the sake of a film. It will **never** be worth it. (But if you ever do, make sure you get it on tape!)

Dealing with PR Reps and Other Media Liaisons

Once you have sold them on your idea, the PR/media liaisons person will be your ambassador to the institution. They will usually arrange everything and instruct you as to who, when, and where you may shoot. They will often inform you of the best visual locations on the property and suggest great interview subjects that you may not have considered. I have found PR people to be helpful allies on many documentary shoots.

Be honest with a PR person or location owner when pitching your story. (For example, don't say your story is about the hospital's new cancer ward if it's really about assisted suicide, and don't agree to not shoot patients, then sneak in some quick shots.) I say this not just because it's ethically questionable, but because you will risk getting kicked out mid-shoot. And from a strictly personal standpoint, you will screw it up for the rest of us who may need to shoot there in the future.

Doc Location Ethics

You can get into slippery ethical territory when you're trying to convince a skeptical location owner (or subject for that matter) who is reluctant to participate in your documentary, but there are ways to do it and still be honest. Empathize, relate, listen, mirror their concerns. Be passionate.

But most of all, focus on everything your documentary has to offer that will appeal to the location owner's best interest and sensibilities—a chance to be heard, a chance to correct a misperception, positive publicity, educating the public, expanding their audience, free advertising. Keep an open mind. Be fair. And be honest. You will sleep well at night and be more respected as a documentary filmmaker.

> ✔ Be upfront about the subject of your project and stick to agreements with location owners.

The Exception to the Rule

Now having said all that, I should also say that there is a notable exception to the above advice. And that is the *investigative* doc. By it's very nature, the investigative doc often calls for filmmakers to gain access to secret, dark, and restricted places to uncover critical social and political situations that usually don't want to be uncovered. Penetrating these places to get at the truth will, more likely than not, require some deception along the way. Shooting under false pretenses, ambush interviews, and hidden cameras are all common tricks of the investigative doc trade. At its very best, the investigative documentary can serve as the catalyst to free people from Death Row, change laws, and help right longstanding wrongs. But at its very worst, it can ruin people's lives and livelihoods unfairly. There is a big difference between profound, hard-hitting video journalism that uncovers serious wrongdoing and sleazy, manipulative video sucker punches that deliberately twist the truth. If you're in the doc game, you need to also be in the truth game, because along with the title "documentary filmmaker" comes great power and responsibility.

A camera can do more damage than a gun. Be responsible about what you point yours at.

HOW *NOT* TO GET YOUR CAMERA JACKED

One of the things that lower budget productions sometimes overlook is security. This is unfortunate because they are the people who can least afford to lose a few thousand dollars worth of equipment. Here are some things you can do to avoid being ripped off in the big city, or anywhere else for that matter:

1 **NEVER LEAVE EQUIPMENT UNATTENDED . . . EVER**
The number one thing you can do to protect your gear is not leave it unattended in vehicles, *especially* overnight, *especially* in cities. (Studies have shown that it only takes a crackhead with a crowbar about 30 seconds to break into *any* locked vehicle.) If you have so much gear that it's not practical to unload your vehicle, make sure you park it in a bonded (i.e., insured) garage or reputable lot with 24-hour attendants. You should be aware that many garages will likely charge more for large vehicles or not accept them at all. Never store valuables where they will be visible (and accessible) through windows. Use a cargo van over a passenger van for storing gear. Even during shooting someone should be with the equipment if it is in, or just outside of, a vehicle.

2 **ALWAYS KEEP YOUR MASTER TAPES SECURE**
Nothing on set is more valuable than the precious footage that you have spent days gathering, because you usually won't have the option to go back and capture those moments again. Once they're gone, they're gone. Master tapes or media should always be kept by the most responsible person on set, either the director, producer, or DP.

3 **TAKE INVENTORY OF EQUIPMENT REGULARLY**
It's very easy for a busy and tired crew to leave some gear behind as you dash from shoot to shoot. Every single time you wrap at a location, you and the crew should double- and triple-check to make sure that you have all of your equipment. Keep a written checklist. Make sure you especially check for easily overlooked parts such as adapters, filters, cables, and especially anything small.

4 **BE WATCHFUL LOADING AND UNLOADING GEAR IN PUBLIC**
Apart from leaving it alone overnight, loading is the most vulnerable time for your equipment because the crew is busy moving gear back and forth or organizing in the back of the vehicle. It's very easy for someone with quick hands to lift an item sitting on the sidewalk and never even be noticed. Always have a dedicated set of eyeballs watching the gear during load in and load out.

BEING PREPARED FOR REMOTE LOCATIONS

ALRICK BROWN—PRODUCER
MICAH SCHAFFER—PRODUCER/DIRECTOR
(Death of Two Sons)

Alrick: Aside from the physical challenges of being in Africa, there were technical challenges even with our small equipment package. I actually produced getting all the equipment together. We made sure we had backup everything, because when you're out there, you don't know what's gonna happen, so we had two cameras. One was our main camera, one was our backup just in case anything happened we'd have an extra camera.

We had two DVX-100s. We had our lav [mics] and we had our mixer, which we didn't have backups for. So if any of those went, we would've ended up just going straight into the camera. We anticipated the kind of scenarios that would come up. We took a crazy amount of batteries . . . enough batteries that would, literally, if we had to run the camera straight, run the lavs straight, we'd have enough batteries to cover the entire three weeks that we were shooting. We made sure we had adaptors so we could charge the batteries any chance we could, we even bought a charger for the car . . . Some of the villages are very remote—no running water, sometimes no electricity, and we just made sure that we had that stuff under lock.

Micah: It didn't take a huge amount of money to have this sort of preparation. We bought used equipment. We got deals on the rental stuff. We had people loan us things, we had a camera loaned to us. It's not like this anal, intensive preparation necessarily has to be expensive. It just has to be *thorough*. So we did the production phase on a very, very small budget, relative to the production value of the film, and it was just our hours that went into it, rather than dollars. Hours making sure everything was straight.

TRANSPORTATION CONSIDERATIONS

Okay, so your locations are all set, you've got a crew, equipment, and a shooting schedule. Now the only question is: "How are you gonna get these people and this stuff to where it's gotta go?" The answer depends primarily on the size of your budget, the size of your crew, and the distance you have to travel. Let's look at a couple of options.

VEHICLE	CAPACITY	RENTAL	COMMENTS
Car	■ 4–5 people ■ Sm./med. package*	$60–100/day	■ Best means for stealth shooting ■ Easiest to drive and park ■ You own or can borrow a car for free ■ Limited trunk space for gear ■ Least comfortable ■ Personal luggage requires a second car
SUV/Mini-Van	■ 6–8 people ■ Sm./med. package*	$80–150/day	■ Good for stealth shooting ■ Larger capacity for people and gear ■ No hidden storage for equipment
Cargo Van	■ 2 people in front ■ Med./lg. equipment package	$100–150/day	■ Can carry all gear plus luggage ■ More difficult to find parking ■ Only 2 passengers can fit in cab ■ Cannot double as crew vehicle
Passenger Van	■ 12–15 people ■ Medium equipment package*	$100–200/day	■ Can carry all gear plus luggage ■ More difficult to find parking ■ 8 gas guzzling cylinders ■ No hidden storage for equipment

*If you're carrying less people, you can fit a larger equipment package in these vehicles.

VEHICLE	CAPACITY	RENTAL	COMMENTS
Cube Truck	■ 2 people in front ■ Any size equipment package	$150–250/day	■ May come with equipment package ■ More difficult and expensive to park ■ Very conspicuous/high profile
RV (Camper)	■ 6–12 people ■ Any size equipment package	$150-$300/day	■ Rolling office/interview location ■ Most comfortable crew travel option ■ Plan/edit while traveling ■ Overnight sleeping space ■ Gas guzzling behemoth ■ Very conspicuous/high profile ■ More difficult/expensive to park/drive ■ More prone to damage/ accidents

STEALTH SHOOTING TACTICS 101

It's always less hassle to do things by the book when possible, but as many broke documentary filmmakers will tell you . . . it ain't always possible. At the end of the day, there's only one golden rule when making a Down and Dirty documentary—get the shot. Here are some of my stealth strategies for overcoming common shooting obstacles.

1 NO PERMITS, NO PROBLEM

Scout the location for security, the best shooting angles, and spots where you are most likely to go unnoticed. Talk and walk through your shots in a nearby location, out of sight, then go to the crucial location ready to roll. Save riskier shots for last. You don't want to get kicked out before you shoot what you came for. Keep a producer on lookout nearby to talk and run interference with authorities if you get busted. (Ultimately, this probably won't get you an okay to shoot, but it will buy you more time to finish getting your shot.) Never get into a big ruckus with a cop, security guard, or other authority figure when you don't have permits or permission. You have nothing to gain but unnecessary trouble once you've been busted. Just pretend you're a clueless film student or hobbyist, apologize, and leave quietly. Find an alternate location or come back another time, when the coast is clear.

2 TRAVEL AND SHOOT LOW PROFILE

This means roll with a skeleton crew of two or three people max: a camera operator, a director/producer, and/or a sound recordist or PA. Use cell phones instead of walkie talkies to communicate with crew members. Wrap the camera up in a large towel for cushioning and use backpacks or gym bags instead of camera bags. Don't take out the camera until you need it. Use **breakaway cables** if you have a separate sound person. Dress and act like the rest of the crowd.

3 RECORD STEALTH SOUND

Nothing attracts attention like an 8-foot pole with a mic waving around on the end. If you're using a shotgun mic, try mounting it on the camera or on a pistol grip instead. This is a rare situation where you should avoid wearing over the ear headphones as they will attract too much attention. Instead, use professional *sound isolating* headphone earbuds or rely on the camera's **auto gain control** (AGC) function, which will usually maintain an acceptable sound level for you.

4 USE STEALTH CAMERAWORK

Set your camera menu, record color bars, and do a test recording *before* you even get out of the car. (Make sure you disable or tape over the red recording light and turn off the recording beep in the menu.) Use auto functions for white balance, iris, gain, and sound. In this instance, you may also want to use autofocus if there is sufficient lighting.

Keep the camera on and at the ready. Cradle the camera or hold it down low when walking. Avoid using tripods. Instead, use a **monopod** or whatever you have to work with to steady your shots. You can set your camera flat or nestle it in a towel or coat on top of a trashcan, mailbox, or car. If you must use a tripod, it's best to use a portable lightweight model that can be quickly set up and moved.

5 ADD PRODUCTION VALUE WITH LOCAL RESOURCES

The greatest asset a Down and Dirty filmmaker has is imagination. Where others see a Ferris wheel, we see a crane shot. Where others see a guy behind the wheel of a taxi, we see a location scout and production vehicle for B-roll. Anything that rolls, moves, lifts, flies, or has a great view that you can sneak onto with a camera could serve to add some free or inexpensive production value to your shoot. For the price of admission (and

This dramatic aerial view is courtesy of a Ferris wheel. Total cost: $3.50.

perhaps a generous tip for a cooperative driver or operator), you can shoot compelling footage, narration, and even interviews from double-decker sightseeing buses, cabs, tourist boat rides, Ferris wheels, rickshaw rides, observation decks, raised subway lines, horse-drawn carriages, helicopter tours, cable cars, public balconies, or even glass elevators. With a little imagination and creativity, the **cranes**, **dollies**, and **jibs** you need are all around you. If it has a dramatic viewpoint, you just need to get on it, bust out your camera, and shoot.

6 ALWAYS HAVE A "PLAN B"

Even if you do all of the above, you still have a good chance of being shut down by "the man" if you don't have permits or permission to shoot at your location. When this happens, make sure you're ready with **Plan B**—an alternative location or something else you can shoot instead. Don't let the whole day's shoot go to crap because of a single setback. There will always be unexpected setbacks. Just be ready to roll with the punches, duck, and punch back.

Location Releases

You should try to get signed **location releases** (also called "location agreements") as soon as possible after a location owner has agreed to let you shoot. This can be done in-person, by fax, e-mail, or standard mail. If you are unable to secure a location agreement before shoot day, it should be at the top of your list *before* you shoot. Location agreements vary, but almost all include:

- ❏ Name of location owner
- ❏ Location address
- ❏ Filmmakers, title of project, and production company
- ❏ Dates and times needed
- ❏ Permission and cost (if any) to use location
- ❏ How any damage or legal claims will be handled
- ❏ Signatures of location owner and filmmaker

> ✔ *Get a signed location release __before__ you shoot.*

Location Insurance

A primary requirement of most locations, particularly commercial and corporate, will be that your production has insurance that covers the location by naming them as "additional insured." It is reasonable and advisable for them to cover their butts in case your lights set the curtains on fire or a customer trips over your tripod and breaks their ankle. They won't want to be held legally liable for any damages to their property or injury to others that result from your production.

Your policy should cover property damage up to $1,000,000.00 (standard). Covering specific locations is usually a simple affair. Basically you notify your insurance company of the name and address of the location(s) you want covered and they will fax and/or mail out the certificates of insurance for you to give to the location owner. You should plan on 24–48 hours for the insurance company to process your request, but I've also worked with companies that would process certificates the same day. Make sure you check with your insurance company for the turn-around time on certificates.

> ✔ *Many locations require that you have insurance.*

INSURANCE ISSUES

Do You Really Need Insurance?

I know that many filmmakers strapped for cash ask this question, especially after they get that first insurance quote. They have a small crew and their location owners haven't asked about an **insurance certificate**, so they ask themselves if they really need production insurance.

The short answer is "No, if you're *sure* that nothing will go wrong." The problem with that answer is that you're never *sure* when or if something is going to go wrong. Having production insurance is like using a seatbelt or having airbags in your car. You don't actually *need* either one 99.9% of the time, but on those unavoidable tragic .1% of occasions when you really do need them, seatbelts, airbags, and *production insurance* are all invaluable. You or your production may not survive without them. I think there is a technical term for what happens when a filmmaker doesn't have insurance and a rare, but all too real catastrophe actually does happen. I believe the term is "totally screwed."

Shooting Without Insurance

Even so, I understand that many documentary makers don't have the luxury of putting their money anywhere else, but on the screen. (I have gotten insurance quotes that actually exceeded my entire project budget!) So they shoot without insurance. This is a common reality. It's also a gamble. Film shoots are magnets for improbable disasters—car wrecks, grand theft, injury—you name it.

Make sure that you fully understand the risks and consequences if there is a catastrophe, and do everything you can to minimize the chance of damage or injury. Consult other filmmakers for their candid advice about your circumstances. My advice is that if you can afford insurance, get it. The very nature of guerrilla filmmaking is risky and sooner or later everyone's luck runs out. With a micro-crew shooting a documentary, you probably won't be dealing with as much risk as a narrative film crew, which usually has more people, equipment, and activity. But you're still dealing with risk, the unpredictable, and the ever-present Murphy's Law: "Anything that can go wrong, will."

Keep in mind, something as simple as a passerby tripping over a cable on the ground could lead to years of messy legal and financial headaches. Insurance is peace of mind, albeit a costly peace. If you genuinely can't afford insurance, you're certainly not alone in the world of indie filmmaking, but you really have to weigh the risks carefully before shooting without insurance. Remember, accepting risks is also accepting consequences.

✔ If you shoot without insurance, you risk liability for property damage, injury, etc. Do what you gotta do to make your film, but understand the risks you are taking.

HOT TIP

SHOOTING IN DA 'HOOD

Standard documentary subject matter such as poverty, social justice, underground culture, etc., will almost always involve at least some shooting in rough areas, euphemistically known as "da 'hood." Documentary filmmaking can be a foolhardy or even dangerous endeavor if you ignore the real-world issues of class, race, and culture. Over the years I've shot extensively in various 'hoods throughout the country. In almost all cases, the crew I was part of was well-received and got the footage we needed without incident. Here are some tips for shooting in 'hoods from Baltimore, Maryland to Kabul, Afghanistan.

1 RESEARCH THE AREA

Before you even think about shooting in a rough or unfamiliar urban area, you need to find out as much as you can about that neighborhood. Try to get a sense of the racial and economic make up of that area, as well as how historical and recent events have affected the neighborhood. Talking to key people from the neighborhood ahead of time could be the difference between you and your crew being greeted with warm smiles or hurling bottles.

2 GET A 'HOOD AMBASSADOR

This is the best move you can make. In Beverly Hills you need a permit. In the 'hood you need an **ambassador**. The ideal person may be a long-time resident, civic leader, a gang member, a beat cop, an outreach worker, a local business owner, etc., anyone that has roots and respect in the neighborhood. Look for a go-between who may carry influence with the people you want on camera. Talk to them in advance (without your camera) and explain what you're doing and why. Really try to connect with them. If they get it and they trust you, they will ultimately become de facto producers on your shoot. They will make introductions, set up interviews, point out significant visuals, alert you to dangers, or even help provide security. They will advise you on how to handle yourself and give you tips on dealing with the people you really seek. If you're down with them, the neighborhood will be much more likely to trust you and open up. In a word, they will give you the Holy Grail of documentary—*access*. If you don't know the culture, the next best thing to an ambassador is an "interpreter." Think of this person as an urban consultant. This is someone who is not necessarily from the area, but who can read the scene and is more familiar with the prevailing culture than you may be.

3 STREET SMARTS

Bodily harm is usually not as likely as someone ripping off your equipment. Instruct all crewmembers to make sure that *nothing* of value is left visible in their cars. Video equipment, CDs, laptops, clothing, and anything else that could command a dollar on the street is fair game for opportunistic criminals. If the equipment is not with you, someone should be with the equipment. (See also "Hot Tip: How Not to Get Your Camera Jacked" on page 59.)

4 RACE MATTERS

While you may be liberal and racially color-blind as a filmmaker, don't kid yourself for a minute—if you want real access to certain places and cultures, race matters. In many areas, the unusual presence of people of other races is often greeted with suspicion at best, and flying insults and debris at worst. It's always better to roll with at least one or preferably several people who are of the same race as your subjects. The more of your crew members who look like the people that live in the area, the better. It's just a fact of life in many cultures that people are more trusting of familiar faces. Of course, you can still win people's trust regardless of race, but plan on it being a longer, slower process—perhaps longer than you have to shoot.

5 TRAVEL AND SHOOT ON THE DL

Travel **on the DL** with a small crew in an unmarked vehicle. Use pistol grips over boom poles for sound. If you mostly need exterior shots, even the roughest areas are usually quiet and relatively safe in the morning hours between 6 a.m. and 11 a.m. You may wish to shoot out of a traveling vehicle or employ a guerrilla stop and shoot strategy using a driver and DP.

6 SHOW RESPECT

Make it a habit to ask before you start shooting anyone or their property. Take the time to explain what you are doing and answer questions as much as practically possible. If you fail to do your research and earn people's trust, you may have to negotiate shooting terms with hostile residents or even slip someone a few bucks or some other tribute to "protect" your crew and equipment. Coughing up twenty bucks is a small price to pay for a few hours of harassment-free shooting.

Remember, you're shooting in someone else's home . . . act like it.

CHAPTER 3
IMAGE CONTROL AND CAMERA WORK

EXPOSURE

Light Is Good

Even though today's DV cameras are more capable than ever of shooting decent images in low light, the simple rule still applies that the more light you have to work with, the better the image you can capture on video. More light gives you more control over your exposure, focus, and **depth-of-field**, and the flexibility to shoot with more filters. A good exposure is absolutely essential to controlling your images. A properly exposed image should clearly show visual details in the scene. Notice how the details of the trees, the model's face, and fountain below are lost to bad exposure.

Underexposed   Good Exposure   Overexposed

Aperture and F-Stops

Apart from the amount of light in the scene, your image's exposure is controlled by turning the camera's **aperture ring**, which controls the amount of light coming into the camera lens. This determines the brightness or darkness of the image. (Some prosumer cameras use a dial wheel instead of an aperture ring, but the rules of exposure apply the same.)

The lens exposure is measured in units called **f-stops**. F-stops go in increments ranging from F1.2 to F22 with most video cameras covering roughly the F2 to F16 range. Here's all I've ever *really* needed to know about f-stops and exposure. Adjusting to lower f-stops is called **opening up the lens** and adjusting the lens to higher f-stops is called **stopping down or closing down the lens**. The lower the f-stop the brighter the picture. The higher the f-stop the darker the image. That's it. (See also, "Hot Tip: Shallow Depth-of-Field," on page 175.)

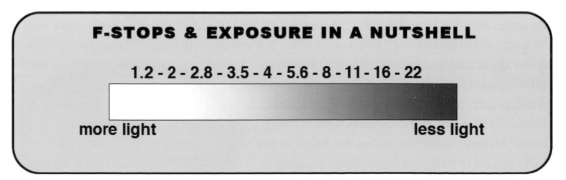

F-STOPS & EXPOSURE IN A NUTSHELL

1.2 - 2 - 2.8 - 3.5 - 4 - 5.6 - 8 - 11 - 16 - 22

more light   less light

F-Stops & Exposure in a Nutshell

Your Friend the Zebra Stripes

Zebra stripes is a camera function that helps you with exposure by superimposing vibrating diagonal stripes on the overexposed parts of the image. *These stripes are only seen on your camera's viewfinder or LCD screen.* Zebra stripes are *not* recorded to tape. Look for a switch or check your camera's menu for a "zebra" function. Set the zebra stripes function to 100%.

Now, whenever you point the camera at something that's *more* than 100% of the acceptable video level (i.e., overexposed), you'll know without guessing. These **blown out** areas of the video will not show any image details, just bright white. Once the details of the overexposed area are lost, they can't be "tweaked back in" during post-production. You don't want to close down the lens to get rid of all of the zebra stripes in the image. There should usually be *some* zebra stripes on the natural highlights in the image such as lamps, jewelry, the sun, shiny objects, etc. Where you *don't* want to have a significant number of zebra stripes is on your subject's face or important details in the frame. If there are zebra stripes on your subject(s) face or on important details of the image, try these remedies: (1) stop down your lens, (2) use an ND filter (or a graduated filter for an overexposed sky), (3) recompose the shot to include less of the overexposed area, or (4) apply powder make-up on shiny faces. (See "Hot Tip: Easy Powder Makeup," page 191).

When in doubt, always get a good exposure on a subject's face.

Using Gain to Boost Exposure

There are two types of **gain** in digital video: sound and video. Gain just refers to digitally boosting the light or sound levels. Both are measured in units called decibels or **dB**. If your image is still too dark after fully opening up your lens, you should turn on your camera's gain function. This will electronically brighten the image, often dramatically. The unfortunate side effect of using gain is video **noise** or static. *The higher you turn up the gain, the grainier your picture will appear.* Your image quality begins to look more like a VHS dub than DV. This is especially noticeable in the blacks and darker colors in the image. In situations such as shooting night exteriors, night clubs or **surveillance video**, you really won't have much choice. Remember, it's always better to get a grainy image than *no* image at all. It's best to add more light if possible, before using the camera's gain. However, this is not always desirable when doing doc work as it may make people more self-conscious and guarded than the low-key natural lighting. Use your own judgment.

> ✔ Use zebra stripes to help judge exposure. Use gain if you need more light, but beware of video "noise."

COLOR TEMPERATURE

Color Temperature Basics (Very Basic)

All light has a color temperature. Color temperature affects what color that light will look like on video. Sunlight, fluorescent lights, and light from **incandescent** bulbs (a.k.a. **tungsten**), all appear as different colors on camera, because they all have different color temperatures.

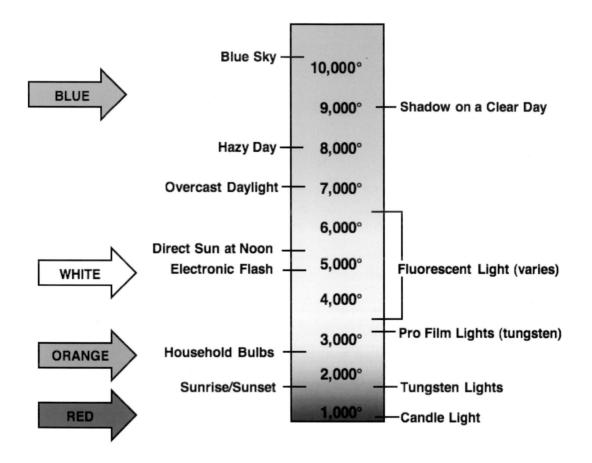

BLUE →	
Blue Sky — 10,000°	
	9,000° — Shadow on a Clear Day
Hazy Day — 8,000°	
Overcast Daylight — 7,000°	
	6,000°
Direct Sun at Noon —	
WHITE → Electronic Flash — 5,000°	Fluorescent Light (varies)
	4,000°
	3,000° — Pro Film Lights (tungsten)
ORANGE → Household Bulbs —	
	2,000°
Sunrise/Sunset —	— Tungsten Lights
RED →	1,000° — Candle Light

Bad   **Good**

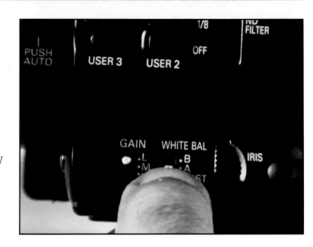

Your camera's white balance function compensates for the variations in color temperature by making the dominant colored light appear as normal white light regardless of its true color. When a camera has not been properly white-balanced, sunlit scenes look hideously blue or indoor scenes look horribly orange. Most cameras have built-in preset functions for daylight and indoor white balance and fairly reliable auto-white balance (AWB) functions. Use these presets or auto if you like the look, but if you want to shoot like the pros, there's only one way to go baby . . . manual.

When to White Balance

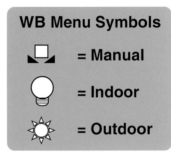

You should always white balance anytime the lighting condition changes, such as the sun is lower in the sky or you turned on some overhead florescent lights. If you even *think* the lighting conditions may have changed, you should re-white-balance just to be sure. Remember to white balance *before* adding gels to your lights or your white balance will not be correct. You should use pure **white cards** or standard bright white paper for normal white balancing. (A crisp white T-shirt will also do in a pinch.) Avoid using off-white and cream-colored paper to white balance.

WB Menu Symbols

= Manual

= Indoor

= Outdoor

White Balance Special Effects

White-balancing on colored cards will produce different looks. The cooler the color you white-balance to, the warmer the look and vice versa. (See Camera Cheat Sheet and Warm Cards in the Crazy Phat Bonus Pages on the Bonus DVD at the back of this book.) Unless you're sure you like the look, it's better to do color effects in *editing*, because you're pretty much stuck with that look once you white balance and it's nearly impossible to restore a normal white balance after the fact.

Mixed Sun and Indoor Lighting

When shooting in mixed lighting sources you can white-balance normally to split the difference or you can gel either light source to match the other. Color temperature orange (CTO) gels are used to make daylight appear as indoor (tungsten) light. Color temperature blue (CTB) gels are used to make indoor light appear the same color temperature as daylight. (See "Down and Dirty DV Gel Guide" on page 108.)

SHUTTER SPEED BASICS

Shutter speed is another reference that comes from the world of still photography where cameras actually have a little shutter or door that opens and closes in a fraction of a second to expose each frame of film to light. A shutter speed of 1/60 means the shutter is open for one sixtieth of a second. Slower shutter speeds keep the shutter open longer. Faster shutter speeds keep the shutter open for less time. Most normal video shooting is done at 1/60, unless you want a special motion effect or will be doing freeze-frame or slow motion in post-production. However, it's also common for shooters to also use normal shutter speeds of 1/48, 1/30, and 1/24 for a more desirable look without causing excessive blur. In video "shutters" are electronic, but the principles of the concept all operate the same.

PRINCIPLE #1 The longer the shutter stays open, the more motion is captured in the frame, the more an object moving on-screen will be *blurred*.

PRINCIPLE #2 The longer the shutter stays open, the more light the frame is exposed to, which means the *brighter* the picture will be.

Motion and Shutter Speed

Remember to adjust your exposure after changing shutter speeds since your exposure will be noticeably different. Although shutter speed also affects exposure and depth-of-field, its primary use is to control how motion is portrayed in each frame of video . . . sharp or blurry. This comes into play if you intend to freeze-frame or slow down a shot later.

Fast-action sports such as hockey and tennis are frequently captured at higher shutter speeds so that slow motion and freeze-frames of the action look sharp and clear. The downside of using higher shutter speeds is that they can also cause a flickering strobe-like effect on the moving video. Sometimes filmmakers intentionally use a high shutter speed to portray a comic, surreal, or horror scene. Similarly, using slower shutter speeds such as 1/4 is useful for creating a surreal, flashback, or hallucinogenic effect. With a very slow shutter speed all of your motion and colors will trail and swirl across the screen when the camera is moved . . . groovy, man.

✔ Normal video is usually shot at a 1/60 shutter speed. Use higher speeds for freeze-frames or slo mo in post.

SHUTTER SPEED AND MOVEMENT

Normal Shutter Speed — 1/60

- Used for most normal shooting
- Appears the way human eye sees
- Slightly blurred movement

High Shutter Speed — 1/1000

- Used for slow mo and freeze FX in post
- Used for fast action sports
- Gives normal footage a surreal feel
- Moving object sharp on paused footage
- Let's less light in lens

Slow Shutter Speed — 1/15

- Creates a dream or hallucinogenic feel
- At a speed of 1/4, motion creates long trails
- Considerable blurring of movement
- Lets more light in lens

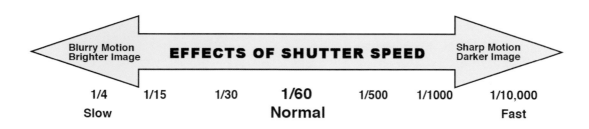

Blurry Motion Brighter Image

EFFECTS OF SHUTTER SPEED

Sharp Motion Darker Image

1/4	1/15	1/30	1/60	1/500	1/1000	1/10,000
Slow			Normal			Fast

CREATING A "FILM LOOK"

1 SHOOT WITH A 24P CAMERA

This is probably the single easiest thing you could do to get that elusive film look. Basically these cameras shoot video at 24 frames per second (fps) or electronically mimic 24 fps, which is the same speed that film runs. (Normal video is shot at 30 fps.) Those few extra frames can make all the difference in the world. 24P prosumer cameras are very capable of delivering a great film look right out of the box when set in their 24P modes. Better yet, you can go 24P *and* HD with the newest generation of HDV cameras.

2 USE FILM LOOK SOFTWARE IN POST

Few things have done as much for the world of DV as software programs such as **Magic Bullet**, which is a plug-in for After Effects that allows you to apply different video filters in post that mimic various film stocks and development processes. There are other programs out there as well, such as Tiffen's DFX Digital Filter Suite.

3 LIGHT IT LIKE FILM

Just because a camera is capable of shooting in low light does not mean that it shoots the *best images* in low light. A BIG part of the reason film looks better than video is the lighting. Avoid low-light situations when possible and use professional lighting gear for controlled setups.

4 USE FILTERS

Here is another cinematographer's secret: There is an entire arsenal of filters that can enhance the look of your DV footage to appear more like those beautiful frames of film. The most common are 1/4 and 1/2 Black Pro Mist Filters, Warming/Enhancing Filters, Graduated Filters, and Fog FX Filters. (You can find more info on filters and their use at Tiffen.com.)

5 SHOOT WITH A TELEPHOTO LENS OR USE A 35 MM ADAPTER

You can rent or buy special adapters that will allow you to use professional 35 mm lens (as in the *same* lens used for 35 mm film) on your camera. These lens offer much greater depth of field (d.o.f) than the standard prosumer video lens. Beautiful crisp professional lens and greater d.o.f. translates into a more filmic look.

35 mm Lens Adapter

MANUAL VS. AUTO FUNCTIONS

Use Manual Controls

A primary difference between pro and amateur shooters is that the pros know how to *manually* control their camera image and many amateurs simply let the camera decide how the shot should look and sound by relying heavily on the camera's auto controls. The hectic and unpredictable nature of documentary shooting makes it tempting to just shoot everything in full auto mode.

The problem is that many of the auto functions on DV cameras are unreliable. Think of it as driving around the city with your car's cruise control turned on . . . it's great until you zip past a police car above the speed limit. The cruise control doesn't know (or care) that you're going to get a speeding ticket. It only works well in the most *ideal* setting–open road with no traffic lights or change in traffic or speed limit. The same is true with most camera auto functions. As soon as anything outside of the ideal recording conditions happens, they become much less reliable.

Your camera isn't nearly as competent as you are. (Or will become by the end of this book.) Don't rely blindly on autofocus, auto-sound levels, or auto-iris. Take the time to learn and understand how to manually control the most important aspects of your video. The buttons and features will vary from camera to camera, but the principles of focus, exposure, and sound will always operate the same.

> ✔ *For professional results, use manual controls. Camera auto functions are often unreliable.*

AUTO FUNCTION DYSFUNCTIONS		
AUTO FUNCTION	**MOST LIKELY TO FAIL WHEN**	**MOST USEFUL WHEN**
Autofocus	■ A person, car, or object crosses in front of your subject ■ Lighting is low ■ Objects are in the foreground (leaves, mic stand, crowd, etc.)	■ You have an inexperienced operator on camera ■ You are having difficulty seeing the viewfinder ■ You are legally blind
Auto-iris	■ A bright object is in frame ■ A scene is backlit ■ There is snow on the ground	■ You are shooting "run and gun" ■ Lighting conditions change frequently or unpredictably
Auto Gain Control (AGC) Sound	■ An audience claps or laughs ■ Naturally sharp/loud sounds (gunshot, subway, scream, etc.) ■ There are silent gaps in sound	■ The sound level does not fluctuate much ■ You are solo in a "run and gun" situation ■ You don't have headphones

WHEN TO USE AUTO FUNCTIONS

Auto Zoom vs. Manual Zoom

One thing most DV cameras *will* do better than you is zoom. The servos (zoom lens motors) on most of the DV cameras made in recent years are pressure-sensitive and capable of very smooth and controlled moves. This is also practical because you will often have to zoom to adjust your frame and manually refocus at the same time.

Surprises and Panics

At some point in production a fleeting moment may come that you need to capture right that second. A protester in the crowd behind you may unfurl a controversial banner. The elusive and rare white leopard is about to pounce on his prey from a tree . . . whatever. Do whatever you gotta do to grab that image. Don't waste time screwing around with menu screens and white-balancing. Just get the shot, man! Your sharp manual focus and perfect white balance mean nothing if the protester has already been dragged away by police or the white leopard has already killed the antelope and made off with the carcass. (In that case, you may as well *be* the protester or the antelope because you blew it.)

If you totally panic or have a brain fart in the moment, it's okay. Just quickly switch the camera into auto-lock or full auto mode. (That's auto-*everything*.) You will most likely still get a pretty decent image and sound. It will be just like using a consumer camcorder. Better to go full auto and sacrifice some image and sound control than to have unusable footage because you forgot to adjust the sound level or re-white-balance the camera. Don't sweat it. Using manual controls will become second nature with practice. Just remember, getting the shot is always numero uno.

Run-and-Gun Shooting

Run-and-gun shooting is when you are on the go and things are happening so quickly or under such confusion that there isn't ample time or calm to concentrate on all the technical details you need to consider. This includes situations such as covering unfolding violence like a riot or shooting in the crowd of a loud rowdy nightclub. Similarly, it may be wise to go with auto functions when covering a short or

sudden event where a lot of action is happening all at once and you need to get full coverage before it all ends. Lastly, anytime you are shooting with unfamiliar equipment, pulling off a tricky camera move, or all by yourself as director, cameraperson, sound recordist, and/or interviewer is also an acceptable time to farm out some of those duties to the auto functions.

Rely on auto-functions when executing tricky camera moves.

✔ *Getting usable shots is numero uno. Use auto functions if necessary to simplify run-and-gun shooting.*

CAPTURING TRUTH

ALBERT MAYSLES — DIRECTOR/DP
(Grey Gardens, Gimme Shelter, Salesman, Lalee's Kin, etc.)

Photo Credit: Kendall Messick

As I see it, and many a documentary filmmaker doesn't live by this creed, I think that we have a great deal of responsibility to set the record straight. To end up with something that's totally authentic, and we turn away from that responsibility when we pre-judge people, when we start out with a particular point of view, which we are determined to support even though it may not be supportable with reality, with fact.

We have a responsibility to tell the truth, and we have the means to do so with a video camera that doesn't run out of tape after ten minutes as with film, a video camera that is not so big and bulky as to scare people. We can do a very decent job of getting the viewer to feel that they are there themselves, even though they weren't present when all of this stuff was going on.

The responsibility is an ethical one: Tell the truth. And sometimes that truth can be extremely hurtful, and you don't want to do that. But at the same time, you don't want to be so protective that what is in the heart and mind of that person that you're filming doesn't get a chance to express itself because you were so overly protective. So the course in the middle is, with a feeling of responsibility, to get material that may be even somewhat embarrassing, but nevertheless, it's something that the person being filmed would feel, "Well, it's embarrassing but I want it to be recorded. I want people to know the tough part of my life as well as some of the better, more satisfying elements."

People would much rather open their minds and hearts to the camera than to keep a secret, that's just human nature. And I think we have an enormous advantage in filming people when we consider that they would prefer to connect in an open fashion with the camera. Now, that doesn't work if the person doesn't trust [the person] who is filming . . . The person filming must be of the kind who takes the responsibility to tell the truth, to care for the person that they're filming through a process of empathy. Without that empathy, there's no poetry. There's no beauty. There's no emotion that is going to come out on the screen.

Adjusting Your Shot

Avoid changing or adjusting your shot while your subject is speaking. The two primary exceptions to this are to refocus a soft-focused shot or to do a **dramatic zoom-in** for emphasis. Other than that, try to make all other shot changes and framing adjustments during the interviewer's question or a pause in the action since these moments can more easily be edited out. Try to make adjustments to your shot as subtle and smooth as possible.

Using the "Digital Zoom" Function

Most DV cameras are capable of "digital zooming" beyond what the lens is optically capable of. Be *very* wary of this function. Despite it's slick sounding name, there's not much desirable about digital zooming. Similar to DV camera's video gain function, digital zooming is the electronic magnification of the image to give the *illusion* of zooming in farther. (Unfortunately, it's a crappy illusion that doesn't fool the eye.)

✔ *Try to adjust shots during a pause in the action, so bad moves can be easily edited out.*

Because it's an electronic effect, the more you zoom in using your digital zoom, the more **noise** or video "static" you will introduce into the image. Unless you are shooting surveillance video or in a situation that is too dangerous or impossible to get the camera closer, digital zooming is strictly for amateurs. Leave it off.

Remember, the more compelling the action on the screen, the more forgiving your audience will be of video noise or poor image quality. The audience will accept grainy dark images of rebels in a shoot out or blurry stop-motion videos of bank robbers in action, but they won't forgive grainy degraded images of mundane scenes.

✔ *The digital zoom function makes video look like crap. Use it only when your subject is too dangerous or you absolutely can't move closer.*

HANDHELD SECRETS OF THE PROS

Forget the Tripod and Go Handheld

Handheld shots can add some real energy and a more subjective point of view to a scene when tripods aren't practical or desirable. The basic technique is simple, but it takes practice to master. You can also use a camera stabilizer such as a Steadicam Jr. or Glidecam (pictured bottom right), which takes even more practice. There are several important things to consider if you want to shoot handheld like the big girls and boys.

How to Shoot Handheld

1. **Brace your camera elbow against your body. Use your free hand to steady your camera hand or to steady the camera by gripping the lens.**
2. **Keep your lens zoomed out to it's widest setting.**
3. **Assume comfortable footing and lower your center of gravity slightly as you twist left or right to follow the action.**
4. **Avoid zooming. Move in closer or farther away to adjust your frame.**

Handheld Editing Considerations

Handheld shots often won't intercut well with tripod shots *in the same scene*—it's like stepping on a boat, then back on the dock, then back in a boat—the audience will accept either shot, but the two probably won't match smoothly. The steadier the camerawork, the more likely you can juxtapose shots in editing.

Motivation and Style

Handheld footage should be a *motivated* stylistic choice that fits with the subject matter. Look at other documentaries and try to analyze when and why they go handheld and what effect it has on the viewer. Is it all handheld or just some scenes? Is the camera movement helping to tell the story? How does it affect viewpoint? Ask yourself these important questions *before* you go handheld.

HANDHELD CAMERA POSITIUNS

Standard

- Elbows braced against body
- Slightly bent knees
- Best all-purpose handheld position

High Angle

- Arms extended overhead
- LCD screen angled down 45°
- Use to shoot over crowds/obstacles

Low Angle

- Hold camera near ground
- Walk smoothly with bent knees
- Mostly for POV and following shots

Cradle

- Cam at waist level with braced elbows
- Ideal for long handheld takes
- Good for "roving" high-energy shots

Introduction

When you need a steady image such as zooming in to shoot something far away or you're doing an interview, put that camera on some "**sticks**" and join the Rock Steady Crew. Smooth pans and tilts and nice even zooms are best accomplished with a good professional-quality tripod. Be warned if you're serious about this DV thing and you're buying a tripod: Cheap consumer-level tripods are far more trouble than they're worth. They simply won't do the job and you'll eventually end up spending more to buy a professional-quality tripod or suffer through one botched camera move after another.

What to Look for in a Tripod

1. **Weight Capacity:** Make sure your tripod is rated to handle your camera's weight.
2. **Fluid Head:** Any tripod that you shoot with should have a "fluid head." Fluid head tripods are made just for film/video work. They are more expensive, but necessary and worth it to pull off smooth professional-quality camerawork. (If you *prefer* whack amateur moves just stick with the rickety plastic consumer models.)
3. **Pan and Tilt Tension Knobs:** Another feature to look for in a professional-quality tripod are knobs to adjust the pan and tilt tension, which will allow you to adjust the tripod to move as fast or slow as you like up and down and left and right.
4. **Quick Release Plate:** A good tripod head will have a quick release plate that will stay attached to the camera during shooting. This will allow you to easily remove and replace the camera on the tripod whenever you need to quickly go handheld or move the camera. This item is a *must* for unpredictable documentary production.

General Tripod Tips

When performing camera moves, be careful not to end up in an awkward yoga-like position. Always start in the least comfortable position, then end in the most comfortable position. Also, don't use your pan or tilt tension knobs to **lock down** shots. Don't use your pan or tilt locks to adjust tripod tension. Doing either will eventually shorten the life of your tripod. If your tripod has one, use the spirit bubble (a.k.a. "level bubble") to make sure you are even with the horizon, but when pressed for time, just check your frame line against the horizon line.

Record Pre-Roll and End-Roll for Each Shot

DV cameras don't just go from stop to record instantly when you hit the record button. It takes your camera a few seconds to get up to recording speed, so allow yourself proper room for editing by padding the start of each take by a few seconds. (Even a Porsche takes a few seconds to get up to speed!) On DV cameras this is called **pre-roll**.

When the record button is hit on most cameras, the record indicator (typically a red light or the letters REC) will appear on-screen as white or flashing text then turn to red or nonflashing text once the camera has reached **speed**. This is the point at which the camera actually begins recording a stable image.

Likewise, you want to allow a few seconds of **end-roll** on each take. Otherwise, you may find yourself cursing in the edit room because you inadvertently cut off the end of a great moment or line. Remember, edit decks, just like cameras, require a certain amount of pre-roll to get up to speed. Padding the start and end of each shot will also make editing considerably less painless, since you will be able to avoid the time code errors that are common with footage shot without any pre- or end-roll. (See also "Time Code and DV Tapes" on page 226.)

> ✔ *Record a few extra seconds at the start and end of each shot to reduce time code problems when editing.*

Filmmaking has its own language and scripts. Film crews have a dialogue to get each new camera **take** up and running. This little script allows filmmakers to ensure that everyone and everything is ready and rolling when the action starts.

PRODUCER/DIRECTOR	TRANSLATION	CREW ACTION	CREW SAYS
1. "LIGHTS!"	Turn on all video lights.	**Gaffer:** "Striking!"	**Gaffer:** Turns on all set lights.
2. "ROLL SOUND!" (when using *separate* sound recording system, otherwise just check that sound op is ready)	Start recording sound.	**Sound:** Starts recording and waits for pre-roll. **Sound:** When the sound device indicates full recording speed.	**Sound:** "Rolling!" **Sound:** "Speed!"
3. "ROLL CAMERA!"	Start recording picture.	**Camera:** Starts recording. **Camera:** Waits for record light to finish blinking to indicate full tape speed.	**Camera:** "Rolling!" **Camera:** "Speed!"
4. "SLATE!"	Put the slate in front of the camera.	**P.A.:** Holds the slate open with shot information. **Camera:** Focuses on slate, if necessary.	**Camera:** "Focused" or **Camera:** "Clap It."
5. "MARK IT!" (Most necessary when using separate sound recording system *or* multiple cameras)	Record the slate text and clap.	**P.A.:** Claps slate, then pulls it out when cued. **Camera:** Resets or refocuses the shot.	**Camera:** "Got it." or "Clear Slate." **Camera:** "Set"
6. "ACTION!"	We're starting.	**Prod./Dir:** Cues talent to start.	

Why You Should Use Color Bars

It's a good practice, and especially important if you are shooting for broadcast, to try to record a minute of color bars at the beginning of each tape. Color bars are the multicolored patterns generated by video equipment that help ensure that your video colors are accurate from one monitor to the next. By recording the color bar pattern at the top of your footage you now have a *standard reference point* that will allow you to more accurately adjust the color on various monitors to look exactly as you intended it to when you recorded it.

Although many of the prosumer DV cameras don't have true professional **SMPTE** color bars (pictured at the end of the section) which are the most accurate and useful, the simple straight-lined color bars found on these cameras are still better than none and will help you judge hue, brightness, and saturation. If you forget to record color bars during production, it's no big deal. Just record them at the end of the tape.

How to Adjust NTSC Color Bars

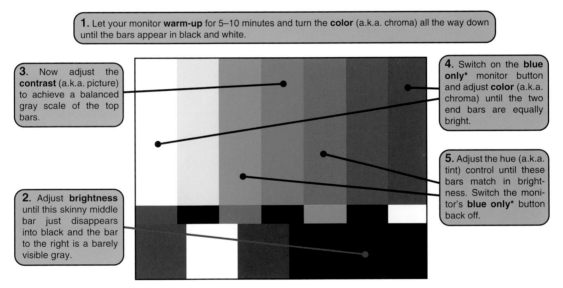

1. Let your monitor **warm-up** for 5–10 minutes and turn the **color** (a.k.a. chroma) all the way down until the bars appear in black and white.

3. Now adjust the **contrast** (a.k.a. picture) to achieve a balanced gray scale of the top bars.

4. Switch on the **blue only*** monitor button and adjust **color** (a.k.a. chroma) until the two end bars are equally bright.

5. Adjust the hue (a.k.a. tint) control until these bars match in brightness. Switch the monitor's **blue only*** button back off.

2. Adjust **brightness** until this skinny middle bar just disappears into black and the bar to the right is a barely visible gray.

*If you are using a TV or a monitor without a "blue only" feature another alternative is to (A) cover your screen with a blue gel or (B) adjust the color (chroma) level until the colors no longer "bleed" into each other, then adjust the hue (tint) level until the yellow bar is lemon yellow, not orange or green, and the magenta bar looks correct, not red or purple.

✔ *Record a minute of color bars at the top of each tape. Use color bars to adjust monitors when screening footage.*

Pre-Labeling Blank Tapes

Before your shoot, you also want to take a little time to pre-label and organize your blank tapes. Once the action is unfolding this little task can easily be screwed up or left undone. This is especially important if you have multiple cameras and shooters. Each camera should have a separate set of pre-labeled blank tapes and each tape should have its own unique number and label that identifies the program, sequence title, and other info that will help with post-production.

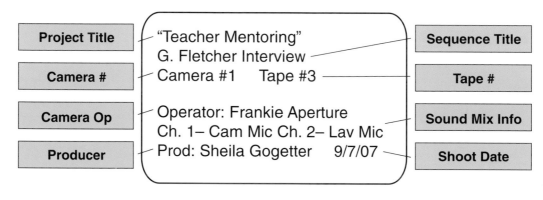

Project Title	"Teacher Mentoring"	Sequence Title
Camera #	G. Fletcher Interview Camera #1 Tape #3	Tape #
Camera Op	Operator: Frankie Aperture Ch. 1– Cam Mic Ch. 2– Lav Mic	Sound Mix Info
Producer	Prod: Sheila Gogetter 9/7/07	Shoot Date

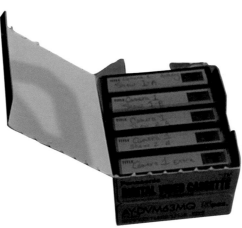

Fill in as much of this information as you know ahead of time, then fill in the blanks while shooting. Pre-labeling tapes is one of many little things that can save you a whole lot of headaches and frustrations in post-production. If you just take a *few minutes* beforehand and organize your tapes, you may save *hours* of frustration scanning tapes trying to locate a particular piece of footage or figuring out which sound channel to use for every clip. Even if you don't get to do this beforehand, label your tapes as soon as possible after you eject them.

Record Tabs

Equally important, remember to switch the little record tab on the spine of the DV tape to the "save" position immediately, so you don't end up accidentally recording over footage you already shot, which is an unforgivable sin on any film set.

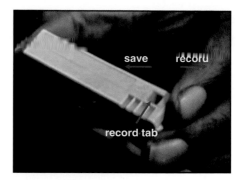

✔ Pre-label your blank tapes with important info. Don't forget to switch record tabs to save immediately after you eject.

CLEANING YOUR LENS

Lens Cleaning Kit:

1. Lens tissue
2. Liquid lens cleaner
3. Blow bulb/brush
4. Optical lens cleaning cloth (optional for dry wiping)

If the hallmark of a pro shooter is a sharp focused picture, the first hallmark of a crisp picture is a clean lens. This is one of those lessons that might still escape you well after you've learned and adopted many of the other professional practices in this book. It will escape you that is, until the day it comes roaring back to bite you on the butt. (Do I sound like a man with experience here?) It's very easy to get caught up in the heat of the moment and not notice or completely forget about regularly checking and cleaning the camera lens, especially when shooting solo.

The dangerous thing about not developing a lens cleaning habit early is that often a dirty lens won't really show up in your footage depending on your lighting, camera angle, and focal length. But whenever the sun or a light shines in the lens, from the right angle—at just the right focal length—a thousand little specks of lint, fiber, fingerprints, and smudges will magically appear in front of your image then disappear again as soon as you change the camera angle or focal length.

So, even if you're looking for dirt, 90% of the time it won't be visible on the LCD screen. Your viewfinder and flip-out LCD screen are just too small and have too low a resolution to catch these tiny details. You have to check the *surface of the lens* itself. (**Note**: Never use Windex, tissues, toilet paper, paper towels, shirt sleeves, etc., to clean a camera lens unless you're actually *trying* to scratch your lens.)

Remove dust using a lens brush/blow bulb.

Lightly moisten wad of lens tissue with lens fluid.

Wipe gently in small circular motions.

Follow with a dry lens tissue to wipe smears.

CHAPTER 4
LIGHTING

Electricity Considerations

Be careful not to overload the electrical circuits on location. (See *How Not to Blow a Circuit*) Check the circuit box before you begin plugging in lights to see which outlets are on which circuits. Kitchens are usually on their own circuit. You should also be aware that outlets on opposite sides of the same wall will often be on the *same* circuit.

If the circuit box is not clearly labeled, a surefire way to check which outlet is on which circuit is to plug a regular household lamp in an outlet and click the circuit breakers on and off. Label the circuit breaker switches as you identify the room(s) they control. If you overload a circuit later, this will make it easy to reset it. If you are shooting in an older location with a fuse box instead of a circuit breaker, make sure you have extra fuses on hand or you may find your entire shoot shut down for lack of a $2.00 part.

✔ Match outlets to circuits and be prepared to reset a tripped circuit breaker or blown fuse if you overload.

Safety Considerations

The most hazardous thing you will encounter on most sets are lights. Professional lighting instruments generally get very hot very fast. Apart from burning careless bare fingers on a regular basis, lights can and do start fires when mishandled. A fire can easily start if lights are placed too close to curtains, ceilings, or anything else flammable. Serious fire hazards can also arise if electrical circuits are overloaded. Not to mention the possibility of exploding bulbs, electrocution, or falling light instruments whenever simple safety measures are ignored.

Just like crossing the street, driving, or handling power tools, lighting *can* be very dangerous. However, by taking some basic precautions and treating lights and electricity with full respect, you can greatly reduce the risks of burning someone's home or business to the ground. Be careful and make safety a primary concern on set and you'll have few worries apart from getting your shot.

✔ Lights can be very dangerous. Proper handling and safety should always be your primary concern.

LIGHTING SAFETY TIP SHEET

Listen up people. This is another one of those bull horn moments:

> *You can't be down and dirty with safety when the potential consequences are serious injury, fire, or an expensive morale-busting disaster.*

Following these safety guidelines will help you avoid most of the worst-case scenarios:

• Use heavy-duty extension cords

Use only heavy-duty extension cords. Check to make sure that the gauge or cable thickness will handle the full number of amps you run through it. (See "Extension Cord Loads" below.) Gauge can usually be found on the extension cord itself and wattage can be found on your light or light bulb base.

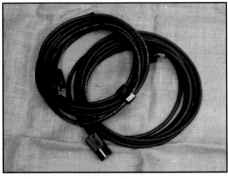

Heavy Duty

• Use gloves to handle hot lights

Film lights get very hot very fast. Go to the hardware store to pick up some inexpensive electrical or work gloves for adjusting hot barn doors and light instruments.

Use Gloves

EXTENSION CORD LOADS		
Gauge*	Length	Will Handle
12	50–100 ft.	10–15 amps
14	up to 50 ft.	10–15 amps
16	up to 100 ft.	10 amps

*It's tricky! The **lower** the gauge number the **more** power the cord will handle.

• Use sandbags to steady lights

Always use sandbags to secure light stands from careless crew members, wind, kids, or anything else that might accidentally walk into or knock over a light.

Hold It Down

• Screen open-faced lights

Make sure open-faced lights such as Omni or Arri Lights have protective screens or full **scrims** covering them to prevent hot shards of glass from scattering across the set if a bulb explodes.

Use Screens

• Stay clear of flammables

Never place a light instrument close to anything flammable or anything that may be damaged by heat, especially curtains, ceilings, and furniture.

Stay Clear!

• Be careful moving hot lights

Turn off lights whenever you aren't shooting or adjusting your lighting. Avoid moving lights when they are turned on. Your bulb **filament** is more likely to break or blow out when it's hot and jostled around. Similarly, be gentle with **spot** and **flood** controls. Any sudden jerk or bump to a hot light could cause a blow-out and cost you a good 15 to 20 minutes of time waiting for the light to cool down and the bulb to be changed. (Also keep in mind that quartz bulbs cost more than $25 each, even for small light units!) Always bring spare bulbs or back-up light gear to a shoot.

Be Gentle!

• Make sure lights are secure

Always double check to make sure that your lights are securely tightened to their stands. A loosely mounted light can easily fall off its stand or swing out of place.

Tight!

• Never operate lights in the rain

If a storm or sudden drizzle catches you off guard, immediately cut off power to your lights, unplug them, and get them out of the rain. DO NOT plug in or use again until *completely* dry. Dry off wet lights as soon as possible to avoid rusting. (A hairdryer is useful for quickly drying out wet gear.)

Dry

• Never touch a quartz bulb

The oil from your skin can dramatically shorten the life of these very expensive bulbs or even cause them to explode in rare cases. Handle bulbs carefully using the protective foam wrapper normally found with the new bulb, gloves, tissue . . . anything, but your bare fingers. Inspect quartz bulbs for telltale bubbles caused by fingerprints or broken porcelain connectors (both pictured right).

Bubble = Trouble

By dividing your total light wattage by the voltage of the electrical outlets you can calculate how many amps of electricity you will need to power your lights and tell whether you're likely to blow a circuit or fuse. Here's the formula:

Watts ÷ Volts = Amps

Most modern houses in the United States have 15 or 20 amp circuits. Check the circuit breaker or fuse box to see what you're dealing with on your location. Voltage in the United States ranges from 110–120 volts. However, rounding the voltage down to 100 makes it much easier for people who suck at math (like me) and, more important, it leaves a comfortable margin of safety when calculating the above formula. Let's run through two examples:

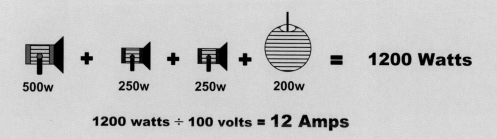

500w + 250w + 250w + 200w = **1200 Watts**

1200 watts ÷ 100 volts = 12 Amps

Conclusion: In this case the total wattage of all lights adds up to less than 15 amps, so we're good to go with room to add up to another 300 watts of lighting on a 15 amp circuit or up to 800 more watts on a 20 amp circuit. (Don't forget to account for any *other* electrical appliances apart from lights that may be plugged into the same circuit, because they are draining precious juice too.)

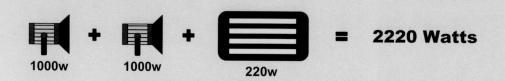

1000w + 1000w + 220w = **2220 Watts**

2220 watts ÷ 100 volts = 22.2 Amps

Conclusion: This would be too many lights, or more correctly, too much *power* to plug into a room with a 20 amp circuit. The solution here would be to plug one of the 1000 watt lights into a heavy-duty extension cord plugged into a different circuit in another room, so that the electrical load on all circuits stayed comfortably under our 20 amp limit.

Fresnel Light 	These lights have a focusable glass lens. The light beam can be focused into a spotted (narrow) or flooded (broader) beam. Mole-Richardson brand Inkie, Baby, and Baby Junior are all examples of Fresnel lights.
Open-Face Light 	These are lights that don't have a glass lens in the front. Instead they have open-faced reflectors. You always want to have a screen or scrim in front of an open-faced light in case the bulb breaks. Examples of open-faced lights include Lowel's Omni and Tota lights.
China Ball 	These are simply your standard, inexpensive, paper Chinese lanterns. They sell for $5.00–30.00, depending on the size you want. You can pick them up at any lighting store. These lights are highly portable since they weigh next to nothing and collapse flat. They create beautiful soft light for interviews using nothing more than a standard household light bulb and a socket unit. These are an indispensable tool for doc guerrillas. Get some.
Fluorescent Light 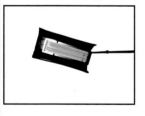	Fluorescent lights, also commonly referred to as **Kino Flo**s, after the most popular brand, are relatively lightweight and cast lots of soft even light. Best of all for guerrillas, they require much less electricity than tungsten lights. You can experiment with homemade fluorescent setups of your own, but beware of potential flicker issues with household fluorescents. (**Note**: Fluorescents won't work properly on an external dimmer.)
Practical Light 	This just refers to any location light fixture that is seen on-camera. Desk lamps, halogen floor lights, track lights, etc., all make excellent practical lights. A practical light can serve as your key, fill, hair, or background light depending on its position and brightness. If you can dim the light, aim it, or swap out different wattage bulbs, it's even more "practical." Using existing lighting should always be the first option you consider for lighting docs since it's natural and requires little or no extra setup time. Experiment with white balance, reflectors, diffusion gel, and different types of bulbs to get a more desirable look.

"El Cheapo" Light 	This is just my own terminology for any type of standard household or utility light that is used for filmmaking purposes. This category would include standard halogen lights, work lights, fluorescents, or novelty lights that are put to use for video production. These are hit or miss. Look around your apartment or hit your local lighting store to experiment with different accessories. (Refer to the previous entry Practical Lights.)
Barn Doors 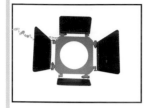	Barn doors are used to control light. And that's the name of the game . . . *light control*. The simple act of turning on a light is not lighting any more than hitting the record button can be called filmmaking. If you are not in *control* of your lights, you're not light-*ing*. You must use barn doors and other accessories such as **blackwrap** (see the next page) to make sure your light goes exactly where you want it and nowhere else.
Reflector Umbrella 	This nifty device mounts onto the front of an open-faced light instrument (to cast a much softer, broad, and evenly diffused light. Reflector umbrellas work great to create **fill light**. They can also be used to form a soft key light. If you want to impress clients for a paid gig, reflector umbrellas are also great for making things look and feel "Hollywood" for them.
Extension Cords 	Get as many heavy-duty extension cords as you can get your hands on. At least one for every light. Standard skinny household extension cords won't cut it. The lower the gauge number on the cord, the more power it can handle safely. Extension cords are necessary to run lights to different circuits of your location, which are usually going to be in different rooms. (See "Extension Cord Loads" chart on page 95.)
Dimmer 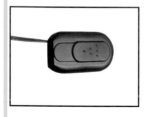	This is one of the most valuable lighting accessories that you can have in your guerrilla kit. A dimmer will allow you to quickly and easily adjust the intensity of any light you plug into it, which will save you immeasurable time moving lights, adjusting scrims, and fussing with **ND gels**. If using household dimmers, make sure that any lights you use don't exceed the maximum wattage listed on the dimmer. (**Note:** Always **white balance** your camera *after* you dim a key light since dimming lights may affect light color temperature.)
Gels 	Gels, which affix to barn doors using clothespins, are another indispensable accessory. At the very least you want to have color temperature blue (**CTB**) and color temperature orange (**CTO**) gels to allow your lighting to mimic daylight or indoor light color temperatures in mixed lighting situations (common) and neutral density (**ND**) gels. After those, you'll want to get an assortment of colors that will allow you to accent and "paint" your lighting compositions to portray different moods and meanings. (See "Down and Dirty Gel Guide" on pages 108–109.)

Diffusion 	You absolutely must have some diffusion if you're using professional film lighting instruments. Diffusion material allows you to turn a hard light source into a **soft light** source. Diffusion material comes in frosted white gels and also heat-resistant cloth-like material called **toughspun,** which resembles dryer sheets. (Please note that you should never use *actual* dryer sheets for diffusion as they will shortly burst into flames . . . Don't ask how I know.)
Snoots 	Snoots mount onto the front of a light to give you a "spotlight" effect by narrowing the size of the beam. They are useful for pinpointing key lights, highlighting props, and tabletop work. If you don't have a snoot, you can pretty much use a piece of blackwrap to the same effect (see entry below).
Blackwrap 	A few good-sized sheets of this handy material will *always* serve you well. Blackwrap is essentially extra heavy-duty aluminum foil coated in a heat resistant flat black paint to absorb light. It is primarily used to control and shape light much like barn doors. However, blackwrap is much more flexible as you can attach it to barn doors and mold it into any shape you desire within seconds to quickly adjust your lighting on the fly.
Flag 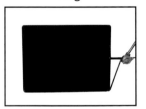	A flag is a piece of heat-resistant black cloth attached to an open frame. Just like blackwrap, flags are used to block light from shining where it's not wanted. A piece of cardboard (at a safe distance) or anything that casts a shadow can also be used to flag out light.
C47s (clothespins) 	A standard lighting tool for decades, *wooden* clothespins—known in the industry as C47s, are the most practical and inexpensive means of attaching gels and diffusion material to the edge of barn doors.

HAIR LIGHT AND BACKLIGHT

Hair Light

A hair light, or **backlight** as it's also known, is not always necessary if your background sufficiently contrasts your subject, but it's one of those nice touches that can add some dimensionality, **production value**, and compliment your subject. This is the light that gives the hair of your favorite Hollywood starlets like Halle Berry or Angelina Jolie (sigh!) that magic glow in their close-ups. A small light source placed above and

just behind your subject on the opposite side of the camera from the key light will work this magic for you. Be careful that your hair light does not spill onto your subject's face or elsewhere. It should only form a nice rim around one side of the head, neck, and shoulders. This will be easy to tell if you are adjusting your lights one at a time . . . as you *should* be.

Background Light

A small or standard hard source will serve you well as a **background light**. One method is to create diagonal slashes of light across the background. These are easily formed by adjusting barn doors or blackwrap to form a small slit. Other popular options are triangular slices of light shooting up or down across the background. This effect can also be created using barn doors or blackwrap to narrow the beam then slightly twisting the light toward or away from the background. Another common method for interviews is to use a cut-out pattern called a **cookie**. Cookies may come as part of a flag kit. You can also easily create your own cookies to cast interesting

shadows by cutting a piece of cardboard or blackwrap to a desired pattern. Experiment to see which effects work best for your project.

The final touch to your background lighting will be to gel the lights an appropriate color that provides some contrast or otherwise compliments your subject. Again, use your own taste. (If you don't have good taste, ask a more fashionable crew member.)

The Cookie Effect

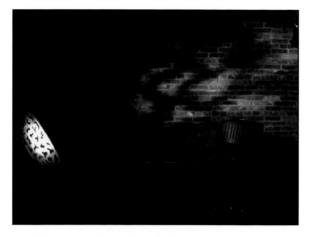

A light aimed through a cookie to create a pattern
on the background

The cookie effect in a close-up

THE FILL LIGHT

Be careful not to just make your whole scene flat with **fill light**. Adjust your fill light to taste. Simply moving or twisting the light source closer or farther away from your subject can control fill light from a lighting instrument.

About half the time I find that I don't really need a fill light. All you want to do is fill in any harsh shadows and bring out some of the details hidden in the shadows, not blast the subject with light that will make your image look flat, two-dimensional, and lifeless.

Subject with "racoon eyes"

Pay attention to the eye sockets of your subject, which often require a fill light to eliminate dark eye shadows known as "raccoon eyes," which is particularly prevalent when your key light is at a high angle or when shooting outdoors in bright, midday sunlight when the sun is at its highest. In the illustration below right notice that the subtle fill light just fills in some of the shadow on the right side of the model's face.

Key Light Only

Key Light + Fill Light

Fill Light Alternatives

Rather than setting up another light for fill, you can usually do just fine and keep it low tech by using a reflector to bounce the key or hair light into dark facial shadows. Similarly, you may find that by simply opening up the camera's aperture a little more you can often eliminate dark facial areas without blowing out other parts of the image.

CONTROLLING LIGHT INTENSITY

In video, there's almost always more than one way to do something. When lights appear too bright or intense there are a variety of solutions that you can mix and match to get just the right look:

Spot and Flood Your Light

Most film lights have a knob or dial to control the intensity of the light beam.

When a light is at its broadest beam setting it's flooded.

When a light beam is at its most intense setting it's spotted.

Add ND Gels

Use clear gray ND gels to cut down light intensity.

Use Different Bulbs

You can also switch bulbs of different wattages to control intensity.

Move the Light

Moving lights closer or farther away is also effective, but more time-consuming and likely to blow hot bulbs.

Use Scrims

Scrims are little screens that are used to cut down light. They come in full or half sizes and single or double thickness.

Diffusion Gel

Color: frosty white

1. This is a must for interviews when using a hard source of light. Diffusion gels soften the texture of a subject's skin and will always look better than hard light shined directly on a subject.
2. Use to soften or diminish harsh shadows.

ND Gel

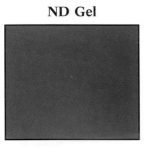

Color: light to dark gray

1. Use to cut down a light that's too bright. These gels come in various shades of light and dark gray and do not affect color temperature.
2. Use on one-half of a light to balance lighting between a light- and dark-skinned subject under the same key light. Adjust your lighting and exposure for the darker subject, then use an ND filter on one side of the light to get a good exposure on the light-skinned subject.
3. ND gel can also be taped to the inside of a lamp or china ball that is too bright on-camera.

CTO

Color: light to dark orange

1. Place CTO (color temperature orange) gel on a daylight-balanced light, such as an HMI, to match it to the color temperature of indoor light.
2. Use a large CTO gel sheet to cover windows in the background or behind your subject to make the normally bluish daylight appear be the same color temperature as tungsten (indoor) light. Carefully tape the gel into the window frame. Composing a tighter shot or using shallow-depth-of-field will make a gelled window less noticeable to the camera.
3. CTO can also be used to "warm up" an interview subject's skin tone. This is an easy cure for pale faces and an all-around simple way to make just about anyone look more healthy and attractive on video.
4. You can use CTO on light instruments when shooting outdoors with your camera balanced for daylight to give subjects a strong warm contrast to their cooler background.

CTB

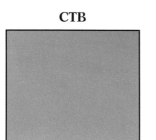

Color: light to medium blue

1. Place CTB (color temperature blue) gel on a tungsten-balanced light indoors to supplement natural sunlight being used in a scene. Place your light outside a window shining in or anywhere off-camera, pointing the same direction as the sunlight.
2. Use to create "artificial sunlight" by placing on any powerful tungsten (indoor) source of light. You can create "sunlight" in a studio or on location in the dead of night with this handy gel. Shine through a set of blinds or cardboard cut out (a.k.a. cookie) in the shape of a window to create a more interesting effect.
3. Place on a tungsten-balanced (indoor) light to match it to the color temperature of daylight when shooting outdoors to supplement daylight without having a blue/orange contrast in color temperatures between your subject and the background.
4. Use to "cool" a scene or subject that looks too warm. You could also white balance the camera to a warm card for a similar effect. (See the Crazy Phat Bonus Pages on the DVD at the back of this book.)

Amber Gel

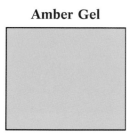

Color: yellow/orange

1. Use these gels to warm up a scene or a subject's face.
2. Use to create a sunrise or early morning sunlight effect. (**Note**: Lighter shades of CTO gels can also be used as a substitute.)

---

1. Use these gels to add a little color to hair/back lights.
2. Use to change the color of the background to match or contrast with your subject's clothing, hair, or skin tone.
3. Use to accent "props" in a scene.
4. Use for coloring any scene where appropriate.

Party Gels

Color: various—reds, greens, purples, etc.

See also "Color Temperature," page 74.

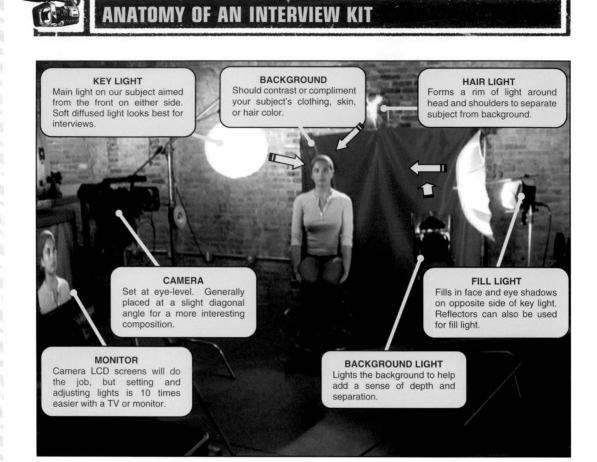

KEY LIGHT
Main light on our subject aimed from the front on either side. Soft diffused light looks best for interviews.

BACKGROUND
Should contrast or compliment your subject's clothing, skin, or hair color.

HAIR LIGHT
Forms a rim of light around head and shoulders to separate subject from background.

CAMERA
Set at eye-level. Generally placed at a slight diagonal angle for a more interesting composition.

FILL LIGHT
Fills in face and eye shadows on opposite side of key light. Reflectors can also be used for fill light.

MONITOR
Camera LCD screens will do the job, but setting and adjusting lights is 10 times easier with a TV or monitor.

BACKGROUND LIGHT
Lights the background to help add a sense of depth and separation.

The cost of your lighting kit is almost irrelevant. The most important factor is your understanding and mastery of your lights. I have consistently achieved great results lighting interviews using a simple, Lowel Omni 3 Light Kit (pictured below), which consists of three 500 watt lights, and supplementing with whatever **practical lights** (lamps, desk lights, etc.) on location that I found useful. I like the Omni 3 Kit for doc work and interviews, because it's highly portable (although still heavy) and pretty much holds everything I need for lighting. The lights are relatively small (about 10″ × 10″ × 8″) and weigh less than 3 pounds each.

For more formal setups using **4-point lighting,** a China ball or fluorescent light is a good addition to a 3 light kit. In addition, a smaller light such as a Pro-light, Inkie, or Pepper light may also be desirable. (See "Lighting Tools of the Trade" on pages 99–101 for detailed descriptions.) These small focusable lights are useful as hair lights, prop lights, or even background lights. With most DV cameras you can even get away with one as your key light for tight shots.

3 TIPS FOR SHOOTING IN LOW LIGHT

One of the unavoidable realities of documentary work is low-light situations. Some subject matters unfold almost entirely in low-light and dark environments. Adding more light or using an onboard camera light is the *technical* ideal, but this often compromises the *natural* action on-screen. What's a Down and Dirty filmmaker to do?

1 USE THE GAIN FUNCTION

All of the 3-chip prosumer cameras have a gain function that artificially brightens the image. The gain can be adjusted in steps from very little brightening (3 to 6 dB) to major brightening (12 to 18 dB). However, the big trade-off that comes with gain is video "noise," resulting in a lower quality grainier video image. Use only as much gain as you need.

"The Education of Shelby Knox"

2 SHOOT WIDE

Telephoto lens settings suck up more light. Shooting with your zoom lens at the widest setting is also another way to get more light into the camera. Rather than zooming in and out to adjust your frame, move the camera closer or farther away from your subject to reframe shots and still stay on a wide lens.

3 DECREASE YOUR SHUTTER SPEED

Taking your shutter speed down a setting or two from the normal 1/60 will increase the amount of light going into your camera, which will brighten your image. The trade-off is that faster motions may appear blurry or surreal if the shutter speed is lowered too much.

Reflectors

A carefully aimed reflector can double your lighting power and substitute for your fill, key, or hair light.

Blackwrap

Blackwrap can be molded to barn doors to act as a flag. Barn doors, blackwrap, and flags all work to keep light only where you want it.

Placing Gels

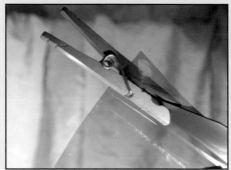

C-47s (a.k.a. clothespins) should be used to attach gels to the very edge of barn doors to avoid melted gels and burning clothespins.

Experimental Lights

Try making your own gear like this home-made fluorescent fixture or experiment with different types of lighting instruments to expand your kit.

Lighting from Below

Lighting subjects from below can make them appear mysterious, spooky, or surreal.

Gold Reflectors

Apart from amber gels, gold reflectors can be used to warm up a subject's skin tone.

1 **Decide Where You Want to Shoot**
Ideally, the scene should communicate something about the person you are interviewing, but practical and technical issues may sometimes trump this desire.

2 **Set Up Your Camera and Monitor and Choose a Frame**
Adjust color bars on your monitor accordingly. (See "How to Adjust NTSC Color Bars" on page 89) It is pointless to adjust lights for video without looking at a monitor, because what your naked eye sees has almost nothing to do with how the scene will actually look on *video*. Use a stand-in model (i.e., crew, P.A. or bystander), preferably one with the same skin tone and height as your subject.

3 **Take Control of the Light In the Room**
Turn off all lights on set (unless you're using them as work lights). Block out any unwanted sunlight using curtains, dark cloth, garbage bags, or newspaper.

4 **Assemble the Lights**
Plug the AC cable into each light, tighten onto a stand, add barn doors, and plug light in. Call out, "Spotting!" to warn crew and test. Set light in desired position and weigh it down with a sandbag. Secure cables on floor with Gaffer's tape.

5 **Adjust the Lights and Set the Final Frame**
Lights should always be set one at a time, so that you can see what *each* light is doing. I'd start with the key light, then background light or prop light, then hair light, and finally the fill light. You want to

a. Aim, spot, and flood each light to desired intensity
b. Adjust the barn doors
c. Add scrims and/or diffusion as desired (NO colored gels yet)
d. Use blackwrap and flags as necessary to control light spill
e. White balance the camera
f. NOW you can add colored gels as your heart desires

I suggest that you set lights in order of importance just in case you run out of time. That way, your subject will still have a good key light if you didn't get to tweak everything else the way you'd like to. Now have your actual subject sit in and tweak the lights one last time to accommodate their height, skin tone, etc. Apply makeup if desired.

Practical Lighting Setup

THE RECIPE:

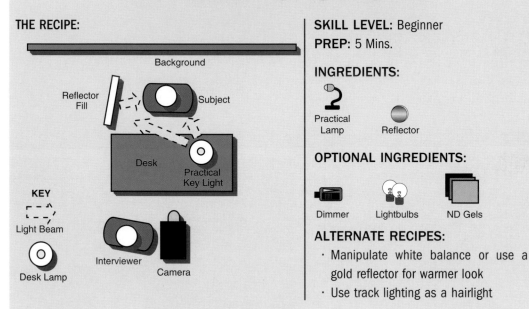

Background

Reflector Fill

Subject

Desk

Practical Key Light

KEY

Light Beam

Desk Lamp

Interviewer

Camera

SKILL LEVEL: Beginner

PREP: 5 Mins.

INGREDIENTS:

2

Practical Lamp

Reflector

OPTIONAL INGREDIENTS:

Dimmer   Lightbulbs   ND Gels

ALTERNATE RECIPES:

· Manipulate white balance or use a gold reflector for warmer look
· Use track lighting as a hairlight

NOTES: Down and Dirty DV is all about keeping it simple, resourceful, and practical. Any light that's already on location and appears on-camera is called a practical light for obvious reasons. Pay attention to the lighting on location and look for lamps or other light fixtures that you can use to your advantage. It doesn't have to be a key light either. Practical lights can be used as background lights, fill lights, or even hair lights in the case of track lighting. Cut and neatly tape a piece of ND gel to the inside of a lamp shade that looks too bright on-camera. If you also carry a few different sized bulbs and/or a dimmer you can easily create a variety of attractive looks with household bulbs.

4-Point Lighting Setup

THE RECIPE:

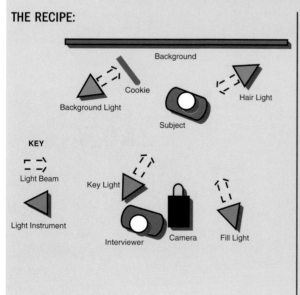

Background

Cookie

Background Light

Subject

Hair Light

KEY

Light Beam

Light Instrument

Key Light

Interviewer

Camera

Fill Light

SKILL LEVEL: Intermediate

PREP: 30–45 mins.

INGREDIENTS:

| Key Light | Fill Light | B.g. Light | Hair Light | Color Gels | Cookie |

OPTIONAL INGREDIENTS:

Dimmer

ALTERNATE RECIPES:

· Omit background light for more isolated subject

· Try slashes or washes of light instead of cookie

· Reflector can be used for fill

NOTES: This is the standard interview setup used by formal documentaries, magazine news shows, and other projects seeking a polished or broadcast look. By using a cookie or other patterns on the background and/or gels on other lights it can be quite stylized and dramatic. These setups add a certain professional production value, but also call more attention to the filmmaking process, look less natural, and take the most time to set up.

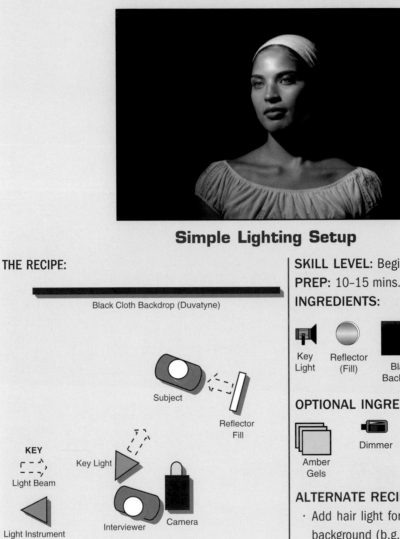

Simple Lighting Setup

THE RECIPE:

Black Cloth Backdrop (Duvatyne)

Subject

Reflector Fill

KEY

Light Beam

Key Light

Light Instrument

Interviewer

Camera

SKILL LEVEL: Beginner

PREP: 10–15 mins.

INGREDIENTS:

Key Light

Reflector (Fill)

Black Backdrop

OPTIONAL INGREDIENTS:

Dimmer

Amber Gels

ALTERNATE RECIPES:

· Add hair light for more separation from background (b.g.)

· Use darkened natural surroundings instead of backdrop

NOTES: Simple, elegant, and natural. In the setup pictured here, we used a single open-faced key light with diffusion gel then propped up a reflector to fill in the shadows on the right side of the model's face. Four-point lighting is great, but one- or two-point lighting can be just as effective, and look more natural. You don't have to get fancy to get great lighting results.

Window Lighting Setup

THE RECIPE:

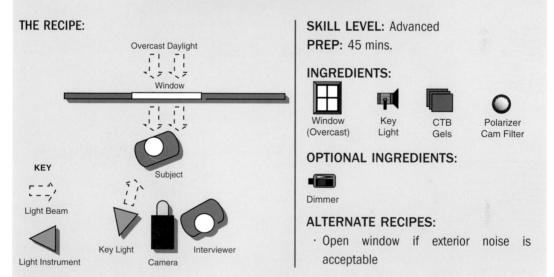

Overcast Daylight

Window

Subject

KEY

Light Beam

Light Instrument

Key Light

Camera

Interviewer

SKILL LEVEL: Advanced

PREP: 45 mins.

INGREDIENTS:

Window (Overcast)

Key Light

CTB Gels

Polarizer Cam Filter

OPTIONAL INGREDIENTS:

Dimmer

ALTERNATE RECIPES:

· Open window if exterior noise is acceptable

NOTES: This setup is a little unorthodox, but it's a perfect example of using creativity to overcome a lame shooting location. This room was just plain white walls and windows, but had a decent view down onto the street. Pulling off this setup is tricky on three accounts: (1) a polarizer camera filter is needed and the key light has to be carefully aimed at the right angle to light the subject to minimize reflections, (2) the camera and interviewer have to be at a high angle to get the street below in the background and maintain a decent eyeline, and (3) the sunlit background had to remain constant, so an overcast day was needed. Using a dimmer will make it easier to balance the key light with the outdoor light.

Anonymous Lighting Setup

THE RECIPE:

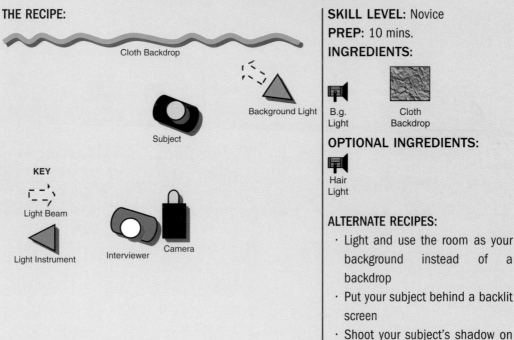

Cloth Backdrop

Background Light

Subject

KEY

Light Beam

Light Instrument

Interviewer

Camera

SKILL LEVEL: Novice

PREP: 10 mins.

INGREDIENTS:

B.g.
Light

Cloth
Backdrop

OPTIONAL INGREDIENTS:

Hair
Light

ALTERNATE RECIPES:

· Light and use the room as your background instead of a backdrop
· Put your subject behind a backlit screen
· Shoot your subject's shadow on the wall

NOTES: This setup is for subjects such as whistle-blowers, victims, or crime figures who agree to an interview, but wish to remain anonymous for reasons of safety, legality, or privacy. The key to this setup is to only light the background. This will produce a sharp dramatic silhouette. You'll probably also want to gel this light a color that works for your scene. Keep in mind that different colors can convey very different messages about your subject to your viewers. You can add a hair light if you'd like a little more definition of your subject, but be careful that it doesn't spill onto her face and reveal her identity. If safety is really a concern, you can also disguise her voice in post-production.

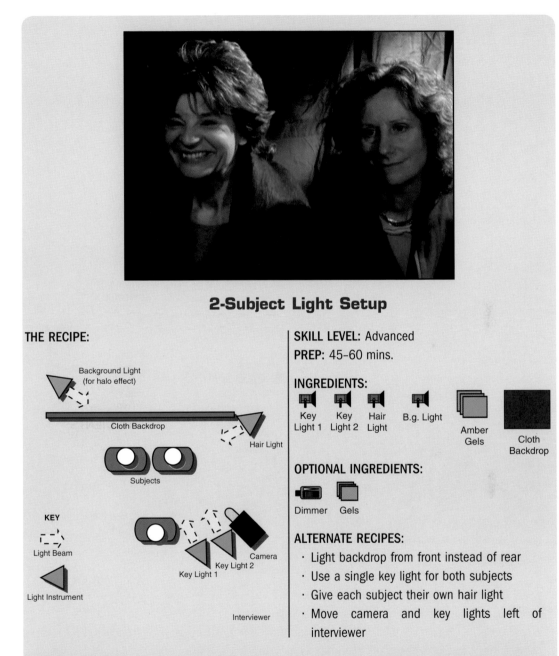

2-Subject Light Setup

THE RECIPE:

Background Light
(for halo effect)

Cloth Backdrop

Hair Light

Subjects

KEY

Light Beam

Light Instrument

Key Light 1

Key Light 2

Camera

Interviewer

SKILL LEVEL: Advanced
PREP: 45–60 mins.

INGREDIENTS:

Key Light 1   Key Light 2   Hair Light   B.g. Light   Amber Gels   Cloth Backdrop

OPTIONAL INGREDIENTS:

Dimmer   Gels

ALTERNATE RECIPES:

· Light backdrop from front instead of rear
· Use a single key light for both subjects
· Give each subject their own hair light
· Move camera and key lights left of interviewer

NOTES: Lighting two-subject interviews with a small light kit calls for one or more of your lights to do double duty to light both subjects at the same time. It's not uncommon to have subject's shoulders touching. If they sat in their normal personal space comfort zones, there would be a huge empty spot in the middle of the frame and I'd need to compose a wider (i.e., less intimate) shot and use a much bigger cloth backdrop to pull off the setup. The backdrop doesn't have to be iridescent like the one pictured above, but you will at least need a translucent material to get a halo effect when lit from behind.

2-Subject Light Setup

Photo: *Paper Chasers* – Son #1 Media

THE RECIPE:

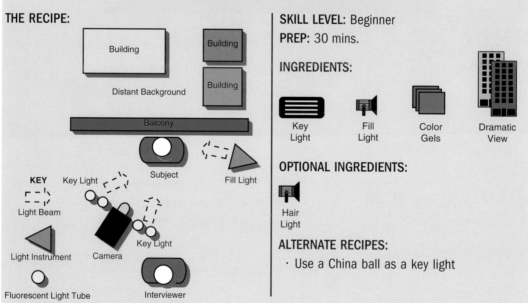

Building

Distant Background

Building

Building

Balcony

Subject

Fill Light

KEY Key Light

Light Beam

Light Instrument Camera Key Light

Fluorescent Light Tube Interviewer

SKILL LEVEL: Beginner
PREP: 30 mins.

INGREDIENTS:

Key Light

Fill Light

Color Gels

Dramatic View

OPTIONAL INGREDIENTS:

Hair Light

ALTERNATE RECIPES:

· Use a China ball as a key light

NOTES: The above setup was lit with a homemade fluorescent unit that consisted of four small fluorescent light tubes attached to an open frame with a space in the middle for the camera lens. You could achieve a similar effect with one or two standard fluorescent units on either side of your camera. Night exterior setups work best with a strong well-lit background. In this case, it's provided by a balcony view of midtown Manhattan. The camera's low angle provides a more dramatic composition that takes full advantage of the vivid nighttime cityscape behind the subject.

2-Subject Light Setup

Photo: *Paper Chasers – Son #1 Media*

THE RECIPE:

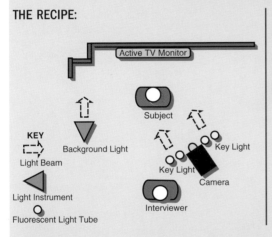

Active TV Monitor

Subject

Background Light

KEY
Light Beam

Light Instrument

Fluorescent Light Tube

Key Light

Key Light

Camera

Interviewer

SKILL LEVEL: Intermediate

PREP: 35 mins.

INGREDIENTS:

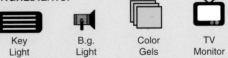

| Key Light | B.g. Light | Color Gels | TV Monitor |

ALTERNATE RECIPES:

· Use a standard tungsten key light
· Window with curtains in place of monitor
· Use shallow depth of field to "soften" background

NOTES: This is another setup using a homemade four-tube fluorescent unit. The pictures on the wall are lit using barn doors on an open-faced light to form a slash of light across the corner. Swap out different colored gels to create different moods and play with subject-background contrasts. The lighting here is easy enough, but using an active tv monitor in the background can be tricky on a few accounts: (1) Your camera has to have a scan synchronization function that allows you to eliminate or decrease flicker common when shooting video monitors (check your menu); (2) you need to be *sure* that you have the legal right to show the video playing on the monitor; (3) the video must be long enough or looped, and, most important; (4) it should not overshadow your subject.

Blacklight Setup

Photo: *Paper Chasers* – Son #1 Media

THE RECIPE:

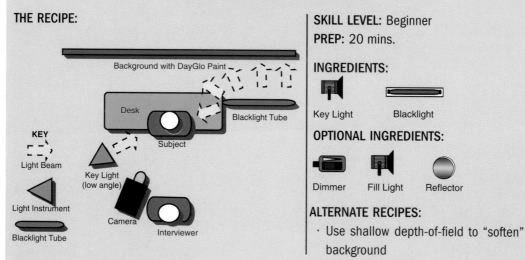

SKILL LEVEL: Beginner

PREP: 20 mins.

INGREDIENTS:

Key Light   Blacklight

OPTIONAL INGREDIENTS:

Dimmer   Fill Light   Reflector

ALTERNATE RECIPES:

· Use shallow depth-of-field to "soften" background

NOTES: You always want to try to take advantage of location lighting first and supplement or add light as necessary to set the right visual mood. In this dark music studio, a practical blacklight on location is acting as a background light and a fill light. DayGlo graffiti on the walls pops a funky burst of color behind our subject and separates him from the neon background to add depth to the shot and set the perfect tone for the interview. A single key light is angled up from below creating a stark contrast to the purple fill light on our subject's face. By carefully observing the creative options on location, you can save time and better portray your subject in their natural environment.

CHAPTER 5
SOUND RECORDING

It's absolutely essential that you have some audio gear apart from the camera's built-in mic. To get professional-quality audio, you're going to need a professional-quality mic at the very least. **You simply can't record good sound from crappy mics.** Buy used sound gear, if you can't afford it new. Unlike cameras, good name-brand professional mics will easily serve you for a decade or more if they are not abused. Here's the minimum gear I recommend for a doc.

Shotgun Mic

You want the best shotgun mic you can afford. These extremely sensitive and directional mics are used to isolate the sound source they are pointed at and minimize background noises. The *Sennheiser 416* shotgun mic pictured here is a popular workhorse among indie filmmakers.

Lav Mic

A lav mic is indispensable for recording interviews and a good choice to mic wide shots. Get at least one. Get two lavs or a wireless lav mic, if you can swing it, but don't get cheap models.

Boom Pole with Shock Mount

The lighter and longer the pole, the better. A decent shock mount is a must for location audio. It's okay to cheap out on the boom pole if you have to. A heavier, homemade paint pole boom will get the mic just as close as the $500.00 models. Search the Internet for do-it-yourself boom pole designs if you go this route.

Headphones

You need the padded kind that completely cover the ear. The Sony 7506 headphones pictured here are an industry standard. Professional-quality headphones should cost at least $50 to $200. Make sure the plug (stereo or mini) is the right one for your mixer or camera. If not, you may need to use an adapter plug. If you need to shoot more low-key, you could go with *professional* sound-isolating earbud headphones which completely plug your earholes.

XLR Cables

Take at least three 6′ cables for every mic. You can't have too many XLR cables. Beware, with rough handling, XLRs may develop shorts, which cause static and sound drop-outs. If you will be recording live events such as concerts or public speakers you will want to use extra-long 25–50′ XLR cables. Test for shorts by linking all your XLR cables together, hooking up to a mic and jiggling the cables while listening for static.

Once you've scrounged up enough cash to get the basics, you'll want to add these items to expand your sound package and take your recording to the next level.

Zeppelin with Pistol Grip

These little mic housings are pricey, but they are hands down the most effective solution for blocking wind noise when shooting exteriors. The pistol grip acts as a sound shock-absorber for the mic and also allows you to use boom-mounted mics in small spaces without a boom pole.

Windjammer

To make your zeppelin even more effective at blocking wind noise, slip on a windjammer (also affectionately known as a "**dead cat**") and you can still shoot on moderately windy days. Use a hairbrush to fluff it before shooting for maximum effect. This is an item that you *can* go cheaper with a guerrilla substitute, if you are handy with a sewing machine and have a piece of faux fur. Look online for DIY windjammer instructions.

Mixer

I like the *Shure FP33* pictured here for doc work, but you can go with any quality mixer as long as it's portable, battery-powered, has the number of inputs you need (3 to 4 inputs is plenty), has a peak meter to read levels, and has the ability to send a reference tone.

Accessories

You'll need an assortment of cable ties, gaffer's tape, and a stack of sound reports. Get gaffer tape from a film/video supply store. Don't use electrical tape as a substitute! It'll leave a sticky residue on everything!

Adapters

These are a must if you'll be mixing equipment from different sources or want to plug into the main sound feed of a live event such as a press conference. Stereo to mini plug adapters, XLR male-to-female adapters, and XLR to RCA adapters and cables are commonly needed. Your local Radio Shack should carry whatever you need. You can also try music supply stores and big box electronics stores.

Introduction

Sound is one of the least appreciated, but most important parts of filmmaking. It's as much a part of telling your story as the cinematography, art direction, or acting. And if you screw it up, the audience won't forgive you. They will forgive a blurry shot, a boom mic in the frame, and they'll even let a weak performance slide, but no one will forgive bad sound. And it's very time-consuming and difficult, if not impossible, to fix most sound mistakes made on location.

There are four basic types of microphones to consider for documentary production: boom mics, lavalier mics, handheld mics, and wireless mics. Each has unique advantages and drawbacks depending on the specific production situation you are in.

Boom Mics

These are mics mounted on a boom pole, which is held by a boom operator. Although you can use any type of mic that will fit on a boom pole, **shotgun mics** (a.k.a. hypercardioid mics), which have a very directional and narrow **pick-up pattern**, are most often used on boom poles. Shotgun mics focus on sound only in the direction they are pointed and greatly diminish most sounds from the rear and sides. Because of this, they are great for isolating your subject's voice from a noisy or crowded environment.

Zeppelin mic housing with wind-jammer for blocking wind noise

Boom mics are handy for "run-and-gun" shooting, when you may have multiple or spontaneous interview subjects, and also when your subject is very active and you don't have a wireless lav. I avoid boom mics for interviews, because they are very distracting to subjects who sometimes have a natural tendency to steal a glance at a phallic object hovering just above their head every few seconds or so.

Carbon fiber boom poles like this one are the most lightweight (and expensive)

8 QUICK TIPS FOR BETTER BOOMING

(1) Check your frame line with the camera person before shooting, then get the mic as close as possible without getting it in the frame.

(2) Keep the mic pointed directly at your subject's mouth.

(3) Always wear over-the-ear headphones.

(4) Regularly check for visual cues and feedback from the mixer and camera person.

(5) Allow enough XLR cable slack to move as freely as necessary, but not enough to trip. Try to get an assistant to wrangle cable if there will be a lot of unpredictable movement.

(6) Anticipate your subject's movement and be prepared to quickly follow. Keep your eyes on the cameraperson and mixer to avoid getting in the shot or yanking the XLR cable.

(7) Spiral XLR cable around boom pole and secure all loose cable to help avoid cable noise, handling noise, and trips.

(8) Assume comfortable feet and arm positions. Relax.

While it may not be rocket science, booming is a skill that can make the difference between professional quality sound and amateur radio hour. A good boom operator must have stamina, a good ear (and eye) for detail, and should keep the following in mind.

This is an example of how NOT to boom. Keep your mic pointed at your subject's mouth.

Pay attention to lighting to avoid boom shadows on your background or subject, especially their face as pictured here.

Booms can often be distracting to subjects. Use a lav mic when possible for controlled setups where your subject is not moving, such as interior interviews.

Spiral the XLR cable around your boom pole. Secure with gaffer tape or elastic hair ties to avoid cables clanking against the boom.

When booming more than one person, gently twist the boom pole to mic each person as they speak.

Use a windjammer on the zeppelin to help cut down wind noise when shooting exteriors.

BOOMING TECHNIQUE

There are a variety of ways you can hold a boom and each has distinct advantages and drawbacks depending on shooting circumstances. Once you try out a few of these stances you will discover what works best for you in different production situations.

Overhead

Pro: Easy to twist mic axis and follow moving subjects
Con: Hard to hold up for long time

Below

Pro: Easy to hold for long time
Con: Prone to plane/vent noise; gets in the way of moving subjects

Shoulder

Pro: Easy to hold/easy to switch to overhead
Con: Clothing noise; slower to move

Pelvic

Pro: Can hold one-handed long time; free to scratch or write
Con: Can cut off frame diagonally

Pistol Grip

Pro: Very mobile, low profile; good for tight spaces
Con: Shorter reach; limited angles

Lavalier Mics

Also known as "lav mics" for short, "lapel mics" (because of where they are commonly placed), or "plant mics" (because they are easily hidden or planted in a scene), the lav mic is another mainstay of documentary production—especially for interviews. These tiny mics mount on a shirt, lapel, or tie and do an excellent job of picking up the speaker's voice because of their proximity to the throat and chest cavity where the sound is being  generated. Lav mics are a good choice for car scenes where they can be taped to a dashboard, rear view mirror, or sun visor to pick up conversations in the front seat. Lavs are also handy for wide shots where their tiny wire and mic can be hidden behind just about any object in the frame that's close to your subject.

Handheld Mics

The term is self-explanatory. These are the mics passed around the audience on talk shows and used by talent on location to do "man-on-the-street" interviews, news, and live events. They are simple and easy to use. Apart from the above they are also good for speakers on stage and open talking forums such as town hall meetings.

Wireless Mics

These little beauties are an indispensable part of any serious documentary sound kit. The most common units come with lav mics, but if you're using a unit with an **XLR** input or XLR adapter cable, you can use it to make boom mics, handheld mics, mixers, or just about *any* sound device wireless. The beauty of going wireless is that your subjects are free to move about, get up, sit down, run, perform, or do just about any other activity completely  unhindered by wires and cables. With wireless lav mics, it is considerably easier to get candid interviews and **B-roll** footage. Your subjects essentially forget that they are wearing a mic because it's so small and unrestrictive. This means a less guarded subject and more candid and honest footage for you.

Time and again, documentary makers and reality TV producers have captured personal scenes, closed-door fights, and whispered conversations with these unobtrusive mics. Using a good wireless unit, the most intimate moments can be recorded from a distance word-for-word with crystal-clear sound even when your subject is behind closed doors, whispering, or in complete darkness. For most guerrillas, the big deterrent to using wireless is price. At $500 to $4000 on up, good wireless units are not cheap. Similarly, rental rates are also higher. Cheap VHF wireless units are not worth bothering with as they get way too much interference from radios, walkie talkies, and other wireless audio signals. If you go wireless, stick with UHF models and don't be cheap. It *won't* pay off.

Out of sight, out of mind. Wireless mics allow you to capture intimate conversations at a distance.

Professional lav mics come with a "tie clip" for mounting them onto your subject. The important thing is that the mounted mic is not too low and doesn't distract the audience. When a clip is put on sloppily and the wire is dangling down the front of your subject, it screams to the audience that this is a haphazard production. The technique outlined below takes a little fussing and practice to get right the first few times, but it's easy once you learn it.

Put the mic into the clip mount, screen side facing out. Form the wire into a loop and place the loop inside the clip.

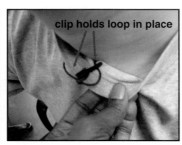

clip holds loop in place

Put the clip into place on a shirt lapel or the neck of pullover shirts. Use the clip to hold your loop in place *inside* the clothing.

Hide the wire by having your subject drop it down *inside* their clothing, then tuck the excess wire into their waistline or pocket.

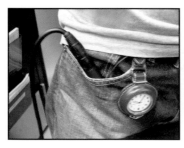

Stash the mic capsule in subject's pocket or on the floor. If they need to get up, disconnect the XLR and leave the mic in place.

This is how you would mount a lav vertically on a jacket, tie, or collar.

For T-shirts and other clothing without a place to mount vertically, just turn the whole thing 45 degrees and mount it sideways.

Handling Subjects

You always want to *ask* a subject if it's okay before you start pulling, clipping, and adjusting things on them. Let subjects know what you need to do and why, especially if you're a guy dealing with a female subject. Give subjects a minute of privacy to run the wires down their clothing, then readjust the mic as necessary.

2 SUBJECTS, BUT ONLY 1 LAV MIC

What do you do when you're shooting solo and need to record two subjects at the same time? A boom mic is well-suited for capturing the back and forth between two subjects, but it requires an operator. A lav for each subject is always ideal, but time or equipment limitations may dictate that you have to make due with one mic. One mic is all you'll need if you get Down and Dirty with it . . .

Solution #1—Mic Opposite the Biggest Mouth: When recording two people with one lav, mount the mic on the softer spoken of the two subjects and on the side closest to the louder person. Make sure your subjects are sitting close to one another. You may have to ask the subject without a mic to speak a little louder, or pay more attention to your mix in post to make sure things even out, but this technique will generally work fine in a pinch.

Solution #2—Hide a Lav in the Scene: You can hide the mic in the scene between the two subjects if you can find an appropriate prop or another object to mount it to—a cup, pencil holder, or desk decoration. Make sure the mic screen is facing your subjects. It's normal and acceptable to see lavs mounted on a subject, but they look like crap just taped onto something in frame. If you have to do so, hide it.

Solution #3—Dangle a Lav from Above: If you have enough XLR cables (and you *should*), you could also dangle the mic just above frame using a mic boom stand or a C-stand and gobo arm. If you're keeping it real down and dirty, you can just string it from any light fixture or other object you find on the ceiling. Make sure the mic is centered and about a foot in front of your subjects with the tiny mic screen facing them. Beware, this configuration is more susceptible to ambient noise because lav mics are omnidirectional. This technique is best suited to quieter locations.

Solution #1   Solution #2   Solution #3

SOUND RECORDING | 133

	BOOM MIC	LAV MIC	HANDHELD MIC
Best Use	■ Run-and-gun shooting ■ Subject can't wear lav ■ Unpredictable or dynamic scenarios	■ Controlled interviews ■ Very wide shots ■ Car interiors ■ Need to hide mic ■ Wireless use	■ Man-on-the-street interviews ■ Open forums (i.e., talk show, town halls, etc.) ■ Live reporting
Pick-up Pattern	■ Hyper-directional (shotgun)	■ Omnidirectional	■ Cardioid (semi-directional)
Advantages	■ Subject free to move ■ Isolates dialogue ■ Can be mounted on camera	■ Low profile ■ Small size ■ Easily hidden in a car or wide shot	■ Easy to use ■ Can cover multiple people in succession
Drawbacks	■ Large and distracting ■ Booming requires another person ■ Sensitive to airplane noise	■ Time-consuming to mount ■ Prone to noise from clothing or touching ■ Easy to break	■ Sound quality usually not as good as boom or lav mics ■ Must be held at correct distance for good sound
Beware	■ Operator and camera going separate directions ■ Improper handling creates noise on sound recording	■ Subject walking away still attached to camera ■ Radio interference (on wireless lavs)	■ Subjects seizing control of mic

Crisp, clean sound can only be achieved by recording at *optimum levels*. You can use a great mic or boom as close as you can get, but if you're not mindful of where that level meter should be on your screen, you may still screw yourself in the end. So where should your levels be? I've got six words for you, baby . . . The Super Happy Fun Sound Zone!

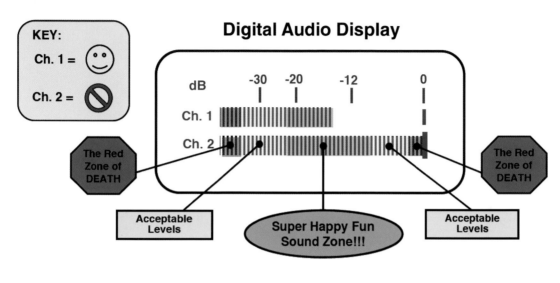

Digital Audio Display

This is where audio levels go to die. If you try to fix low levels in post by simply boosting the volume, you will *also* be boosting the level of any background noise and hiss. Over-modulated audio is distorted and unintelligible. Badly recorded audio is almost always unfixable in post. It's fine to let naturally sharp loud sounds (i.e., gunshots, a slammed door, etc.) "kiss" this zone for a quick moment, but anything more is problematic.

It's okay to have your levels hang out in this zone for a while during recording, but it's preferable to keep them more toward the center. If this is where most of your audio is recorded, you can still work with it in post, but count on spending more time tweaking levels and mixing audio.

Super Happy Fun Sound Zone!!!

Hey, the name says it all. Between –20 dB and –12 dB is the good stuff. This is where crisp, clean audio is recorded. You will have much more flexibility to raise or lower these healthy audio levels in post. Moreover, you'll have super happy fun sound!

Riding Levels

The term "riding levels" just means adjusting your sound levels during recording. Don't make the novice mistake of *constantly* adjusting levels for every minor fluctuation in sound level. Most people's conversation and speech fluctuates in volume to a predictable degree. Try to set levels while people carry on with *normal* conversation rather than doing the old "Mic check 1-2-3." This will make it easier to hone in on subject's *natural* speech pattern and volume levels.

Digital equipment should peak at −12 dB, but analog equipment with peaking needles like this mixer should peak at 0 dB.

If you've done your job right, you should only have to adjust your levels sparingly during most recording. Pay attention to what's being said and the tone of the conversation so you can anticipate when things are going to get softer or louder.

Where Should Your Needle Peak?

On digital cameras and digital sound equipment you want the levels to peak at around −12 dB. That is to say, the meter should just "kiss" −12 dB at the highest points of speech. (On analog devices that have peaking needles instead of digital meters your levels should peak at 0.) It's okay, if during the quieter reflective moments your levels hang out near −30 dB. And it's also okay if during animated storytelling or normal laughter they jump a little over −12 dB. What you're primarily concerned about are loud bursts of laughter, shouting, quiet whispers, or very soft-spoken comments . . . basically anything that lingers in the red zones of death at either end of the spectrum.

Beware of Prosumer Camera Audio Meters

Some prosumer cameras don't show decibel indicators on their display. Instead they just have a digital meter that rises and falls and turns red at the far right end whenever the audio **over-modulates**. With these cameras you should pretty much just "eyeball" the meter and try to keep levels near the middle, a few bars below the red zone of death. Also note that some prosumer camera models have awkward designs for adjusting levels

Prosumer camera with audio meter peaking in the red zone of death. A big no-no.

during shooting. Some cameras bring up an audio control display screen that makes it much harder to see the image on the monitor. (It's not a popular feature with camera people.) With these models, use a mixer to adjust levels or tough it out.

WHY USE A MIXER?

You may ask yourself: "Why would anyone ever *want* to use a mixer when the camera already has two XLR mic inputs and audio level control?" Ask no more...

Separate Sound from Camera

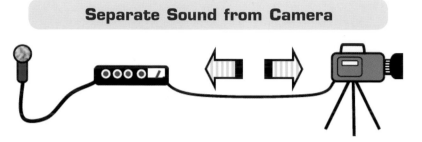

A mixer serves as an extension of the camera's audio controls by allowing a sound person to monitor and adjust audio without having to touch (i.e., shake) the camera or get in the camera person's way during shooting. It thus preserves the delicate relationship between the sound department and the camera department.

Use Multiple Mics/Devices

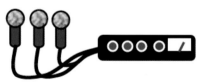

Mixers allow you to use and power multiple microphones or other sound sources, usually three or four, at the same time. Using a DV camera alone you are limited to just two sound sources and audio is much trickier to monitor and adjust using camera controls, which often cause you to shake the camera *during* shooting!

Control Over Sound Quality

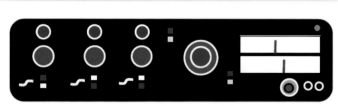

A field mixer will give you control of the volume (gain) of each mic or sound source that you feed into it, and it may also permit you to pan the sound to the left or right channels, filter out background noises, use a **limiter** to prevent distortion, and hook up a second set of headphones for a boom operator. Most DV cameras don't offer any of these options, because cameras were made to record great images. Mixers, on the other hand, were made to help you record great *sound*.

USING A FIELD MIXER

These instructions are for the *Shure FP33* field mixer shown on page 125. However, you can follow these same steps for any mixer that has similar features such as tone and mic/line settings.

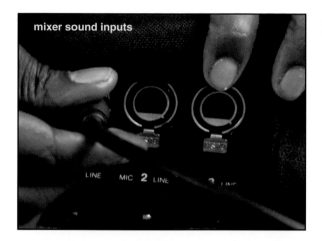

mixer sound inputs

camera sound inputs

mic-line switches

STEP 1: Hook Up Mics

1. Use XLR cable to plug each mic (or sound source) into a mixer input.
2. If your mic needs power to operate, turn on the mixer's "phantom power" switch.
3. Set your input signal level to "mic" for microphones and set it to "line" for most other devices.
4. Plug in your headphones. Turn mixer power on. Use only fresh premium brand batteries and keep at least two extra sets of batteries on standby.

STEP 2: Hook Up Camera

1. Run XLR cables from the mixer's right and left outputs into the matching camera inputs. (*On DV cameras left is Channel 1 and right is Channel 2.)
2. Set the mixer output signal level to mic or line.
3. Next, set your camera signal level the same as the mixer output at either mic or line.

(*If you are ever unsure of which type of signal level to use, listen to your headphones as you switch between mic and line. Only one will sound normal, the other will sound very soft and faint or very loud and distorted. Go with the normal one.)

camera sound meter

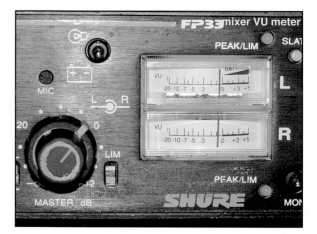

FP33 mixer VU meter

mixer inputs and master gain

STEP 3: Send Out "Tone"

1. Turn on your mixer's "tone" function. This will send an electronic tone from the mixer's output.
2. Adjust the mixer's master gain until the needle on the VU meter stays at 0. Next, adjust the gain on your DV camera until the meter reads −20 dB.*
3. Once set, turn off tone, and don't touch the camera sound controls again.
4. You will now use the input and master level controls on the mixer to control all sound.

STEP 4: Adjust Audio Levels

1. Set the input pan knob: (a) all the way left to send the mic only to the left output, (b) all the way right to send the mic only to the right output, or (c) somewhere in between to send it out to both outputs.
2. Set the mixers master level to about 3 or 4.
3. Have each speaker talk into their mic at his or her normal voice level. Adjust the input level for the mic as they speak, so that the mixer needle mostly lingers in the area just before the 0.
4. Repeat for each mic input. The general rule is to keep your input levels high (at 7 or 8) and your master level low (at 3 or 4).

(*If your camera's meter doesn't have numbers for decibel levels, but does have an automatic gain function, you can turn on this function in the camera's menu, observe the level that auto gain sets for the mixer tone, then manually adjust your camera's gain to the same level.)

OTHER MIXER FEATURES

Limiter

The limiter is a function on the mixer and other sound devices that keeps your sound from getting so loud that it distorts. All limiters are not created equal. Some limiters will sharply cut off loud sounds rather than smoothly dampen them down. (Shown in the off position here.)

Lo-Cut Filter

This little switch, also found on some mics, helps filter out low-frequency background noises such as wind, idling engines, air conditioners, etc. (Shown in the off position here.)

Pan Knob

Use to assign the sound from each input to the left sound channel (output 1), or the right sound channel (output 2), or anywhere in between (both outputs).

Monitor In

This is where you would plug in a mini to mini stereo cable (See "Cable Guide" on pages 147–149.) from your camera's headphone jack to listen to the sound recorded by the *camera*, rather than the sound coming out of the mixer, through your headphones.

Tone Generator

Use to send a **reference tone** to the camera. Adjust the master volume until the needle is at 0. Then adjust the volume on your DV camera until the meter is just below the red zone (or at about –20 dB if your audio meter has decibel markings).

Slate

Use to insert a little electronic beep to "slate" the beginning of each new sound take so it's easier to locate during editing. On some mixers, such as the FP33, there is also an internal mic so that you can make verbal comments for each take as well.

(Also see "Jump Start–FP33 Mixer" in the Crazy Phat Bonus Pages on the DVD at the back of this book.)

5 SOUND RULES TO LIVE BY

Some rules were meant to be broken. The following were NOT. Break these rules at your own risk.

RULE #1   Get the Mic as Close as Possible

The most basic rule for recording dialogue is to get the mic as close to the action as possible without being in the shot. The closer the mic, the better the quality of the recording. This is why boom mics so often end up creeping into scenes; the sound person was trying to get as close as possible and accidentally allowed the mic to enter the frame. The sound person should always confirm the **frame line** with the DP *before* shooting starts to avoid this problem.

RULE #2   Always Use Headphones . . . Always

There are a wide variety of things that can ruin your sound that can *only* be heard by listening to your sound with professional over-the-ear headphones. Simply watching sound levels on a meter or relying on your naked ear will not reveal the following: a cable clunking against the boom pole, air conditioner noise, hum from a computer, a distant plane, a loose mic in the zeppelin, excessive street noise, etc.

If using a mixer, you should monitor the sound being recorded by *the camera*, as opposed to monitoring the sound coming from the mixer. The sound could come out of the mixer perfectly, but still be ruined by bad levels or other settings on your camera. Many mixers have a setting to monitor sound from the camera. The bottom line is to always listen to the sound from it's *final recording destination*, regardless of whether you run through a mixer or other sound equipment.

RULE #3	Monitor the Sound Levels from the Camera

Not even the most skilled sound technician can do anything to fix over-modulated sound in post. If you record sound that is too loud, you've just jumped on a one-way train to Stinktown. If you are using a mixer, remember to match levels between the camera and mixer. Once your levels are set, use the mixer controls. Be sure to monitor sound from the camera by feeding it back to your mixer through the "monitor in" jack, because *that's* what's actually being recorded to tape and *that's* what counts. If you can't feed it back, keep an eye on the sound levels on the camera LCD.

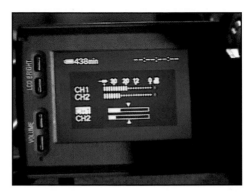

Audio level display on a Sony PD 150

RULE #4	Scout Your Locations for Sound

It is vital to carefully observe every location, inside and out, for any source of noise or sound problems that could interfere with your shoot. Murphy's Law—whatever can go wrong will go wrong—is always in full effect when it comes to location shooting. If you don't take sound into full consideration when location scouting, or even worse, if you haven't observed your location beforehand, you are personally inviting Murphy to wreak further havoc on your shoot.

Always think about sound in addition to those beautiful images in your head. Do that cool director viewfinder thing with your hands . . . then cup your ears and *listen* to your location.

Recording **wild sound** or **room tone** is simply recording the natural sound of any location—all the little buzzes, hums, birds, traffic, and background noises that often go unnoticed in production. The purpose of recording wild sound is to smooth out audio inconsistencies in editing. This comes into play in two primary situations:

Situation A: You need to do additional dialogue recording (**ADR**) after a scene was already shot. The ambient sound under the dialogue that you record during ADR will not match the shots you recorded on location unless you lay in the ambient sound from location or "room tone."

Situation B: During location recording, background noise elements that you have no control over or failed to notice, such as air conditioners or computers, were there for certain takes but not for others. You'll need to restore that particular noise for certain shots for them to sound the same as the other shots when edited together in the same scene.

The procedure is simple. During a break or as soon as picture is wrapped, have everyone on location be silent and freeze where they are. No packing or adjusting equipment—no nothing for at least one full minute while the sound recordist captures the natural ambient sound of the location that will save your butt in the edit room.

LOCATION SOUND RECORDING

Don't Just Look, *Listen* to Your Location

You can generally dress up even the lamest of locations by using a combination of interesting background lighting, tight framing, and/or shallow depth-of-field. However, one area you CANNOT compensate for is sound. If you're recording dialogue and your location is a noisy factory, an apartment over a loud bar, or next to the airport, you might as well find another location or pack it in for the day, because your audio is *more* important than your video.

✔ **Your audio is more important than your video.**

Did I just blow your mind? Did the needle just skip off the record? For some people this notion is filmmaking heresy and I would be run out of town on the first train (probably headed to Stinktown). But let me break it down real simple: There are probably a dozen different things you can do in editing to cover up, cut out, or cut around bad video. However, bad *audio* (i.e., audio that is too loud, too soft, too noisy) is pretty much unfixable, not to mention unbearable on the ears.

Bad sound sabotages everything else, even compelling content. People can't enjoy your compelling content, if the sound is too awful to ignore. If you have whack sound, you have a whack project. Your location *has* to be good for sound. Period. Careful attention to sound always separates the pros from the hacks and the festival winners from the festival selections. The only thing more effective at telling your story than the camerawork, lighting, editing, and location is the voice of your subject who actually is *telling the story*. If the audience can't hear what they have to say, crisp and clean, what's the point?

The chart on the next page will help you anticipate and resolve some of the most common location sound problems.

The lake pictured here is beautiful to *look* at, but it's next to a noisy highway near an airport flight path, which makes it horrible for *sound*.

✔ **Don't just look at your location. Listen for anything that may cause sound problems when shooting.**

SOURCE	PROBLEM	SOLUTIONS (IN ORDER OF PREFERENCE)
Refrigerator	■ Cycle on and off creating low rumble noise	■ Unplug, but don't forget to plug back in ■ Use low cut mic/mixer filter to reduce rumble
Air Conditioners	■ Cycle on and off or make a continuous hum	■ Turn off when shooting ■ Try low cut filter on mic or mixer
Fluorescent Light	■ Can sometimes emit a buzz if mics are close or pointed at light	■ Keep mic away from lights ■ Avoid booming from below ■ Turn off the fluorescents
Subway Train	■ Periodic train noise or rumble	■ Change locations ■ Stop whenever train passes ■ If train runs under building, placing sound blankets on floor may help soften train noise
Traffic Noise	■ Excessive car/plane traffic outside of location	■ Close all windows ■ Put sound blankets over windows ■ Change locations
Noisy Pet	■ Yipe! Yipe! Yipe! ■ Meeeow! Meeeow! ■ Hoooooowl!	■ Put pet outside ■ Take the pet for a long walk ■ Have crew hold and comfort pet ■ Let subject hold pet on camera
Noisy Neighbors	■ Talking, watching TV, playing music or video games loudly	■ Politely ask them to lower volume, turn off or use headphones ■ Sweet talk/negotiate ■ Send them out for a walk ■ Flat out bribe them

The world of prosumer video has matured considerably over the last decade, leaving us with a wide variety of groovy gadgets and digital do-dads. If you're going to do this video thing for real, you're going to need to call on a variety of cables to help you connect your various cameras, decks, mics, mixers, hard drives, and computers. Knowing and having the proper cable can make the difference between being the project hero or the project heel and save you time and frustration. So Down and Dirty DV is giving you the hook-up—the cable hook-up that is. Here's a guide to the most common audio and video cables/connectors:

CABLE	PORT	AUDIO	VIDEO	CONNECTS TO	COMMENTS/ USAGE
RCA		A	V	■ Cameras ■ Monitors/TVs ■ Projectors ■ Consumer A/V gear	■ Yellow = Video ■ White = Left audio ■ Red = Right audio ■ Analog—NOT digital signal
BNC			V	■ Cameras ■ Monitors/TVs ■ Projectors ■ Professional video gear	■ Mostly used for high-end broadcast equipment and cameras
Firewire 4-pin 6-pin		A	V	■ Cameras (4-pin) ■ Small electronics (4-pin) ■ Hard drives (6-pin)	■ Also known as IEEE 1394a or Firewire 400 ■ Fast transfer of video files ■ Use 4-pin to 6-pin cable to connect camera to computer ■ 6-pin connects Firewire drives together
S-Video			V	■ Cameras ■ Monitors/TVs ■ Computers ■ High-end video gear	■ Does NOT carry audio info ■ High-quality analog video signal

CABLE	PORT	AUDIO	VIDEO	CONNECTS TO	COMMENTS/ USAGE
Firewire 800		A	V	■ Newer hard drives ■ Newer computers	■ Twice as fast as standard Firewire (IEEE 1394) ■ Buying equipment with Firewire 800 or USB 2.0 is a good option for "future-proofing"
Coaxial		A	V	■ Monitors/TVs ■ Cable boxes ■ Older analog cameras	■ Screw-on or push-on types
USB2.0/USB mini standard		A	V	■ DV cameras (USB 2.0) ■ Hard drives (USB 2.0) ■ Printers ■ Flash drives ■ Computers ■ Small electronics	■ Mini and standard connectors ■ USB 2.0 format is even FASTER than Firewire ■ Standard USB format is too slow to carry DV signals, but can be used for very slow file transfers
Component			V	■ HD/HDV cameras ■ HD Monitors/ TVs ■ DVD Players ■ HD Cable Boxes	■ Next best thing to HDMI cables for best quality display ■ Best option for standard DVD picture quality
HDMI			V	■ HD/HDV cameras ■ HD Monitors/ TVs ■ HD Cable Boxes	■ Used to view HD footage on HD display at full HD resolution ■ Best HD signal possible ■ Very expensive cable

CABLE	PORT	AUDIO	VIDEO	CONNECTS TO	COMMENTS/ USAGE
XLR		A	V	■ Pro cameras ■ Mixers ■ Most pro audio gear	■ Most common pro audio cable ■ Use adapter such as Beechtek DXA box to go from XLR—1/8″ stereo
1/8″ Stereo		A		■ Headphones ■ Cameras ■ Small electronics ■ Wide range of pro A/V gear	■ a.k.a. "mini-stereo" ■ Get a 1/4″ adapter for more versatility
1/4″ Stereo		A		■ Headphones ■ Some pro audio gear ■ Musical instruments	■ Standard on older audio gear ■ Get a 1/8″ adapter for more versatility

Breakaway Cables

These are strands of two XLR cables, coupled with a headphone extension cable, that separate with a single twist to allow the sound operator to quickly breakaway from the camera operator when necessary. They are very handy for run-and-gun doc shooting and preferred by camera ops who often hate being "married" to sound.

Coiling Cables

Knowing how to coil cables properly is something that separates the wannabes from the pros. (You won't even be able to keep a P.A. gig if you don't know how to correctly coil cables!) The most important thing to keep in mind is that the cable must be able to unravel quickly without getting tangled up. The second thing to remember is that every cable has a natural coil known as the cable's

"history." In other words, it will only coil and uncoil neatly and correctly in that direction and will ultimately become a tangled mess if you coil it any other way. Here's how to do it.

1	2	3	4
Find the natural "history" of the cable by seeing which way it forms and holds a 1 to 2′ foot loop easiest.	Give the cable a slight twist at the top of each loop to form a spiral and keep its "history."	Repeat, stacking each loop in your hand so it will easily unravel without snagging.	Secure the coiled cable with Velcro, a twist tie, or small piece of sash rope.

Hiding Mics

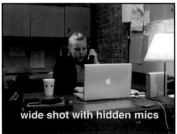

wide shot with hidden mics

shotgun mic

lav mic

lav screen facing out at subject

Often it won't be possible to use a boom, particularly for wide shots. In these scenarios consider hiding a lav, table, or even a shotgun mic within the scene.	The possibilities for hiding mics are as open as your imagination. Any object in frame can be used to obscure a mic.	Lav mics are tiny and can be taped or mounted to almost anything. Make sure the screen on the lav mic is facing your subject or else you'll just be recording a cup of coffee!

Shooting in Rooms with Echo

Bathrooms have perhaps the worst acoustics of any interior you will ever shoot in. Because there is often no furniture, curtains, or rugs to absorb sound, bathrooms are hollow echo chambers of hard surfaces that bounce sound off the tiles, floor, and ceiling.

The quick and easy solution to recording sound in bathrooms or any other echo-y space is to simply hang or lay some **sound blankets**. These are the same thick, rough, quilted blankets that movers use to wrap furniture. (If you're keeping it down and dirty, a thick household quilt or blanket will also serve the exact same purpose.) Use as many sound blankets as necessary to cover large hard surfaces and "soften" echo-plagued rooms by the desired amount. If you need to steal a power nap during down time, a few sound blankets can also be fashioned into a cozy guerrilla bed.

How to Mount a Sound Blanket

Method 1: Clamp or drape the sound blanket over the top of a stall or shower curtain rod (bathrooms).

Method 2: Clamp blanket onto a frame of two C-stands with long gobo arms locked together (pictured above).

Method 3: Use gaffer's tape to hang it on the wall.

Method 4: Simply lay it on the floor like a rug.

How to Eggroll a Sound Blanket

Here's a cool trick for efficiently packing and storing sound blankets.

1
Lay blanket out flat.

2
Fold into thirds.

3
Roll up tightly on floor.

4
Tuck the rolled end into the open end.

5
**Bam! You've got yourself an eggroll! Strike
a pose.**

CHAPTER 6
COMPOSITION AND COVERAGE

ASPECT RATIOS

Which Aspect Ratio Should You Shoot?

The first major composition decision you will make is which **aspect ratio** you will shoot in. Aspect ratio is a term that refers to the shape or dimensions of your image. In its simplest terms, just think of video aspect ratios as the difference between standard and widescreen DVDs.

The decision to shoot standard 4:3 or widescreen 16:9 should take into account two key factors: (1) Where is the final project going to be distributed? In theaters? Direct to DVD? Broadcast on TV? and (2) What will work best artistically? Does your subject matter cry out for widescreen or would it play just the same in a standard video ratio? In other words, a theatrical feature about desert nomads that involves sweeping aerial vistas of the Saharan desert is very different than a television doc about artists with HIV that will be streamed from a Web site.

Widescreen Options

16:9 Cameras: If you want to shoot with a widescreen aspect ratio, your easiest and best bet is to use a camera that has a set of native 16:9 CCDs or image sensors. This means the camera's image sensors are rectangular in shape and naturally capture 16:9 widescreen images. Many high-end DV Cam and DVC Pro cameras come with native 16:9 CCDs. All HD and HDV cameras have native 16:9 aspect ratios. (Like everything else, the best quality solution is also the most expensive.)

Anamorphic Lens: This is the best quality option for getting a widescreen image on a 4:3 camera. An **anamorphic** lens is a specially made and expensive (at least $800.00) lens attachment for your camera that essentially squeezes a 16:9 widescreen picture onto a standard 4:3 image sensor. The recorded image is stretched vertically like an image in a funhouse mirror. This effect can be annoying and take some getting used to when shooting. However, through the magic of post-production, the image can be unstretched to form a bona fide 16:9 widescreen image.

In-Camera Letterbox Mode: Most prosumer DV cameras have some sort of built-in widescreen mode that can be switched on and off in the menu. However, beware that some cameras have a "fake" 16:9 mode, which should be avoided. This wannabe widescreen mode will give you a 16:9 widescreen image on a standard 4:3 CCD chip *at the expense of screen resolution*. It simply chops off the top and bottom of the more squared 4:3 image to make a rectangular 16:9 image.

The two boxes contain:

Standard Video **4:3** Aspect Ratio

Widescreen Video **16:9** Aspect Ratio

There are several different ways you can get a widescreen frame when shooting DV. They are presented here in order from most to least desirable (which also happens to be most to least expensive). *Always* consult your editor or post-production facility, and shoot tests before committing to a particular widescreen method. Note that *electronic* 16:9 methods vary from model to model and should be researched thoroughly before shooting. (All images here are simulated still photos.)

Standard 4:3 Image

This is the standard frame for most consumer and prosumer video cameras and television sets; however, the world is rapidly moving to 16:9 HDTV.

True 16:9 Widescreen Image

Achieved by shooting on a video camera with a native 16:9 CCD including the HDV and HD formats, which all have native 16:9 CCDs. Naturally, these cameras are the most expensive of the DV family.

Anamorphic 16:9 Image

Anamorphic lens adapters "squish" a 16:9 image onto a 4:3 CCD. Editing software is used to stretch the image out to 16:9 on an HDTV or letterbox it on a standard 4:3 TV.

Electronic 16:9 Image on HDTV

Some in-camera "letterbox" modes simply chop off the top and bottom of a 4:3 frame to display the above image on an HD monitor. It's an inferior image to true 16:9 because it electronically enlarges a smaller area of a 4:3 chip, causing a loss of resolution.

Electronic 16:9 on 4:3 TV

This in-camera widescreen mode simply chops off the top and bottom of the frame, which sacrifices 25% of your resolution. This is how it would look on your standard 4:3 TV screen.

DOWN AND DIRTY WIDESCREEN

Many 4:3 aspect ratio cameras don't offer a 16:9 widescreen mode. And many of those that do, offer inferior widescreen modes that simply chop off the top and bottom of the frame and 25% of your precious video resolution along with it. Here's a simple method that will allow you to get a widescreen aspect ratio using any 4:3 camera.

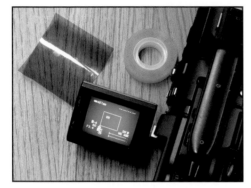

First you'll need some tape, scissors, and a small piece of lighting gel. Turn on your camera's widescreen mode, so that black bars appear at the top and bottom of the screen to make it a 16:9 aspect ratio.

Cut out 2 strips of gel as long as your LCD display and about a 1/2″ thick. Tape them down over the black bars on the LCD. (You can approximate if your camera doesn't have a widescreen mode.)

Turn off the camera's widescreen mode. You can now shoot using the gels to frame for widescreen and still keep a "TV safe" frame if you need it.

In your editing program, superimpose black bars over your footage to make your image letterboxed 16:9 with no loss of resolution! And, if you ever need to, you still have the option of going back to standard 4:3!

COMPOSITION BASICS

Introduction

Your composition (i.e., framing) and choice of images are the main elements of visual storytelling. How you frame your shot will help communicate to your audience the tone of the scene, the perspective of the piece, and how they should feel about your subject, just to name a few. Below are some basics to keep in mind when shooting docs.

When framing your shots you want to follow the "rule of thirds" wherein the screen is divided into thirds, horizontally and vertically, forming a tic-tac-toe pattern. Your subject should be framed so that they fall on one of those lines, ideally at a point where two lines intersect. In close-ups, it is also important that your subject's eyes be framed along the upper horizontal line as well.

Not Enough Look Room

Good Look Room

Make sure you leave enough "look room," or extra space, in the direction your subject is facing. If you don't allow for this, your subject will appear crowded and the composition may subconsiously bug your audience. (Which is okay if that's what you *meant* to do.)

Too Much Head Room

Good Look Room

Similar to look room, mind your "head room," or the space above your subject's head. Too much head room will make your subject appear diminished, insignificant, and lost in the frame. Again, using the rule of thirds will help you avoid poor head room.

Cut Off at the Knees

Better Framing

Be careful not to cut off your subject at the knees or in other ways that unbalance your frame or awkwardly "sever" body parts.

COMPOSITION TRICKS

Hiding Undesirable Backgrounds

In documentary, you will often have to make do with the settings you have to work with. However, there are a few tricks you can use to make those settings work better for you. Distracting or undesirable objects such as the boathouse (circled) can be "flagged" out using a foreground object such as a leaf or sign. This also has the added benefit of creating a more interesting composition. If you need to block out a crowd of people, an ugly setting, or other large area, you can always raise your subject or lower the camera and shoot tilting up so the sky is your background. (Be aware that this technique could also have the effect of making your subject more imposing and possibly backlit, but either is less distracting than some kid making faces in the background!)

Cheating Backgrounds

Sometimes you will need to "cheat" or move a piece of furniture to get a more pleasing shot. In the illustrations above I was stuck with the doc maker's worst nightmare—a plain room with white walls. My best option was to find a way to use the scene outside, but I thought showing just the building fronts was a boring composition. So I raised up the camera tripod high enough to tilt down to the more dynamic street background with people and cars and used the window as a **frame-within-a-frame**. Then, I cheated my subject's chair by raising it on some apple boxes. Finally, I raised my own chair to maintain the same **eyeline** as my subject during our interview.

LENS FOCAL LENGTH

A sometimes overlooked, but major factor of composition is your choice of lens **focal length**. Although some of the 3-chip prosumer cameras have removable lenses, most offer a single zoom lens permanently affixed to the camera. To adjust focal length on these cameras you simply zoom in or out. Focal lengths are generally categorized as wide, normal, or **telephoto**. In the footage below, the model stood in the same spot while I adjusted the zoom lens, then moved the camera forward or backward to maintain the same subject framing.

Normal

Technique: Zoom lens to midpoint

❏ Both foreground and background remain in focus
❏ Most resembles the eye's natural perspective

Telephoto Lens

Technique: Zoom fully in

❏ Background soft-focused
❏ Much less of the background is visible
❏ Distant objects appear closer and more compressed

Wide-Angle Lens

Technique: Zoom fully out

❏ Objects close to lens are distorted
❏ Distance greatly exaggerated
❏ Much more background is visible
❏ Background objects shrink in size

TELEPHOTO AND WIDE-ANGLE LENSES

While the lenses found on prosumer DV cameras lack the shallow depth-of-field found on broadcast and film cameras, you can still get a very cinematic *simulation* of shallow d.o.f. by shooting with your lens at full telephoto (i.e., zoomed all the way in). Move the camera closer or farther away to frame up your desired composition. Keeping the camera at a greater distance can be an awkward way to shoot, but it will work for many shots, especially B-roll and establishing shots. Telephoto shots that involve dialogue will likely require: (1) using a wireless mic or (2) a stationary subject and a good deal of sound cable to run all the way to the camera.

NORMAL **TELEPHOTO** **WIDE**

Your choice of focal length is as much a creative choice as your framing or location. You can make the same street seem congested and teaming with cars or desolate and empty. The previous shots were all taken during a one-minute period shooting the same group of cars coming down the street from the same camera position. However, notice the dramatic difference in the images and the way that distant and foreground objects are portrayed at each focal length.

CAMERA'S WIDEST ANGLE

WITH WIDE-ANGLE ADAPTER

If you can only afford one camera accessory, a screw-on wide-angle lens adapter is a great investment. In tight quarters and crowd scenes it can greatly increase your camera's field of view. A wide-angle adapter is indispensable for shooting car interiors and can really add drama to landscapes and crowds. But beware of wide adapters that distort the edges of the picture or that are too heavy for your camera.

WIDE SHOTS (WS)

Wide shots or master shots are your conservative "safety" shots that will save your scene if that funky creative framing you tried doesn't work out. It's the one shot that you can always count on to cover all the action. No matter who's speaking or what happens—it's in the master shot. Looking at a master shot we should get some sense of the setting and a full sense of the scale of the main action whether it's children playing in a stream or simply a subject talking on the phone. If two or more subjects are interacting, try to get an angle that includes all the participants.

Until you fully understand the visual language of docs (and probably even after that) you should make it a habit to get a good master shot *first*. Then go in for tighter and more creative angles as the scene dictates. Ask yourself this question on location: "If I had to communicate this whole scene to an audience with only one shot—what would that shot be?" Whatever you frame up in your monitor in response to that question will probably make for a good master shot.

MEDIUM SHOTS (MS)

Paper Chasers   *Death of Two Sons*

Medium shots are basically framed from the waist up. Medium shots bring the audience in closer to further inform them of what people are wearing or doing. Most notably, medium shots show us a subject's gestures and body language. You should never underestimate the incredible power of body language in storytelling. Body language and gestures communicate more information in a matter of seconds than speech alone ever could. (That's why us New Yorkers always gesture to other drivers with one hand when we get cut off on the road . . . it's more communicative.)

CLOSE UPS (CU)

Medium Close Up (MCU)
Framed from the shoulders up.

Close Up (CU)
Framed from the neck up.

Extreme Close Up (ECU)
Framed tight on facial features.

Now that you've told the audience where you are with the establishing shot, and you gave them a medium shot to show them your subject's dress, action, and gestures, it's time to get intimate with some close-ups. Close-up shots range from the chest or shoulders up and are often used to capture dialogue, show expression, and otherwise bring your audience close to the character or object on screen. Apart from intimacy, close-ups draw our attention to specific details onscreen. (See below.)

Death of Two Sons

1-SHOTS

1-shots are shots of a single person. These are generally going to be the master shot of your subject. For interviews, 1-shots are usually medium close ups (MCUs) with enough room at the bottom of the screen to overlay a graphic of their name and title. Within this shot you can also zoom in to a CU or ECU when appropriate.

2-SHOTS

Any medium or close shot that frames two people at the same time is generally referred to as a 2-shot. A 2-shot is an ideal master for covering the interaction between two people.

OVER THE SHOULDER SHOTS

The name says it all here. This is another shot designed to help the audience determine the positioning and eyeline of the people on the screen. Over the shoulder (OTS) shots show the perspective of one side of a situation and highlight the reactions of subjects to each other. During interviews you can steal these shots whenever there is just chit chat, a break in the shooting, or a question is being asked, then smoothly push in for a tighter shot on your subject. Apart from interviews, OTS shots are a good choice for any conversation or interaction between people and for showing a character's point of view (POV).

REACTION/REVERSE SHOTS

These shots show how a subject responds to a person, thing, or situation. For interviews, you may wish to "cheat" these after the interview by having the interviewer restate specific questions, or just recreate a series of their responses (nodding, smiling, etc.) for the camera. Similarly, a reverse shot shows the opposite angle or viewpoint of the shot before it.

DUTCH ANGLES

If you're going for something stylistic or edgy or trying to portray a subject in an unusual way, a Dutch angle, where the frame is slightly diagonal, can be used to create tension in the frame or impose a flashy artsy look. MTV, reality shows, and some high-energy sports and entertainment shows frequently use this technique. Nothing's more imposing than a 360-lb. linebacker ready to charge onto the field, than a 360-lb. linebacker ready to charge onto the field shot in a Dutch angle!

DOLLY SHOTS

The Losmandy Spider dolly breaks down into a suitcase and is designed to roll on rubber Flextrak, which can be laid down in minutes.

Any shot that rolls the camera on wheels is a dolly shot. **Dolly** shots smoothly follow a moving subject or roll to reveal a character, object, or some other new visual in a scene. They can go left or right, in or out, or weave a fluid path through scenes. Well-executed dolly moves are a guaranteed way to break up static camerawork and make your film look and feel like it actually has a budget.

You can use any variety of portable and lightweight DV dolly systems, make your own, or create dolly moves by putting your camera on almost anything with wheels and a smooth enough ride. One Down and Dirty mantra is "a dolly is as a dolly does." Wheelchairs, cars, subway trains, skateboards, rollerblades, bikes, shopping carts, and more can all be made to serve as dollies with some practice and the right surface. When it comes to dolly surfaces, the smoother the better. Soft rubber tires are also best for more textured surfaces.

The Classic NYC Subway Dolly

The Skateboard Dolly   **The "Rollercam" Dolly**   **The Drive-by Dolly Shot**

Regardless of your equipment, dolly shots will almost always take more time to get right. Plan it out carefully. Estimate how long you *think* it will take—then *double it*. But when you do eventually get that smooth few seconds of hot moving footage, it's pure filmmaking gold called production value.

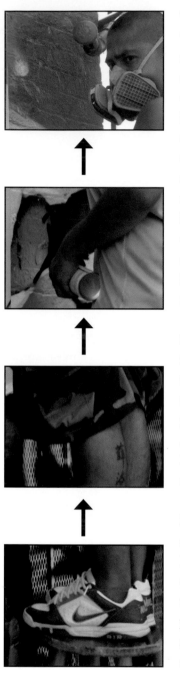

The Full Tilt Boogey

Tilt shots are camera moves that scan the scene up or down. Tilts can be used to: (1) follow action vertically as in an elevator going up, (2) emphasize or take in height as in scanning the length of a redwood tree, (3) reveal new information in a shot as in the example on the left, or (4) open a scene with a more dramatic establishing shot as in look at the shot on the right.

Left: The camera tilts up from a stool on the sidewalk to reveal a pair of sneakers, then a mysterious masked youth. Is he a rebel soldier? A toxic clean up worker? No, wait, he's got a spray can in his hand. It's an artist.

Right: "Death of Two Sons" cinematographer, Cary Fukunaga, imparts an ominous mood with a gentle tilt down from an eerie yellow sky to a wide-angle shot of a rural hospital to open this scene in which a doctor discusses a tragic accident.

DRAMATIC ZOOMS

Zoom moves in or out should be motivated. Amateur video is typically full of pointless dizzying zooms in and out on a subject without any clear rhyme or reason. Apart from adjusting your frame, zooming camera moves should be used sparingly and only when they will add some dramatic effect and help to tell (here's that word again) the *story* unfolding before the lens. For example, your documentary subject is telling you the sad tale of how their puppy, Scrappy, fell through the thin ice on a pond and how helpless they felt watching little Scrappy bravely struggle. Just as that tear begins to well up in their eye you're going to ever so gently zoom in, slow and steady, from your medium shot to a close-up as the tear rolls down her cheek. If you've zoomed just right and look very closely at that tear, you may even see the reflection of your own Sundance Award for Best Cinematography.

To pull this off you have to be able to anticipate and time where your subject is going with a story *before* they get there then meet them at just the perfect moment for the height of drama. (Basketball fans should think of it as a video alley-oop.) Even if you don't win anything it's still extremely gratifying to pull off a smooth and perfectly timed dramatic zoom.

Executing the Move

It's easy to botch a zoom by stopping too soon or zooming in too close to a bad composition. Make sure you practice this move and are familiar with the sensitivity of your camera's zoom control. Keep your pan and tilt tripod controls comfortably loose and use the tripod handle to smoothly adjust the frame as you zoom in. Otherwise, if the tripod is locked into place and you do a dramatic zoom-in you may end up on a close-up of your subject's forehead!

Other than the above, your zoom control should be used primarily for readjusting your frame with the intention of editing out the zoom movement itself. However, when shooting live events, it's a good idea to always zoom as though you may have to use the whole shot just in case some unexpected, but crucial action unfolds in the middle of your move.

> ✔ When shooting interviews and B-roll use zoom moves sparingly to heighten drama and intimacy.

CUTAWAYS

CU cutaway shots allow you to condense interviews by giving you a transition shot.

To smoothly edit your subject's comments and condense time without using **jump cuts**, you will need to insert completely different shots during the editing process that will allow you to cut away from one part of the interview and move to another. Hence, we get the term "cutaway."

I can't say enough about the importance of cutaways. If you want to avoid suicidal thoughts in the edit room, get lots and lots of cutaways. Time after time they will help you out of difficult problems during editing. They take such little effort to shoot, but can add so much to a finished scene.

Cutaways are generally individual shots of anything relevant to your interview or location. Most often they are close-ups, but medium and wide shots can also work. A family picture on the wall, your subject's nervous hand gestures, the trophy case behind them, the scene nearby . . . anything that captures the character of your location, says something about your subject, communicates more info about the scene, or helps you tell your story more effectively will make for a good cutaway. Shoot as many and as much as you can, even if they seem mediocre or don't really seem to help you tell your story, because you will always need *something* to cut away to in editing.

I've often shot what I thought were too many cutaways only to find that I needed every single one in the final cut to make a project work. Listen, there is no such thing as *too many cutaways*! If you don't shoot enough cutaways you'll find yourself doing one or all of the following: (1) using the same one or two decent shots repeatedly, (2) putting in jump cuts out of necessity, rather than as a creative choice, or (3) dressing a corner of your bedroom to shoot a "fake" cutaway. Say it and live it: Cutaways. Cutaways. Cutaways . . . Always.

Subject's hand gestures make great all-purpose cutaways.

CUTAWAY	COULD COMMUNICATE
Reaction shots of others in the room	How the subject is received
Family photos	Happier days in a failed marriage
A factory billowing smoke	Living in a blue collar town
A nervous hand gesture	Subject is uncomfortable with topic
Shaky hands cracking open a beer	Subject has tremors Subject is shaken up about something Subject is a drinker
A clock	Subject is late for appointment It's unusually late A certain amount of time has passed
A big toe poking out of ragged shoes	Subject's financial/social status Subject's trendy fashion Subject's humble nature
A political bumper sticker	Subject's politics or sense of humor

How to Shoot Cutaways

If there's one golden rule of cutaways, it's to hold any shot for at least 10 seconds *after* you're focused and adjusted. When I shoot cutaways I always get several different shots, because I'm never quite sure how they're going to be used in editing. The more choices the better.

STILLS

CU, MED, WIDE, hold each for 10 seconds. Vary by racking focus at front and end of each shot.

ZOOMS

Zoom in and out at various speeds. Hold on end shots. (These holds can double as your still shots.)

PANS

Pan left, then right, letting subject enter and exit the frame *cleanly*. Pan left then right holding on subject in frame for each. Pan at various speeds.

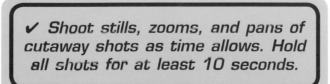

✔ Shoot stills, zooms, and pans of cutaway shots as time allows. Hold all shots for at least 10 seconds.

The term "B-roll" comes from the world of film where editors used to use an "A" and a "B" roll of identical footage, before the digital age changed everything. B-roll shots are similar to cutaways in that they help break up the static interview shots, but B-roll plays a more major role in telling a visual documentary story.

A long-time documentary filmmaker I know actually refuses to use the term B-roll, because she feels it diminishes the importance of these visuals—and she's right. B-roll should not be a secondary or low priority. It really should be thought of as "A-roll," because it is the *action* of your story, which serves to reveal character. Without it, you've just got a bunch of talking heads . . . booor-ing.

Even with an engaging storyteller speaking, the audience still needs to see visuals of the scene, settings, characters, and action of the story. An interview or voice-over itself is the narration or literal *telling* of the story. The B-roll is the *showing* of the story. Together they can complement each other by painting a more complete picture.

That amazing guitarist could *tell* us what it was like to play Woodstock (the real one), but we've only got half the story until we cut in the B-roll shots that *show* the multitudes of free-spirited, mud-covered hippies swirling to the music as far as the camera lens can see. A soldier could tell us what it's like to be in combat, but when we cut in a shot of explosions and a chaotic firefight, his story takes on real human meaning. Now we've got a much stronger sense of story than either an interview or B-roll footage alone could have given us.

If you only have a short time with your subject, you're going to have to figure out how to best get some supporting images. Often, I'll try to grab some B-roll, immediately before and after the interview, of the subject doing whatever they would naturally do in the environment. As with cutaway shots, any B-roll you shoot may be needed by your editor to make a problem segment work, to cover up a problem with another shot, or it may be just the right shot to make visual poetry.

Ideally, the B-roll relates directly to the topic at hand, but often you'll have to settle for mundane activity that just shows your subject in action in their environment(s). The best-case scenario is to schedule some separate or additional time to follow your subject and shoot action shots. If you arrange this with them ahead of time, you'll be able to determine the most appropriate and visual activities and events to capture for your project.

> ✔ *Shoot lots of B-roll and cutaways.*
> ✔ *Look for visuals that help tell your story.*

Think of ways to have subjects *demonstrate* the subject matter. If he's a chef, show him cooking. If she's a vet, show her treating an animal. Show us the A-roll . . . the *action* of your story.

DOC STORYTELLING WITH ANIMATION

JOHN CANEMAKER—ANIMATOR/FILM HISTORIAN
(*The Moon and the Son:* An Imagined Conversation)

"Documations" or "Animentaries" (to coin a bad term or two) are wonderful hybrids that can challenge filmmakers and keep audiences on their toes. Mixing moving images of reality and fantasy is yet another way to find the truth.

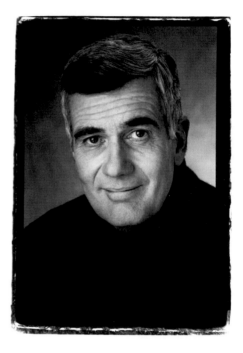

I think audiences are more accepting, less guarded, more open to information and subject matter via animation. The fun and good feelings received from animated fare when we were kids holds over to adult years. Serious subject matter can be broached through this trust held over from childhood, and the material can be understood more easily (and deeply) through animation with its penetrating concentration of energy and design.

Animation can go places live-action cannot. For example, it can personify abstract thought and emotions in a direct, immediate way. It can use symbols to get under the skin of the viewer, or into his or her mind and heart. It can discuss and explore subject matter that might be too personal or sensitive or complex for a live camera. It can deepen perceptions of the truth.

I warn potential clients that they must have a good reason to use animation in a doc; the animation should push beyond where live-action can or should go, not reiterate or imitate reality, but move forward into new areas of believable visualization. It was easier for me to do *The Moon and the Son* (2005 Academy Award—Best Animated Short) in animation since that is the medium I know best. I think the film would work in live-action as a documentary, or as a straight, live-action dramatic narrative. But I wanted to push the perimeters of the animation medium to encompass documentary-like storytelling. I wanted to go beyond the physical limitations of live-action.

"Shallow depth-of-field" refers to the visual effect where your subject is in sharp focus, but the background and/or foreground is soft-focused or vice versa. It's a very pleasing and dramatic cinematic effect that goes a long way to making video look more like film, which more naturally has a shallow depth-of-field. The term "depth-of-field" simply refers to how much (deep depth-of-field) or how little (shallow depth-of-field) of the picture in front of and behind the subject is in focus. In addition to just looking cool, using shallow depth-of-field keeps your audience's attention focused on the subject and blurs out distracting backgrounds.

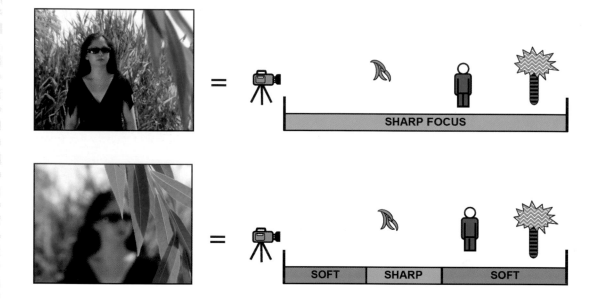

Racking Focus

Shifting focus between a foreground subject to a background subject using shallow depth-of-field is known as **racking focus**. It's a potent storytelling device for filmmakers to reveal new, information, introduce a character, or shift the audience's attention.

SHALLOW DEPTH-OF-FIELD

So now that you know what shallow depth-of-field is, how do you get your camera to do it? Contrary to popular belief, even low-budget guerrillas can simulate or get impressive shallow depth-of-field from any regular old prosumer camera. Here are several different ways to pull it off. And most won't cost you an extra dime.

Open Up Aperture

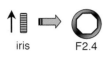

iris   F2.4

If you **open up** your lens aperture (iris) to a low f-stop such as f/1.6 or f/2.4, you can get dramatic depth-of-field over shooting at higher f-stops. Increasing your shutter speed slightly or using an ND filter will also allow you to shoot at a lower f-stop to get a more shallow depth-of-field.

Zoom In to Telephoto

Zooming all the way in to the lens telephoto setting is the easiest way to simulate shallow depth-of-field with prosumer cameras. This method requires moving the camera farther away from your subject to get a normal composition. You may also need a wireless mic or extra cable to run from the camera to your subject's mic. For the effect to work best, place your subject as far from the background as possible to help create depth.

Move Camera Closer

The closer the camera is to your subject, the more shallow the depth-of-field. Used in combination with a telephoto lens and an open aperture, this is a sure-fire recipe for cinematic shallow d.o.f.

Shoot on Big CCD's

CCDs or imaging chips are the actual electronic gizmos that capture an image in video. Image chip size can be thought of like negative size in still photography. The bigger the chip, the better the image (and the more expensive the camera). Prosumer CCDs are typically 1/4″ or 1/3″. Prosumer cameras with 1/3″ CCDs or larger have a more shallow (i.e., cinematic) depth-of-field than models with smaller 1/4″ chips.

Use a 35 mm Adapter

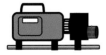

Another way to add a more filmic look to video is to pimp out your 24P DV camera with a pricey—but effective—35mm adapter, which allows you to shoot with a 35mm still camera lens on fixed lens prosumer cameras. While you are still limited to the image quality of your camera's fixed lens, you will get a dramatic increase in shallow depth-of-field, which is a key ingredient of a "film look."

One of the more fun challenges you may encounter is shooting live events. Whether it's a stage show, concert, wedding, or speaker at a podium, there are some basic tips you should apply every time.

1. Scout the Venue First

Before the event, try to scope out the venue. Most events will usually have some type of rehearsal beforehand. The earlier you can get a look at the venue and/or performance, the better. Before you shoot, take notes on the performance, available electrical outlets, best camera placements, venue layout, lighting changes, sound system, venue rules, etc. Write down all of your questions and any ideas for coverage as they come to mind. Find out who the technical point people are in case you have questions or need adjustments to the lighting or audio. Think and walk yourself through every step of the production from setup to show to wrap. Will you need a wide-angle adapter to shoot the whole stage? Is the lighting too dark or bright? Is there an outlet you can plug into or will you need enough batteries to last the entire show? If possible, try to shoot some test footage. This may be your only chance to discover and fix major issues *beforehand*.

2. Arrive Early and Get Establishing Shots

Give yourself ample time to set up, speak with organizers, and scout the venue if you haven't already done so. As soon as you have your camera ready, go outside and pop off some exterior and establishing shots while you still have daylight and things are quiet. Simple establishing shots are easily forgotten in the hurried energy of a live event. I will often shoot exteriors before I even walk into the venue. If the actual event is taking place in the evening,

Remember to shoot establishing shots of the venue.

you'll probably want to get more establishing shots of the venue after sundown with the audience arriving.

3. Know the Agenda

Make sure you get a program, set list, or whatever script they're using that will tell you what's happening, when it's happening, and who's involved. Frantic organizers will often forget to tell you about last minute changes, so pay close attention to changes or additions during rehearsals and warm-ups. Write notes on your agenda and keep it in your pocket at all times. One key to successfully covering any live event is *anticipating* what's going to happen and being prepared to cover it. If you don't know where and how the performers are entering, when the vows are going to be said, or when the pyrotechnics are going to go off during the big finale, you're probably going to blow some of the most important shots of the event.

4. Shoot Like a Video Ninja

Wearing all black helps you blend into the dark and avoid distracting the performers or audience as you move around to get your shots. When placing stationary cameras, try to shoot from vantage points that allow you to get a good shot, but also allow the audience to have a clear view. If you have to set up your tripod among the audience to get the best viewpoint, ask if it's possible to block off the immediate seating area around your camera to prevent people from bumping your tripod.

Note the visibility of the photographer in gray vs. the DP wearing black next to him.

Beware of venue areas that become shaky when filled with people moving, dancing, stomping, or tapping their feet. A tripod planted on a shaky surface is pointless. The other alternative is to go handheld. Keep moving when doing handheld work so you don't block any one person's view for too long. For long events, vary your handheld camera positions and use stationary objects to steady the camera to give your arms a break. Plot and time move across the stage to minimize distraction.

5. Check Sound Early and Often

Most shooters will tell you that picture is usually not too much of a hassle to set up, but *audio* at live events and performances can drive you insane. Strange hums, low levels, or simply no sound are common issues when setting up for these types of shoots. The culprit in these instances is usually an incorrect setting, crossed wires, weak batteries, close proximity to other electronics, or incompatible equipment. It may take significant time to diagnose and fix an unexpected sound problem, so set up and check your audio *early and often*. If you've arranged to plug into the main sound feed, make sure you have enough XLR cables to run from the main mixer to your camera position. If you're using wireless mics, you want to allow yourself extra

When possible, try to plug into an output from the main mixing board for the best quality sound.

time to deal with any sound interference or problems mounting the mics on performers' costumes. Always use brand new premium batteries (Duracell or Energizer) for wireless units and don't commit the cardinal sin of forgetting to turn on a performer's mic before they walk out! Someone in the wings should be dedicated to making sure all wireless mics are turned on (and off) when necessary.

6. Shoot with Multiple Cameras

It's difficult to cover a concert or other dynamic live event adequately with a single camera. Shooting with two or three cameras will help ensure plenty of creative choices in the edit room. Decide and communicate what each cameraperson will cover (i.e., main performer, audience, master shot, close-ups, instruments only, etc.). It's best if (1) all the cameras are the same brand/model, (2) all the camera menus are on the same settings, (3) all cameras are white-balanced on the *same*

Use identical menu settings and white-balance all cameras at the same time for picture continuity.

card in the *same light*, and (4) all cameras are shooting at the same f-stop, if possible. If you can't do these things, count on living with inconsistent images between cameras or spending a lot of time tweaking the video during editing. You will also need to decide how you're going to sync up footage from the different cameras, particularly if you're recording any event involving music. You can use a time code generator to "slave" or sync up most higher end cameras. On the prosumer side you may have to sync up cameras by using a film **slate** (a.k.a. clapper board) to mark the beginning of the performance then keep all cameras rolling until the end of the performance, so that you'll only have to sync each tape once during editing.

7. Beware of Tape Changes

Properly timing the changing of tapes involves planning, skill, and a little luck. Even if you can change tapes as fast as Clint Eastwood can draw a gun, you're still going to miss anywhere from 20 to 40 full seconds of the action because camera gears eject and insert tapes slowly. If it's during the big show number, the kissing of the bride, or any other crucial moment, you're screwed. Follow the agenda and anticipate when important moments are coming up. Keep a vigilant eye on your

Keep an eye on tape remaining and strategically plan the changing of tapes when shooting live events.

"tape remaining" indicator on the LCD screen. Always have an unwrapped tape ready to go in your pocket as your current tape nears the end. It's best to pop out a tape at the first break in the action during the last 3 to 5 minutes of tape, than to get stuck changing in the middle of a crucial shot. You can always shoot some B-roll on the end of the tape later.

8. Cover the Whole Event

Don't just shoot the main event or performance itself. You are a documentarian. You are a storyteller. The real story of the event involves more than just what happens between curtain up and curtain close. Use your camera to tell the story of the *whole* event from A to Z. Even if the performance is all you're really interested in, you should still get a few decent shots of the setup, audience, backstage activity, and anything else of interest that will help your editor tell the

Shots such as the audience arriving help communicate more about the event.

whole story in pictures. Before the event, make a shot list of all the action you'll want to cover. If you do this, take a breath mint when you screen your **dailies**, because I promise you that your editor will kiss you for having such foresight! (See also "Live Event Gig Sheet" on the DVD at the back of this book.)

9. Inventory Your Gear at Wrap

It's not uncommon for there to be several different sets of technical equipment or gear on a shoot like this: your own personal gear, rented gear, the venue's gear, and other video crews' gear. It's also not uncommon for this equipment to get mixed up or misplaced during a long day of shooting in a large space. Use labels, tape, paint, or engraving to clearly identify your equipment. Try to keep all of your gear together near your location or in a secure staging area. Make sure all items

Mark your gear and do inventory at wrap to avoid mix-ups with other equipment on site.

that you'll need for the main event are on your person or at arm's reach. Keep a checklist of all the equipment that you brought with you and check your gear against this list as soon as you finish breaking down. Also, make sure you return any cables, adapters, or other gear you may have borrowed from the venue or other shooters.

10. Follow Up With Copies

One of the things that turns many people off to working with amateur film and video makers is their failure to follow through on the simplest of promises—a copy of the finished project. If you promised a venue owner, crew member, client, performer, or anyone involved with your project a copy of the edited piece, you need to deliver. Every time you promise someone a finished tape or DVD and don't deliver, you've not only burned your own bridge with that person, but you've also added yet another hurdle for any other filmmaker, TV crew, or videographer who wants to work with that person in the future. Delivering what you promised to collaborators is a key part of building a down and dirty filmmaking network. Follow through.

CHAPTER 7
INTERVIEW PREP

Introduction

If everything was properly thought out and prepared ahead of time (and I'm sure it was, now that you've read this far), shooting interviews should be the easiest part.

If you've got a good crew that you trust, you probably won't need to worry as much about your sound and picture. However, if your crew is inexperienced or (worse) you just showed your reluctant roommate how to use a mixer or operate the camera the night before, you better keep a close eye on the monitor and sound levels.

> ✔ You should only be focused on two things: your subject's answers and the technical quality of your sound and picture.

Basic Considerations of Shooting Interviews

1. Writing list of questions
2. Choice of location
3. Equipment prep and travel
4. Prepping subject
5. Framing and background
6. Getting coverage
7. Monitoring technical problems
8. Asking questions and responding

Get Yourself Together

Remember, your subject is taking all their cues from *you*, so relax. Take a drink of water. Glance over your opening questions. Smile, if it's appropriate. Make sure all your crew is ready. (I like to imagine that I am *channeling* Oprah Winfrey, but you should do whatever works for you.) Briefly meditate on the goal of your interview, but most important . . .

> ✔ Relax and have a real conversation with your subject.

Equipment Prep

You should always thoroughly check and test shoot with your rig before any type of shoot, especially documentary. The absolute last place you want to find out that you have a problem with a piece of gear is on location during your shoot. In the best case scenario, you will just be thrown a little off your rhythm. However, in the *worst case scenario*, you may not be able to shoot at all and you could lose your only opportunity to get that interview. This is easily avoided by checking and double-checking everything beforehand.
(See "Documentary Shoot Checklist" on the DVD at the back of this book.)

✔ Check and double check all equipment beforehand.

Travel

Make sure you know where you are going. Use an online service like Google Maps or Mapquest.com, or better yet, always carry a local map with you. If you're driving make sure you've got gas or time to get it. And most important, arrive on time or a little early. Your best bet for a big interview is to arrive an hour early and sit

Always take directions *and* a map to a shoot.
(Source: Google Maps)

down at a local coffee shop, review your questions and crew details, and gather your thoughts. You will be much more relaxed than if you scramble out of the car 15 minutes late apologizing to your subject and rushing your setup. I have done both more than once and I can tell you that the former makes for a much better and enjoyable interview.

✔ Know where you're going and allow time for traffic. Arrive early and gather your thoughts.

The first thing you should do when you arrive is greet your subject, preferably without the equipment and never with the cameras rolling (unless this has been previously discussed with your subject).

Introduce your crew members, then do a quick walk-through with your crew. Discuss where you want to set up and any furniture or props that will need to be adjusted. Always *ask first* and explain if you need to do any major adjustments like move a sofa or take a picture off the wall.

Setup Time

Be realistic about your setup time. This will largely depend on the size and experience of your crew. I generally like to allow an hour to get lights, camera, and sound all set up, but I have often had to do it in half that time when pressed. Lights will always take the longest, so once you've got your camera picture up, start with the lighting.

Adjusting your lighting should be done with a stand-in whenever possible (usually a crew member), preferably one with the same skin tone and height as your subject.

> ✔ Greet your subject, then walk through the location with your crew and decide where you want to set up.

Warm 'Em Up

If you aren't too involved with the setup, this time should be spent just "warming up" and briefing your subject. If they seem particularly anxious, save the briefing for the last minute and just have a normal friendly conversation to help put them at ease. Be careful not to get too deep into the topic of your interview during this time. You don't want your subject to give his best answers and responses before the camera even rolls, because their answers are rarely as good the second time around.

Once the tape is rolling the first thing you want to do is get your subject to state their name and title and spell their name out for you. (You'd be surprised how often I've gone into the edit room two weeks later and couldn't remember who an interview subject was, let alone how to spell their name!) If you're not around, your editor will still have all the info they need for titles. I also always get them on tape saying that I have permission to use the video for my project even though I usually have a written release as well. Cover your butt.

> ✔ Before you start, warm up your subject with some casual conversation. get them to relax.

Storytelling Through Framing

Many times, the very first time we get to see the location is an hour (or less!) before our scheduled interview, in which case an office or living room is generally the best you can expect under the circumstances. No sweat. The same goal applies—try to find some element(s) of that space that help visually tell your story and get them in the frame.

Going back to our earlier example, if your subject is a boxer, get her trophies in the background. Frame that autographed poster of Muhammad Ali so it's partially visible behind her. Turn out the lights in the basement and light the punching bag in the frame just over her shoulder. Use your awesome guerrilla skills of observation and imagination to help tell your story. You get the point.

Using Props and Cheating Furniture

Use whatever visual elements you have on location to help tell your story. Don't force the issue or rearrange the whole room, but if it's already there, move it or frame it and use it. Don't worry, the Documentary Police won't come to arrest you. No one will know where that poster was before and it's a long accepted practice to do a *little* creative art direction on location.

Remember, if the props or visual elements aren't lit they won't be seen and, effectively, aren't in the frame. You may find that you have to **cheat** your background light or a practical light to illuminate your props if you are short on lighting gear. Ideally, you would also have a smaller light fixture to highlight props.

A chair "cheated" to show view of street

Using Depth and Busy Backgrounds

Another way to spice up your interview is to stage it so that the shot has a lot of depth behind your subject. However, be very careful when using distracting or busy backgrounds such as television sets, crowd scenes, bright flashing lights, etc. Generally, these should be avoided, but this isn't a hard and fast rule since having greater depth and action in the background of your shot can be a great aid in storytelling and a more dynamic composition as long as it doesn't overshadow your subject. If you really think a particularly busy background will aid your story, follow the procedures from "Hot Tip: Shallow Depth-of-Field" on page 175 to throw the background out of focus and minimize the distraction.

✔ Use and light the "props" in your shot. Avoid shooting busy or distracting backgrounds.

EASY DO-IT-YOURSELF BACKDROPS

A large piece of fabric will make a great and inexpensive all-purpose background. It'll come in handy especially when you don't have a decent location to work with or want to create a uniform look to your interviews even though they take place at a variety of different locations. The network shows use this technique all the time. I think so-called "professional" backdrops are an overpriced waste of money. Any fabric store will yield a multitude of more attractive artistic choices, one of which is sure to work for you. Look for something that's at least 12 × 12 feet that has an interesting texture or pattern. The bigger the piece of fabric, the wider the shots you can compose with it. The possibility of the looks you can achieve are endless.

Lighter colored fabrics such as standard canvas are more flexible because you can gel the lights on them so they appear any color you like. Darker fabrics such as rich red or blue velvets will give you a more formal look, but will require more light. Reflective fabrics also create an attractive and dynamic look. You probably even have some old Ikea curtains lying around that might do the trick. Thicker, more opaque fabrics look better. Bed sheets and other thin fabrics are usually pretty cheesy looking, but you may be able to get away with it if they are wrinkle-free, rigged and lit well, and sufficiently out of focus.

Unless your fabric has an intentional wrinkled look, you're going to need to have an iron handy. Allow time to iron out wrinkles on smooth fabrics such as satins. (Check the iron for the proper setting for your type of fabric.) Use spring clamps to hang backdrops between two C-stands, on a portable clothing rack, or whatever else you've got to work with. Make sure you've arranged it to create some interesting ripples in the fabric. These ripples will add to the overall texture by creating some depth and interesting bands of shadow.

Light your fabric from an angle for the best results. You can use barn doors to create a diagonal slash or oval pattern. Some fabrics will also look good lit from behind. Experiment with different light positions and cloth ruffles. Each will create a unique pattern of light and shadow. You can also place a cookie on a light to create an interesting pattern if the fabric is still too boring.

Finally, you might try out different gels to see what best contrasts or compliments your subject's clothing and skin tone and decide if you want to use shallow depth-of-field to throw the backdrop a little out of focus. The last step is to place your subject at least five feet from the backdrop. Set up your camera and experiment at home.

Subject Positioning

You should generally position your subject facing slightly left or right. A dead-on angle makes for a more flat and boring *visual* aesthetic. However, a subject looking and speaking dead-on into the camera can also make a more stark and powerful *emotional* connection with the audience. Ideally, you want to place them 5–10 feet from the background to avoid their shadow or to achieve a shallow depth-of-field as discussed earlier. The closer your subject is to the background the more you will have to raise your key light to angle shadows down out of the shot. Also, avoid swivel chairs.

Interviewer Positioning and Eyeline

It's important when framing that you pay attention to your subject's "eyeline," which is simply a term to describe where your subject *appears* to be looking in the frame. You should instruct your subject to look at the interviewer not the camera (unless they are directly addressing the audience). Eyeline issues can be avoided by placing the interviewer very close to either side of the camera lens. I have found that between the key light and the camera works best. (It's a tight fit for the interviewer and it will be more difficult for the subject to see you next to the light, but man that eyeline looks good!)

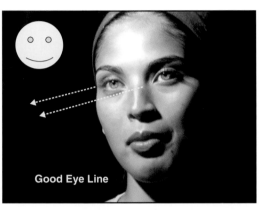

Good Eyeline

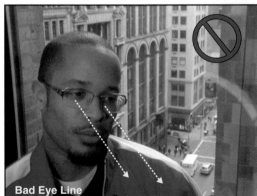

Bad Eyeline

And it's of equal importance that the interviewer's eyes are at the same level as the camera. A few inches of difference between the interviewer's eyeline and camera angle can also make it appear that the subject is looking awkwardly off camera. You generally want them to look just off to the side of the lens they are facing. For example, if your subject is framed more on the right side of the frame, they should be looking just to the left side of the camera and vice versa. This will appear most natural.

Otherwise your audience will completely forget about the subject of your interview and just keep asking themselves, "What the heck is that guy looking at?!" They will want to see it too.

✔ Check your frame to make sure your subject's eyeline appears natural and not too off camera

Improving a subject's appearance in documentary work is a stylistic, or arguably, even an ethical choice. You have to decide what's right for your project and what, if any, impact it will have on your audience and story. In my experience, otherwise perfectly composed people, even those used to being in front of a live audience, are often somewhat nervous and self-conscious in front of a video camera, even with a tiny crew. One of the things these subjects are most concerned about is their appearance. With this being the case, a subject will inevitably ask you how they look. The correct answer is always, "Great!" And with a little bit of Down and Dirty DV know-how, you will be able to say it and mean it.

Clothing

If it's appropriate for your project, you may want to suggest specific clothing to your subject, such as a uniform or traditional costume. However, it is very important that you tell subjects what type of clothing NOT to wear when you speak to them ahead of time to make your arrangements. There are a few types of clothing and accessories that are very uncamera-friendly to video. Clothing with logos is obviously a potential legal issue and may need to be blurred out in post, particularly if your piece will

eventually be broadcast or released theatrically. However, a much bigger problem is certain patterns and colors, usually found on shirts, that can be very problematic for video.

Often these problems are unfixable in post-production, so whenever possible they should be avoided like a bill collector. However, there will inevitably come a time when you'll have to tape someone wearing problematic clothing. The chart on the next page will help you figure out how to handle it on set.

Subjects with glasses or hats can be tricky to shoot.

HAZARD	VIDEO PROBLEM	SOLUTIONS
Bright White	May "blow out" under the lights making it hard to get a good exposure without making your subject's face underexposed, especially, with darker skin tones	■ Wardrobe change ■ Tone down with a jacket, vest, or sweater ■ Frame most of it out
Bright Red	Bright saturated reds can "bleed" or glow on video (darker reds such as burgundy are usually okay)	■ Wardrobe change ■ Frame it out ■ Cover up with a jacket or sweater
Thin Stripes	Will cause your video to produce a "moiré effect," which is a crazy, vibrating, rainbow-like pattern; ditto for herringbone patterns as well	■ Wardrobe change ■ Frame it out ■ Cover up completely with sweater
Hats	Will put your subject's eyes and face in shadow	■ Remove ■ Move key light to lower position ■ Fill shadow with reflector or light ■ Tilt brim up ■ Turn around backward
Sunglasses	Will obscure subject's eyes and reflect lights and crew	■ Remove sunglasses ■ Adjust to minimize reflection ■ Try polarizer filter on camera
Glasses	Will obscure subject's eyes and reflect lights and crew	■ Adjust to minimize reflection ■ Have subject wear contact lenses ■ Try polarazier filter on camera

> ✔ *Brief your subject about video-appropriate clothing in advance. Know how to resolve clothing problems.*

Hey, everybody can't look as good as me and you. Thankfully for them, there are several simple techniques that you can employ to make any subject look more attractive to the camera using a combination of lighting, makeup, camera angles, and filters.

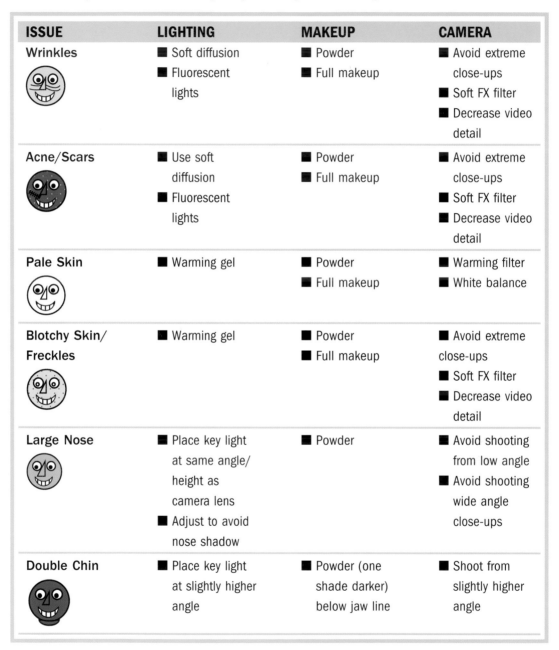

ISSUE	LIGHTING	MAKEUP	CAMERA
Wrinkles	■ Soft diffusion ■ Fluorescent lights	■ Powder ■ Full makeup	■ Avoid extreme close-ups ■ Soft FX filter ■ Decrease video detail
Acne/Scars	■ Use soft diffusion ■ Fluorescent lights	■ Powder ■ Full makeup	■ Avoid extreme close-ups ■ Soft FX filter ■ Decrease video detail
Pale Skin	■ Warming gel	■ Powder ■ Full makeup	■ Warming filter ■ White balance
Blotchy Skin/ Freckles	■ Warming gel	■ Powder ■ Full makeup	■ Avoid extreme close-ups ■ Soft FX filter ■ Decrease video detail
Large Nose	■ Place key light at same angle/ height as camera lens ■ Adjust to avoid nose shadow	■ Powder	■ Avoid shooting from low angle ■ Avoid shooting wide angle close-ups
Double Chin	■ Place key light at slightly higher angle	■ Powder (one shade darker) below jaw line	■ Shoot from slightly higher angle

EASY POWDER MAKEUP

Always carry some professional-quality, translucent powder makeup in a few different skin tones when shooting interviews. If your subject's face or head is shiny, a few quick brushes of this magic dust will take care of it quickly. If they (or you) are concerned about how they look, dust on some professional translucent powder makeup.

I swear it takes off 5 to 10 years of age, helps to mask blemishes, and gives subjects a natural more even complexion that doesn't look too made up. Moreover, it's just powder, so you don't need any special training or hours of practice to apply it. And it comes off easily with soap and water. First, cover up your subject's clothes with a makeup apron or towel. Ask them to close their eyes and very lightly dust their face with the powder.

Keep your powder nearby during the shoot. Your first application will probably start to wear off after 20 to 30 minutes under the lights or as your subject begins to sweat. If there is a P.A. or someone else on the set who knows how, have them quickly reapply the powder to the shiny spots, usually the nose and forehead.

A little makeup can work wonders on subjects who are nervous about how they will look on video. When I show them the final picture on the monitor, subjects often can't believe how *good* they look. However, make sure you've got the right skin tone or else you could easily make them look like a madeup corpse! (I've done that, too.)

I like the Ben Nye theatrical makeup brand, but lots of companies make professional-quality translucent powder. Just don't get anything cheap. You will also need a few good powder puffs or pony hair brushes to apply it. Brushes are much better, but some subjects will be picky about using a brush that's been used on someone else's face. For this reason, it's also a good idea to keep disposable powder puffs at the ready. Yet another solution is to buy little books of disposable paper sheets of powdered makeup.

Before Makeup

After Makeup

Get a Signed Talent Release Form

It's crucial that you get a signed talent release form from your subject. These forms give you legal permission to use the person's physical likeness and voice for your project. It's always a smart practice to get releases signed *before* the interview. Doing so will ensure that you don't forget and the subject won't get cold feet and deny permission after the interview. There is a sample talent release in the back of this book. Consult an entertainment attorney to draft a release form to fit your needs.

Talent Release Form Essentials

- ❏ Name of subject
- ❏ Subject contact info
- ❏ Title of project
- ❏ Producer and production company
- ❏ Compensation (usually none for subjects)
- ❏ Usage (documentary, Web site, ads, etc.)
- ❏ Signature of subject
- ❏ Signature of filmmaker
- ❏ Date

Getting Releases from Major Figures

Sometimes you will be fortunate enough to score a big interview on the spot with a major celebrity or important figure. In this case, you may have to wait and contact your subject for a release after the fact, as such figures aren't keen on signing anything (apart from an autograph) on the spot. They have agents, managers, assistants, and lawyers (a.k.a. "people") that screen and handle this type of paperwork. If you don't already know, casually ask them who you should forward the release form to so that you can use the interview. If they are amenable to signing it they will do so, or tell you whom to contact. They may want to see a copy first.

Verbal Releases

Either way, I try to always get a **verbal release** from my subjects as soon as the camera starts rolling. To get a verbal release, have your subject state and spell their name, then say something to the effect of "Does [name of production company and filmmaker] have your permission to use this interview for [title of your documentary]?" Whether or not this will hold up in court is another story, but it's far better than *no* release at all and a good extra measure even with a signed release.

> ✔ Try to get a signed release form beforehand when possible. Always get a "verbal release" on camera.

FAIR SUBJECT PORTRAYAL AND RELEASES

Photo Credit: Kendall Messick

ALBERT MAYSLES—DIRECTOR/DP
(Grey Gardens, Gimme Shelter, Salesman, Lalee's Kin, etc.)

I think that it's important to feel confident that you're gonna get the release. When we made *Salesman*, each time we'd film in another person's house we waited until the end to ask for the release and we didn't have any problem. But you can run into that problem. That's why [it's best] earlier on, rather than later on to get the release. But basically, you don't want to get a release from a person who feels that they don't want to be in the film. You'd rather not show the film if they're unhappy with it . . .

You don't want to cut off yourself from the opportunity to film somebody in a very profound way because it's a little embarrassing or whatever. But at the same time, there are moments where it would be exploitive, where it would be a damage to that person to film them, and I don't film under those circumstances. Sometimes you're in a borderline situation where it might be damaging, might not, and you go ahead and film it, knowing that you have the responsibility in the editing not to include it if it's embarrassing. Oftentimes it's a good idea to show the film to the person in the film before the film is finally released, because there may be something in that film that you didn't know would hurt that person and you wouldn't want it as much as he wouldn't want it either.

The basic thing is that I believe in what I'm doing, in that I believe that I'm not going to do harm to the people that I'm filming, but rather that it will be a benefit to them. Several years ago I helped to make a film of a very poor black family in the south, (*Lalee's Kin*), and they had everything to be embarrassed by . . . but, because I shot with love in my heart and with an open mind, I ended up with a film that when I showed it to Grandma, she turned to me having just seen it and said, "That's the truth." Then she went on to say, "But couldn't you have made it longer?"

That kind of affirmation is what I get all the time because what I do is good for the people that I film. It sort of is an answer to Arthur Miller's plea, "Attention must be paid." I think we have to pay attention to our neighbors, and to people far from us as well. And in paying attention to end up understanding them and loving them because of the desire to understand them and the love that we give people in filming them.

Remind your subject of the focus of your interview and tell them approximately how long the interview is going to be. Be considerate of any time constraints they give you. Be forthright and honest about your approach and what is expected of the subject in terms of answers and candidness. If there are sensitive personal issues at hand, discuss how they will be treated.

If complete spontaneity is not necessary for your interview, you might even tell your subject a few of the questions you will be asking ahead of time to allow them time to think of how they will respond. The more they know in advance, the more comfortable they will feel with the interview process. Just before the interview starts, give your subject some basic instructions that will help them relax and, more important, keep you from pulling out your hair in the editing room.

Also, don't forget to ask your subject and everyone else in the room to turn off their cell phones. However, if your subject doesn't turn off their phone and they take a call, keep the camera rolling. You never know what you might capture in that little human moment—an angry tirade to a lawyer, a tender moment with their kid, a big deal going down, good news, bad news . . . drama. See "Instructing Subjects" on the next page for specific instructions to give to your subject just before an interview.

> ✔ Before you shoot, give your subject instructions that will help you to shoot and edit the interview smoothly.

All phones should be off, but if your subject takes a phone call keep the camera rolling. You never know what you might get.

1   Just relax. Ignore the camera and lights and just talk to me. Don't look into the camera. Just look at me.

You want to impress upon your subject that the interview process is just a *conversation* between you and them. Looking directly into the camera or stealing glances is disturbing to the audience, which is accustomed to people looking at the interviewer, just off camera. (In certain situations, such as introductions, confessionals, and emotional pleas, addressing the camera directly is acceptable, but when a subject does both in the same shot it bugs people.)

2   Please wait until I complete my question to answer, then answer in complete sentences. For example, if I ask you where you're from, instead of just saying "Chicago," you would say "I'm from Chicago."

This will give you the ability to isolate the subject's answer in post-production and omit your own question/voice from the edited segment. This will keep the focus on your subject and give you more choices in the editing process. It's also always a good idea to mic yourself as well, so you can clearly hear your own questions and preserve the option to add them in later if you change your mind.

3   Don't worry if you make a mistake or misspeak. This is all going to be edited down for the final piece.

Remind your subjects that nothing they say is being broadcast live (unless it actually is!) and that you will be cutting out any obvious mistakes, misspoken words, or anything else that would portray them unfairly or is irrelevant to your film. So they should just reeelaaax.

4   Would you like some water or anything else before we begin?

Even if they say no, keep some water at the ready. Talking for twenty minutes straight or longer will test anyone's voice. They may want some other creature comforts such as a cigarette or a beer. The more relaxed a subject is the more they're going to talk freely, but be careful here—shooting someone who's under the influence poses ethical questions. Use your own ethical meter to decide what's appropriate for your project and for a fair portrayal of your subject. You can say no or ask that they keep the item in question off camera, if their request is not appropriate. Also, keep some tissues handy if you think things could get emotional.

KEEPIN' IT "REAL"

1 SHOOT WITH THE RECORD LIGHT AND BEEP OFF

One of the keys to getting good doc footage is to get people to be more natural and less self-conscious. Whenever you hit the record button, most video cameras beep and activate a little red light on the front of the camera. This makes people even more aware that they're being videotaped. Turn both of these functions off in the camera menu.

2 USE LAVS FOR INTERVIEWS

Boom mics are large and distracting and generally require someone else to hold them. Interview subjects not used to being on camera may be considerably more self-conscious with a large boom mic swinging a foot or two from their head. A tiny lav mic on a subject's lapel has the *opposite* effect. They more easily forget that they are being recorded and are more likely to relax and open up.

3 GO WIRELESS

The only thing better than using a lav mic to keep subjects relaxed and natural

is to use a wireless lav mic. When you go wireless, subjects are free to move about a considerable distance from the camera and still be heard clearly. You can get crisp audio of conversations that take place yards away from the camera, or even behind closed doors. This is a doc staple for capturing unguarded, intimate moments.

A good UHF wireless mic kit like the one above will cost at least $500.

4 KEEP THE CAMERA AT A DISTANCE

Another technique you can use to record more natural doc footage is to keep the camera at a healthy distance from your subject. This is most practical when you are doing a sit-down interview or using wireless mics to shoot cinema verité style. This technique, coupled with a wireless mic, is the easiest way to capture intimate, personal moments on DV. Out if sight, out of mind.

WHEN SUBJECTS WANT TO WALK

ROSE ROSENBLATT & MARION LIPSCHUTZ PRODUCERS/ DIRECTORS

(The Education of Shelby Knox, The Abortion Pill)

Rose: So you're an outsider, and you start out as an outsider and you can't help that. You are the outsider and they have all their prejudices, and here's what happens . . . there are stages to cross. And this has happened in every one of our films. At first they're really interested, they want to do it, and then you move into their house in a matter of speaking, I mean, you're shooting a lot, and you want to get good stuff—and then they freak, they're freaked . . . "Uh oh, I didn't, this is, like, too much."

Marion: And then they want you out and they're pissed. Meanwhile you're thinking, "I shot all this, they can't walk."

Rose: Right. And it looks like they're walking. You know, everybody gets to a point it looks like they're walking, and you go, "My God, I just spent, ten thousand, fifteen, whatever, five thousand, whatever, all the money I had, and they're walking." And you flip . . . And that's the test. You see, at that point, you don't give up. At that point you go, "OK, now I gotta really convince them that I'm really there on their side." And as you do that . . .

Marion: You know but they may get that way, because once we move in, we may be the uninvited guest, but once we're there, we're so there. This may not be the case with everyone, but there's always this point when they're like, "What do you mean you're here? Please, outta my life." And then we behave and then it's fine.

Rose: And everybody has a different way that they'll do that. But that's what you have to do. You can't be scared off by that. You gotta know, this is supposed to happen, it's happening now, I'm at step two or step three and now this is the next hurdle. And then you make friends with them. And after you do that, they start to direct the film. And you gotta let them direct the film. They call you and say, "Oh you shoulda been here yesterday. Come here next week. This is happening, this is happening. You should do this. You should . . . "And it's part of the process to incorporate them, and their suggestions, because that's where their enthusiasm, that's where their energy is.

INTERVIEWING RESISTANT SUBJECTS

SAFIYA MCCLINTON—PRODUCER

(Diamonds: The Price of Ice, Assoc. Prod.—Brown vs. Board of Ed.)

. . . You have to kind of go through it—not ask leading questions, but get them involved in a conversation, and then they divulge more information when they know that you're not trying to catch them or trick them, but you're really just interested in hearing their side of the story: "How do *you* see things? How do *you* walk this earth?" You have to really put on this empathetic side of yourself and not the judgmental side, which is probably hard for a lot of people who are really tied into the mission of their documentary. They're like, "We are going to show that the whales off the coast of this country are being treated poorly, and we're going to go to these people and talk to them, and they're the ones who are responsible." You can't approach people that way. They're going to be defensive . . .

I think that with a [resistant] subject, oftentimes they *know* that you're on the opposing side, and the fact that they even granted you an interview is amazing, because a lot of times, they'll just write you a very well-worded legal letter stating that they will not participate. If they are participating, it's usually because they have a very good public relations answer for anything that you're going to say. So, you do have to work with that, and . . . I think a lot of documentary filmmakers think that they need to have this person spill their guts and say, kind of like on *Murder, She Wrote*, "I'm the one who did it!" They're not going to do that, but what they are going to do is cover their butts so much that it's going to *look* like what it is, and so that's really all you need. You just need someone to look like they're trying to disguise something or hide something, or that they have something so well-worded that you can't punch a hole in it, which means that they have something to hide, and that's all that you really wanted to prove. They're not going to say, "I have something to hide." They're just going to hide it.

And you should really just let them stand on their own; stand as the person they are, and the audience will judge them, not on what they say, but on their body language. They'll judge them on the way that they say it, and that's what you really want. You want people to have a visceral response to the players in this documentary, to the characters, to the people that were instrumental in whatever story you're trying to tell, whether it's an historical one, or cinema verité. So, you just let them be themselves.

HOW TO WORK A PRESS CONFERENCE

The opposite of a one-on-one interview is the press conference, premiere, or public opening. In these situations, you're competing with other media in a crowded room and are lucky to get in one question that matters to your project. Below are some ways to maximize the experience.

1 GET INVITED

Once you've identified the press event that you want to attend, send a written request (via mail, fax, or e-mail) including basic info about your project to the organizers. Follow up with a phone call or e-mail if you don't hear back in time to prepare for the event. If you have some graphic design skills, you might also want to make some laminated "press passes" with your company logo and/or project title. Understand that these press passes give you no legal or official capacity whatsoever. However, they will make you and your crew *look* more legit and you'll be more likely to score an interview.

2 ARRIVE EARLY AND STAKE OUT A GOOD SPOT

You need time to scope out the event, read the press packet, set up the best camera angle, and set up sound. If you arrive less than a half hour before an event, you will find yourself scrambling to figure out what's going to happen when and trying to shoot over the heads of other camera crews from the back row of the designated camera area.

3 PLUG IN TO THE MAIN MIX AND SET UP YOUR OWN MIC

Your best bet for sound is plugging into the main sound feed if it's provided. Ask the event sound engineer. Just run an XLR cable from the main mixer or feed box to your camera's mic input. (Ask, or switch between mic and line level on your camera to find the appropriate setting.) The other option is to set up your own mic at the podium along with the rest. When short on time (or mic stands) you can just quickly tape a lav mic onto or near the bundle of other mics facing the speakers podium.

4 TRY TO SNAG THE ONE-ON-ONE

After the main press conference there will sometimes be an opportunity to catch the featured CEO, celebrity, or public figure for an impromptu stand-up interview. They can't talk to everyone individually, so you need to "sell" your project to their handlers or catch their ear with something appealing: "Mr. Mayor, do you have a quick minute to address Latino voters?" Try to be charming, then jump right to your main questions. You'll probably have 1 to 3 minutes tops. Make them count.

Let subjects know you're listening. While interviewing your subjects you should give them verbal and nonverbal feedback to let them know you're paying attention, encourage them, and/or elicit a stronger emotional response. Obviously your verbal feedback should be geared toward your subject's previous comments, but there are a variety of common gestures, expressions, and brief comments that you can use to encourage your subjects and get them to explain more and do so with more passion and detail.

If you want to get a stronger narrative or more in-depth explanation from your subject, slightly embellish your feedback or "challenge" their answer (i.e., "Get outta here!"). If you amplify your feedback, your subject will naturally amplify his answer. Applying these everyday phrases and social behaviors as conscious interview techniques will help turn a perceived interrogation into a real and lively two-way conversation. (Hey, there's that word again!)

Give verbal feedback only when you're sure your subject is finished talking. You want to be careful not to "step on" your subject's answers, because he may have more to say and you won't be able to isolate the subject's answer from your comment in the editing process if necessary.

Don't rush to fill in every moment of silence. Your subject will naturally want to fill in the gaps by elaborating on their answer. Encourage your subjects to speak and explain more with verbal and nonverbal cues.

> ✔ Respond to your subject. Use verbal feedback and facial expressions to engage them in the interview.

GIVING FEEDBACK

NONVERBAL FEEDBACK	VERBAL FEEDBACK
■ Good eye contact	■ "Amazing! You were only 9 years old?!"
■ Facial expressions (shock, delight, etc.)	■ "I can't believe they did that to you."
■ Head nodding	■ "No way!"
■ Hand gestures	■ "Get outta here! That really happened?!"
■ Head shaking (in disbelief or disgust)	■ "Hold on, are you saying that . . . ?"
■ Smile	■ "I don't believe you!"
■ Inquisitive look (like you don't understand)	■ "That *must've* been really hard on your family."
■ Comforting hand pat	■ "I can't imagine ever being in that situation."

THE THIN LINE OF EXPLOITATION

SAM POLLARD—PRODUCER/EDITOR

(4 Little Girls, Jim Brown All-American, Eyes on the Prize II, When the Levees Broke . . .)

You know it's a delicate thing, sometimes you can cross the line if you ask a person "So tell me how come your mother hated you so much?" . . . And sometimes you can cross the line . . . even when you're the most sensitive.

For example when I was working on a project, initially I had a segment I was going to do about Attica. I interviewed one of the ex-prisoners, a guy named Frank "Big Black" Smith. And he was like 280 pounds and bald and he had been taken by the authorities when they re-took the prison. They had stripped him naked put him out on a big table in the courtyard, burnt matches and cigarettes into his body and stuff, really tortured the guy. So part of my interview was to have him relive that moment. So when we asked him the first time on camera to relive that moment he did it like rote, something he had done a hundred times.

We said it was over. I said to my cameraman, "Cut." I turn to my assistant, my associate producer and camera and I said, "Do you think he really gave us his story? Did he really go back and relive that moment?" And they said, "No, he really didn't." So I turn to him and I say "Black, if you want this audience out there in Television Land to understand really what happened to you at Attica, really the struggle and the pain and the torture that you went through and how it affected you emotionally and psychologically, you've gotta really go back and really relive that. Just don't do it like rote, like you've done it a hundred times, really go back and live the experience again. Live it . . . if you can do it, then this will be fine. If you really want us to really understand what you went through . . . live it."

So we started the cameras again, I asked him a question about that day when they re-took the prison and we sat back and he gave it to us, and he gave it to us. My associate producer started crying, my camera person started crying, I started crying. Then it was over, we said cut. It was powerful. But when we wrapped up that shoot I felt like a real exploiter, even though he gave me my story, part of me was exploiting him. So it's a really thin line you can walk sometimes.

Once you've exhausted all your questions, you always want to give your subject a "soapbox question." Essentially, you're going to ask them: "Is there anything we didn't cover or anything that you'd like to say to people about [the topic]?" This is *your subject's* chance to get up on their "soapbox" and deliver an opinion or commentary about any aspect of the topic. I have found that the soapbox question is often the most passionate part of the interview with the best quotes. (Sometimes it will lead to a whole new segment of the interview and I'll actually start a new tape.)

Even with a great set of well thought out questions, you're inevitably leading the conversation from *your* perspective. Your subject will probably still have at least one or two things she'd like to say that she thinks is important or may have been missed in earlier conversation. And ultimately, the subject's perspective is the one you really want to capture. The soapbox question also provides an opportunity for your subject to further explain any answer that was given earlier that she feels was unclear or incomplete.

> ✔ *After you've exhausted your questions give your subject an opportunity to say whatever she wants about the topic.*

INTERVIEWING CELEBRITIES

I freely admit that as long as I've been in this business I still get excited when I interview certain celebrities. However, for the celebrities themselves, the excitement just isn't there. Most of them have been interviewed a thousand times (some literally), especially if they're promoting a new project. And it's generally a tedious and boring exercise from their side of the microphone. However, I have found that by mostly avoiding the standard questions that they get ad nauseam, you can bring them to life and get past the standard canned answers.

My simplest technique to get celebrities to open up is to do my homework on their passions and just talk about the actual *substance* of what they do. So many celebrity interviews are about their social lives, salary, and lifestyle aspects, that actors rarely get asked about acting and musicians rarely actually talk about music. The audience has heard all of the other stuff before and it's just plain boring, not to mention none of our business.

A little bit of research—reading old interviews and articles, combing through their bio for interesting facts, studying their work—can go a long way to finding some obscure fact or some topic that that person feels strongly about, but has rarely had a chance to speak about. You'll know when this happens, because their eyes and voice will light up. More than once I've been on projects where some VIP who was very adamant that he only had 20 minutes for an interview, then went on to converse for an hour or more (and sometimes well after the camera was off), because the interview tapped into issues he felt passionately about but has rarely been asked about. And that's what people want to talk about most, *their* passions, the things about which they feel strongest.

Even if your goal is more shallow, touch on those passions *first* and they're much more likely to open up and maybe share something new about a juicier aspect of their personal life or their new secret project once they know you've done your homework and respect and *know* them as a musician, actor, athlete, etc., and not just as a celebrity. Remember, a good interview is just an engaging conversation. Ask the questions that no one else has asked. Make people think. Demonstrate your deep knowledge and sincere interest in what they do and the things *they* love and you will get better results almost every time.

CORF—The Education Channel

Paper Chasers—Son #1 Media

MONITORING TECHNICAL ISSUES

Interrupting Your Interview to Solve Problems

Please do NOT be afraid to momentarily stop the interview and address any serious technical problems. If you have technical problems at the last minute or during your interview (and you *will* sooner or later), just play it cool. Reassure your subject and work with your crew to resolve problems quickly and *professionally*. Ideally, you want to wait and interrupt after your subject has completed their thought. However, if it's an emotional moment, a crucial point, or the climax of a story, it may be best to interrupt before they are done speaking, then ask the question again building back up to the moment and resetting the mood.

That great story they are telling, or that emotional moment you have carefully led them to, could be completely *unusable* if all we hear is the lav mic brushing against their scarf or all we see is a blinding reflection of lights in their glasses! I say it's much better to interrupt the flow and get it right than to capture something that's completely crappy or unusable. These issues will usually reveal themselves in the first few minutes of shooting, so the impact of an interruption will often be minimal.

Make sure you communicate to your sound and cameraperson that they should notify you, even if it means interrupting the interview, if any technical issue occurs that might make a shot unusable. This is particularly important if you don't have a monitor and/or headphones. (It may be frustrating to be interrupted when you're on a roll, but it will be *infuriating* to discover an unfixable technical issue in the editing room long after the fact!) Here's another tip: If you and the crew agree beforehand on a simple set of hand signals for things like "pull out," "focus," "raise the boom," etc., you may not have to stop your flow at all.

✔ *Don't be afraid to stop and fix technical issues once you've started shooting. Your footage must be usable.*

Using a Monitor and Headphones

I highly recommend that directors use both a monitor and headphones whenever possible. Any television with RCA jacks will work as an impromptu monitor in a pinch. While a TV set won't do much in the way of representing your true colors or showing you the exact edge of your frame, it will be fine for looking out for many common problems. Remember to just glance over at the monitor periodically. You want to maintain good eye contact with your subject. And definitely keep the monitor out of your subject's view once the interview gets rolling.

Your sound operator should always have earphones, but whenever possible, you should don a pair as well. Use only professional earphones that completely cover the ears and block out other sound. They may be awkward to keep on at first, but they will ensure that you pick up on the myriad of sounds that go unnoticed by the naked ear, but are picked up by mics and can easily ruin an interview.

✔ Always use a monitor and headphones to check the technical quality of your interview when possible.

Other Things to Look Out For

Once the interview has begun you need to be mindful of a few possible issues that could still crop up. It's common, especially during long interviews, that a camera or sound person may just get tired and zone out for a few moments, or even become so captivated by what's being said that they miss some technical issue that occurs during shooting. (I confess that I have been personally guilty of both.) The following chart lists some common things to look out for when the camera is rolling and gives some practical solutions for keeping your interview looking and sounding tight.

HAZARD	POSSIBLE PROBLEMS	SOLUTIONS
Shifting or Animated Subject	■ Subject shifts position causing focus to go soft or throwing off the framing ■ Subjects moves out of light	■ Instruct subject to limit movement ■ Signal cameraperson to watch focus ■ Loosen tripod pan and tilt and "roam" with subject ■ Readjust framing or lights to cover movement
Boom	■ The boom drifts into the shot or casts a shadow	■ Signal boom operator ■ Tighten frame
Loose Tripod	■ A loose tripod allows the camera to slowly tilt up or down	■ Signal cameraperson to readjust shot ■ Lock down tripod
Hitting Mic	■ Subject repeatedly gestures or scratches causing clothing noise on the lav mic	■ Instruct subject to be mindful of mic ■ Move lav mic to better position ■ Use boom instead of lav
Location Noise	■ Refrigerators, A.C. units ■ Traffic, planes, subway ■ Noisy neighbors, pets	■ See "Location Sound Hazards" on page 146
Reflections	■ Subject shifts causing an unwanted reflection on glasses ■ Picture frames on wall ■ Lighting is adjusted causing an unwanted reflection	■ Use polarizer filter on camera ■ Tilt glasses down by raising slightly above ears ■ Adjust angle of frame ■ Tape a small wad of paper behind frames hanging on a wall ■ Adjust angle of lights

Before You Call a "Wrap"

The **wrap out** is the last step of production where you pack up everything and tie up any loose ends. Before you officially instruct your crew to wrap, you want to make sure that you got all the coverage that you'll need to edit. Do you need any **reaction shots**? How about an establishing shot of the location? Did something come up in the interview that suggests a cutaway or B-roll shot? Check

your shot list and notes, then take a moment to think it through before you give the okay to wrap.

Thank Everyone . . . Profusely

Once you're confident you've got everything, profusely thank your subject for the interview. Subjects always want to know when a piece will be finished or broadcasted and whether they will get a copy of the finished DVD. You should have these answers at the ready for them. If they don't already have one, you should leave them your card or contact info. If you're a TV producer or produce a regular online show, a classy move would be to create a simple business card with the dates and times the program will air in addition to your contact info. (This will save you from having to keep repeating the same info for every interviewee, especially for "man-on-the-street" segments.)

Equally important, don't forget to thank your crew, especially if they're working for free or dirt cheap. (Within a few days after you wrap on your project, you should also send your crew a small gift, gift certificate, or at a minimum a simple thank you card.) You'd be surprised how much a sincere and heartfelt thanks can mean to crew members who are often ignored once a project wraps. If people went above and beyond the call of duty, let them know how much you appreciated their help. You'll want to keep them on file for your next shoot. (You do plan on shooting *another* project, don't you?) Lastly, thank your location owner, again, profusely, for helping you make your film. Here's another golden tidbit: Two of the most powerful phrases you can ever use on-set are "please" and "thank you."

> ✔ *Make sure you have all your shots before you call a wrap.*

Packing Up

Make sure your crew is careful and pays attention to details as they pack up. This is one of those times where novice filmmakers let their guard down, because they're exhausted and ecstatic that they pulled off the shoot. Everyone starts patting each other on the back and haphazardly rushes gear into the car, meanwhile some vital piece of equipment is left behind or the location is left in much worse condition than they found it.

The pros know that the shoot is *almost* done after the last shot, but it ain't done yet. You still have to account for and pack all of your equipment and restore the location to the same or better condition than you entered it. Always check your packed equipment against your original list from the rental house. Be extra careful removing tape and place all furniture and props back where you found them. (If you took digital stills or notes before you started, this will be easy.)

> ✔ *Always leave your location in the same or better condition than you found it.*

CHAPTER 9
POST-PRODUCTION

"Success is the ability to go from one failure to another with no loss of enthusiasm."

—Sir Winston Churchill

Basic Elements of Post-Production

1. Viewing footage and taking notes
2. Logging footage and making transcripts
3. Paper outline and/or edit
4. Rough cut
5. Archival and stock footage
6. Animation and artwork
7. Narration
8. Fine cut
9. Music

It's All About Post

How do you know when you're done shooting a doc? This is always a tricky question. The practical answer could depend on your budget, your visa status, your production deadline or, more hopefully, on your story. But at some point, whether by choice or force, you must call an end to production and begin to lay out your story through the process of editing. This is where your project comes together or falls apart. The essence of documentary storytelling ultimately comes down to not so much how a story was shot, but rather how that footage is selected, edited, and treated during post-production.

Given the same 40 hours of raw-footage, any three directors would likely come up with three very different stories if faced with the task of creating a 90-minute film. A great micro-illustration of this concept is the phenomenon of online video "mash-ups" found on Web sites such as YouTube.com where the same raw footage is edited by different people to show multiple meanings and levels of artistry (and idiocy) depending on the editor and their intent. Post-production or editing is the greatest responsibility of the documentary process. It's the final phase where emphasis, meaning, mood, context, structure, and story are all assigned to your footage. It's the final phase where *your footage* is transformed into *your film*.

> ✔ *Editing is the greatest responsibility of the documentary. It's the phase when "your footage" becomes "your film."*

Viewing All Your Footage

Even if you've been viewing **dailies** as you go, you should still sit down once more after the dust clears from shooting to view all of your footage at one time. If you have a lot of footage, you'll want to schedule several sessions of 3 to 4 hours. Anything over that and your eyes start to glaze over. You may or may not want to have your editor or crew with you for this very first full viewing, but they should each be invited to view the raw footage at some point shortly after shooting. Zap some popcorn, dim the lights, and see what you've created. This is the moment of truth.

The treatment you wrote up is now irrelevant. Put it in your scrapbook. The film you wanted to make, planned to make, or thought you were making no longer matters–fugeddaboutit! What you watch now is the film you actually *made*. And it's all you've got to work with, baby. Now it's all about evaluating what you can do with it. The goal is to use your footage to create a compelling, dramatic, interesting, edge-of-your-seat, tear-jerking, awe-inspiring, and insightful documentary (or, at the very least, a coherent story).

> ✔ The film you wanted to make no longer matters. What you watch now is the film you actually made.

Taking Notes

First impressions count. Record your gut reactions to the footage as you view it. It's a good idea to speak your notes into a voice recorder, or have someone else take notes as you say them, so you don't miss some golden subtle moment onscreen. Note anything that makes you laugh, cry, smirk or otherwise draws an immediate emotional reaction. If something about a scene bugs you, write that down too. Your first impressions will often match those of your audience. Don't censor yourself or think too hard about it. Just note all your first impressions on the spot. You can mull them over later.

If watching with others, also note *their* first reactions and comments–the good, bad, and ugly. Also note favorite sound bites and any creative ideas you have for editing, music, or narration. Later, all these notes will help you make crucial decisions and refocus when you've lost perspective from days or weeks of staring at the same footage.

> ✔ First impressions count. Record your gut reactions to your footage when you view it all for the first time.

LOGGING FOOTAGE

Why We Log

One of the most daunting tasks in documentary is **logging** and transcribing footage. Once you have somehow survived production and captured those magical moments on video, you will be left with a feeling of great satisfaction as you lovingly pet your pile of master video tapes (or P2 cards, or hard drives, etc.). That feeling will last for about two minutes until you realize that you have no idea exactly where those magical scenes are. It's time to go through each minute of footage and take notes as to what topics are covered, which shots are best, and most important, the exact tape (or folder) and time code of these scenes.

If you don't have a time code reference for each shot, you'll waste countless hours of post-production fast-forwarding and rewinding trying to find the specific shots and sound bites you need, because so much of what you shoot will likely be interviews and dialogue that have no visual cues as to what is actually being said.

Logging tapes isn't daunting because it's hard to do. It's daunting because it can be tedious and time-consuming, especially when you put it all off until the very end of shooting. The best way to avoid logging fatigue is to *log your footage as you go* and spread the task out into manageable sessions. It's also common for filmmakers to hand off their tapes to an editor, assistant, or intern who can begin logging while the project is still shooting. However, even if you farm it out to someone else, it's still wise to log the most crucial tapes yourself. Logging is the perfect opportunity to become more familiar with your footage before making countless editing decisions.

Organizing Your Shots

Label and organize your footage in a way that helps you begin to form a story. There are no strict rules here. Just find a way that works for you and your editor. Here are some suggestions.

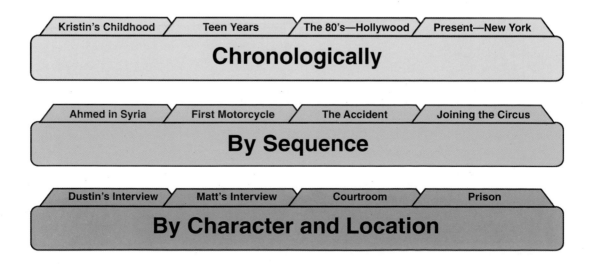

| Kristin's Childhood | Teen Years | The 80's—Hollywood | Present—New York |

Chronologically

| Ahmed in Syria | First Motorcycle | The Accident | Joining the Circus |

By Sequence

| Dustin's Interview | Matt's Interview | Courtroom | Prison |

By Character and Location

The Log Sheet

You can easily whip up your own **log sheet** in MS Word or Excel. Your log sheet should include all the information listed below. You could also add two columns to take notes about the quality of audio and video for each shot.

TAPE #	TC IN	TC OUT	COMMENT	RUN TIME
1	01:53:10:02	01:56:40:07	Pit crew meeting (noisy take)	3:30
1	01:58:35:20	01:58:54:10	Dale putting on helmet	0:19
2A	02:01:20:24	02:14:26:09	Dale's test laps (great shots)	13:06
Starting time code	Ending time code	Description of shot and commentary	Total screen time in minutes and seconds	

Technological Advances in Logging

The chart above is the old-school manual form. However, most non-linear edit programs (a.k.a. NLEs), such as Premiere and Final Cut Pro, will have a built-in feature for logging clips that only requires you to push a key to set the in and out points and type in a description. These more advanced editing programs will automatically record the tape number and calculate the run time for you.

At least two other recent breakthroughs in technology have made the task of logging footage considerably easier. The first is the advent of cameras and camera-mounted hard drives that allow you to digitally record video directly to a hard drive or flash card and bypass tape altogether, such as Panasonic's Hi-Def P2 cameras, Sony's XD-Cams, and the **FireStore** DV Capture Drive. These allow you to mark and title the beginning of each shot as you go and some even provide thumbnail pictures of each shot. Best of all, these tools all eliminate the tedious task of capturing each tape into your computer in real-time, because they record in *edit-ready* digital file formats. This is the future of digital video. Tapes are on their way out and new digital forms of capture are rolling in.

Cameras and devices that capture video directly to hard drives or computer cards simplify editing. The Red One 4K Camera is pictured here.

"AUTOMATIC" TAPE LOGGING

Logging tapes can be tedious and time-consuming. The process traditionally involves: (1) looking at the footage on a tape, (2) setting in and out points for each shot, (3) performing an edit to create a clip for that shot, and (4) labeling the clip. Then you do it all over again for EACH and EVERY shot on EACH and EVERY tape until you've logged all of the footage you shot.

Solution #1: Use Editing Software to "Automatically Log" Tapes

The latest versions of Final Cut Pro, Avid, and iMovie all have a great, relatively new feature called "scene detection" that automatically does steps 1 through 3 of the logging process by detecting the start and stop of each shot (i.e., whenever you hit the record button when shooting) then separating the footage into clips. Simply hook up your camera or deck to your computer, make sure your preferences are set to "start a new clip at each scene break" (Look on the menu under PREFERENCES—IMPORT), then start your camera or deck and hit the IMPORT button. Now you can walk away from your computer, go for a jog, have lunch, or whatever. When you come back in an hour your computer will have logged your entire tape for you separating it into numerically numbered video clips. All you'll have to do is label them or break them into smaller clips if you like. Shoot with this in mind each time you hit the record button and life will be so much easier. (Note: The camera's internal clock must be *set* during recording for this function to work.)

Solution #2: Use a Digital Capture Device When Shooting

The second solution to the tediousness of logging requires you to lay out a little cash, but will save you even more time. In recent years there have been a number of new software/ hardware products that allow you to record video directly to a hard drive or flash card. The most popular is a product called the FireStore, which is a little hard drive that mounts on DV cameras and captures footage as you shoot. I have also recently tried a PC-based software program called DVRack, which requires a laptop computer for fieldwork and allows you to capture your footage to your computer or an external hard drive. Yet another solution is the latest generation of HD cameras that record directly to hard drives or computer cards such as Panasonic's HVX-200 or Sony's XDCam. In all three cases, you can label and begin editing your footage a few moments after you've just shot it. That is an incredible savings in time and efficiency.

Sony's XDCamEX camera captures video directly to a PC card

A simple edit log and notes are sufficient for many smaller projects. However, feature-length docs, reality TV, and other large projects will call for full **transcripts** that contain every word said, who said it, and the time code at which it was said. Making a transcript is the single easiest way to put together a final script and get a handle on your exact contents. You will be able to easily cut and paste sound bites into a **paper edit** and experiment with your story and structure.

Make sure you make dubs of your master first. Don't risk the possibility of harming your precious master tapes while transcribing. The back and forth rewinding during transcription is murder on master tapes and camcorders. If you have a lot of hard drive storage space and you want to avoid making dubs, you could also first **digitize** all your footage onto a hard drive and transcribe it using your computer to view the footage. This will save you a step since you have to digitize anyway. However, this method might not be practical if you have huge amounts of footage.

Another option for bigger budgets and quick turn-around projects is using a professional transcription company. For a fee, transcription companies will give you a fully typed printout and/or file of the contents and time code of each and every one of your taped interviews. Some transcription companies will even include thumbnail pictures of your footage within the transcript. If you want to trim some off the budget,

> ✔ *Always make dubs or digitize your tapes before transcribing. Never transcribe using your master tapes.*

transcribe some or all of the interviews yourself. Better yet, have an intern or assistant transcribe some tapes for you. (Remember, how something plays on paper can still be very different than how it plays on video. You still have to *watch* your clips.)

In addition to helping you piece together a final script, a transcript of your interviews will make sure that you have not misrepresented what a subject said by editing it out of context. When you're pulling sound bites from interviews and juxtaposing them with other material, it's easy to inadvertently apply a different meaning than the one originally intended by the subject. Similarly, if you have everything down on paper, it'll be much easier to check the accuracy of the narration, statements made by subjects, and implied conclusions. So transcripts are also invaluable for fact-checking your final piece. If a company is interested in distributing your doc theatrically or on TV, they will almost always require a transcript of your finished project.

> ✔ *Make a transcript of your interviews noting who said what and the exact time code when they said it.*

This is perhaps the single most important decision you will make on your doc. Think it over long and hard, because the essence of documentary is *editing*. This is where the story is actually told. Up until this point, you've only got a collection of pretty pictures and talking heads. How you juxtapose that material, what info you leave out, what shots and comments you put in, the music you use, the prevailing viewpoints, pacing, all of these things are decided in editing and will make or break your story in the end. This isn't a decision to be taken lightly.

You have three basic choices when it's time to edit your project: cut it yourself, work with a technical editor, or hand it off to a creative editor. Just like many choices in filmmaking, there aren't necessarily right or wrong decisions, simply choices that will or won't work best for your particular project, skill level, and/or resources. Here's my advice, pros and cons. Decide for yourself.

Cutting It Yourself

Pros:
- ❏ Work from comfort of home
- ❏ You know the footage better than anyone
- ❏ You can save money by not hiring an editor
- ❏ No pressure to finish
- ❏ You can edit anywhere on a laptop

Cons:
- ❏ Will take 2 to 10 times longer than a pro editor
- ❏ No second opinion on crucial decisions
- ❏ Need a good computer and large hard drive
- ❏ All the distractions of home
- ❏ Need at least average computer skills
- ❏ You may get stuck for months or never finish at all

Recommended Tools: Final Cut Pro, Avid Xpress, or Premiere with camera as deck.

Preparation: Learn the software, practice editing, write script/outline, organize, log, and digitize tapes.

Advice: This is a realistic option for those with previous editing experience. If you've never edited before in your life and have no formal training, it's a bad idea to *start* with a major project. Cut your teeth on some home movies or helping a friend edit their DV project. Keep your footage organized! Even if you edit yourself, regularly show segments to trusted colleagues and friends and get feedback. The best suggestions often come from the simplest of outside observations. It's common for new filmmakers to get frustrated editing their own work and let their project languish on a shelf for months or even years. There are probably hundreds of half-documentaries buried in closets across the country that will never see the light of day. If you get stuck, consult an experienced editor or filmmaker. Be honest with yourself if it's just not coming together and consider working with or handing your project over to someone with more experience.

Working Closely with a Technical Editor

Pros:

❏ Much faster than doing it yourself
❏ Provides a second opinion
❏ You can just think and be creative
❏ Companionship on those long editing shifts
❏ Editor can cut some sequences without you

Cons:

❏ Your editing sensibilities may clash
❏ Two people in a small room
❏ Will probably have to pay them
❏ Will probably travel to edit in *their* space

Best Person for the Job:

❏ An assistant editor
❏ An intermediate or advanced film student
❏ A bored corporate editor
❏ Professional editors with small egos

Recommended Tools: Final Cut Pro, Avid Xpress, Premiere with edit deck or camera.

Preparation: Write script/outline. Organize and log tapes. Meet to discuss edit style, influential films, and story beforehand.

Advice: You basically need someone who is technically proficient with one of the major DV editing programs such as Avid, Final Cut Pro, Liquid, Premiere, etc. You also want someone who understands your doc project and your goals. Make sure they understand that you're primarily looking for someone to do the "mechanical" edit work and that you'll be present for most sessions to direct most of the edits. You should still allow them some space to do their thing and offer advice. Nobody wants to be just a robot taking orders. Give them first crack at a few scenes. You may be pleasantly surprised. Many editors will hate to work this way, but some will love it because it's easy for them and they're getting paid. Also, make sure they are comfortable with your subject matter if it's controversial. And don't forget, you're going to be spending several long days, if not weeks or months, in a small room with this person. Personality and hygiene definitely count.

Handing It Off to a Creative Editor

Pros:

- ❏ A good editor will take the ball and run
- ❏ Pros work much faster than amateurs
- ❏ Can easily analyze and solve edit problems
- ❏ More familiar with broadcast standards
- ❏ Access to high-end systems
- ❏ Access to more post-production tools
- ❏ May work wonders with mediocre material

Cons:

- ❏ You're a control freak and it kills you to hand over your project
- ❏ Good editors usually cost good money
- ❏ Editor may be making a very different film
- ❏ You may have different editing sensibilities

Best Person for Job:

- ❏ An experienced editor
- ❏ Someone who fully understands your project goals
- ❏ Someone with new ideas about presenting the material
- ❏ Someone with a demo reel that kicks butt
- ❏ Someone who cut a film/video that you liked
- ❏ Someone whose creative judgment you trust
- ❏ An exceptional advanced film student

Preparation: Write script, outline, or detailed notes. Organize and log tapes. Meet to discuss edit style, influential films, and story beforehand.

Recommended Tools: High End Final Cut Pro or Avid System with Deck

Advice: Don't just look at reels, interview people, more than once if necessary. Look for an editor that's excited about the project and has creative ideas about how to communicate with the footage you've got. You want an editor with enthusiasm for the project who brings thoughtful debate and questions to the table. Be realistic and discuss deadlines and how often you'll meet to review sequences. Stay true to your vision, but give them some room to experiment and run with it and bring new storytelling ideas. That's what the best editors do—take your vision, in whatever state it's in, and make it *better*. If it's whack to begin with, they can make it okay. If it's okay to begin with, they can make it good. And if it's already good, they can really make it great!

WORKING WITH EDITORS

SAM POLLARD—PRODUCER/EDITOR
(4 Little Girls, Jim Brown All-American, Eyes on the Prize II, When the Levees Broke)

You know, I was very fortunate with Victor Kanefsky [Sam's Mentor]. What Victor Kanefsky taught me from the very beginning as a young editor, young assistant, young apprentice, was that part of my responsibility as an editor was to have no preconceived notions about the material that a director or producer brings to you. Well I wasn't looking for it to be perfectly shot or every camera angle to be perfectly right, what he or she brought to me as producers was material that said here's material with realms of possibility.

Some producers will come in and say, "Here's material with realms of possibility and here's an outline to help you understand how I think the film should go together."

Then there are some producers who will come in and say, "Here's material with realms of possibility, here's a script—a really thought out script—of how I think the film should come together."

Then there are some producers who come in and say, "Here's material with realms of possibilities, but to tell you the truth Sam, I don't have a clue how to put the damn thing together, I need your help."

Personally for me, because of the way I was taught by Victor, my ego prefers the third. I say, "Oh, now I can show you what I can do." But I'm open to work any way a producer wants to work. Part of my job is . . . to excavate from that material and find again, that word . . . the *story*.

A Quick Lesson on DV Tape

There are four vital tracks of information that are laid down when you hit your DV camera's record button: one track of video, two separate tracks of audio, and one track of time code (TC). The **time code** track on DV tape contains a digital signal, recorded by the camera, that maintains consistent playback by tracking the precise time down to seconds and frames (1 second = 30 frames of video). Time code is what editing programs use to mark the exact start and stop points of an edit.

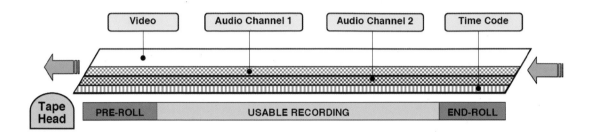

Time Code Problems

Now the video and audio tracks aren't usually problematic. However, time code problems are probably responsible for more editor headaches and receding hairlines than most other issues. There are two common problems that you'll likely encounter sooner or later:

Time Code Problem/Solution #1:

The first likely problem is that during the starting and stopping of recording, the camera's record head skips just a few frames of tape, which leads to a break in time code. This is usually just the price of dealing with the Mini-DV format as opposed to it's more stable and much more expensive digital cousins, DVC Pro or DV Cam. If you keep **playback** during shooting to a minimum, it will help avoid this type of time code break, but your camera and quality of tape will still dictate if and how often you will get these types of time code breaks. Always using fresh tapes will also help you avoid time code errors.

Time Code Problem/Solution #2:

The second problem that may occur is not allowing enough **pre-roll** and **end-roll** for a shot. When this happens, a video deck is searching for the **in-point** or **out-point** of a specific shot, but encounters a time code break and cancels the edit. To avoid these type of breaks, allow a few extra seconds at the beginning and end of each shot when shooting. If you're stuck with this problem, the simple solution is to select a later in-point or an earlier out-point that skips the break in the time code. If this isn't possible, you will have to dub that shot onto another tape with new clean time code.

STOCK FOOTAGE AND MUSIC

Once you've shot all your interviews, B-roll, and cutaways, you may find that you still have a number of visual "holes" in your story. That's to say, you have all the *words* you need, but not enough *images* to support it. That's where **stock footage** and **archival footage** come in. This is essentially any footage that wasn't *originally* shot for your documentary. It can be anything from relevant still photos from a local newspaper to clips of old movies that tie in to your topic. Here are just some examples commonly featured in docs.

Suggested Archival Footage

- ✔ Childhood photos of subjects
- ✔ Photos of subjects family members
- ✔ Home movies
- ✔ Footage from other docs and movies
- ✔ Television news stories
- ✔ Newspaper Articles
- ✔ Government film/TV archives
- ✔ Historical paintings and illustrations
- ✔ Stills of relevant historical relics
- ✔ Digital maps and charts

Any or all of these can be sources of visuals to help tell your story. The real question is where do you get them and how much do they cost? Like almost everything else in filmmaking the answer depends on where you look and who you deal with among other factors.

There are two main sources for stock footage: your subject(s) and stock footage houses. Some stock footage houses now offer all or part of their libraries online. Not only can you preview clips of their footage, you can actually purchase and download a broadcast-quality digital file and start editing–all without leaving your computer. Ask your subjects if they have any photos they will allow you to use. (You'll probably get better results if you wait until you've built up a good level of trust with them.) Ideally you want them to give you shoeboxes and albums of photos, but you may have to settle for whatever they are willing to give you. Handle these with care. If necessary, set up and shoot the photos at your subject's home so you never even have to take them. Another common technique is to have your subject flip through photo albums and comment on relevant pictures. Similarly, yearbooks, scrapbooks, and old diaries may all help your subjects to tell their stories better–with greater recollection and visual detail.

7 COMMANDMENTS OF ARCHIVAL FOOTAGE

BY RICK PRELINGER

The last decade has been good to film archives and stock footage libraries. Increased interest in archive and library holdings has exposed many hidden treasures. At the same time, the artifacts have stimulated reexamination of this century's history and preconceptions. Some independent film and videomakers make good use of these resources, but many others are intimidated by high prices, arcane policies, and complex procedures. Here are a few navigational hints designed to demystify the process of locating and using archival footage.

Many difficulties producers encounter in trying to locate and use archival footage can be avoided through careful planning and a willingness to be flexible. When starting any project that may employ archival footage, it's imperative to obey seven basic commandments:

1 **If the success or failure of the production depends on the inclusion of specific scenes or images, determine at the outset whether the images actually exist, who holds them, and whether you can afford to duplicate and license them.**

Some "famous" stock shots don't in fact exist, including Khrushchev's shoe-banging at the United Nations and the bespectacled 3-D movie audience (which are actually both still photographs). If feature film clips are necessary for your portrait of an activist actor, make sure that the actor's studio(s) will release the clips and get an idea of the costs involved.

2 **Seriously consider hiring an archival researcher with expertise in the area of your production.**

Quite frequently researchers can find more alternatives more quickly for less money. Their experience can make them valuable collaborators and even reshapers of your original concept.

3 **Negotiate your licensing deals as soon as you think you know the footage you want to use.**

Film libraries dislike extending discounts after a production is finished, and they have no incentive to do so.

4 Before your final cut, define your primary distribution media, markets, and territory. Decide which rights you can afford to clear.

As the number of distribution outlets have multiplied, rights have too. Contracts now cite such rights such "nonstandard television," "laser disc," "pay-per-view," "audio visual," and "multimedia." Territory is also a consideration in pricing rights. Distribution territory may be broadly defined to cover the United States or North America/Europe, or one may choose to narrowly target an audience, such as French-speaking Belgium. Many rights holders require full payment before releasing master material. A production with foreign sales or home video potential is useless if it must be shelved for want of license fees.

5 Get all the rights and clearances you need.

In order to reuse certain footage, you may need to obtain special rights. This is especially important when reusing footage from feature films, television programs, and musical and theatrical performances. Remember to clear music rights, get the consent of recognizable individuals appearing in the footage (or their estates), and possibly that of certain unions (Directors Guild of America and Writers Guild of America). Ultimately, you must decide between putting everything you want in your show and having it sit on the shelf, or clearing what you can afford and having a product to distribute legally.

6 Investigate the actual costs of research and duplication.

Libraries charge for their research time and generally mark up duplication costs. Costs may be surprisingly high if the footage you need is dispersed in several repositories, if your editing ratio is high, or if master material is expensive to duplicate.

7 Filmmakers: Choose your duplication format and, in cooperation with your lab, flowchart the handling procedure for different kinds of original material.

The preproduction phase is the time to decide between negative and positive, 35 mm and 16 mm, black and white and color, and all other options.

(From the article "Archival Survival: The Fundamentals of Using Film Archives and Stock Footage Libraries" by Rick Prelinger. More info is available at www.archive. org/details/prelinger.)

5 REASONS TO GET DOWN WITH PODCASTING AND VIDEO SHARING

1 GET PEOPLE TO SEE YOUR TRAILER

If you've got a trailer for your project, there's no better way to get it out to the masses than online. You can just post a straight trailer as a podcast or YouTube video. Or you can get creative and dole it out in pieces, show entire scenes, or add additional content, similar to DVD extras, to entice people to check out your film. Because podcasts are portable the chances of people sharing a trailer with like-minded people is much greater. If you're really smart with your promotion and people respond to the material, your clip could even become "viral" and begin to spread on it's own momentum driving traffic and media attention to your project.

2 GET PEOPLE TO SEE YOUR MOVIE

If you have a short that you want to get out there, podcasting and video sharing are the best things to happen since Ifilm.com. However, the potential for *feature* documentaries is just being tapped. If you have a project that's languishing on the shelf, it could find a whole new audience online. You can dole out your movie in pieces, tease the audience with just the first 10 minutes, or show the whole enchilada. While it's admittedly a long shot, it's quite possible that in the best-case scenario you could even get a distribution deal out of it. If you've got a "calling card" film, a podcast could help you get funding for the next project or gigs as a director for hire. Most important, it's a free way for you to get direct access, feedback, and start to build an audience.

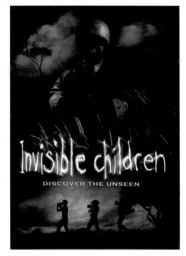

Invisible Children was promoted by a series of podcasts and spawned a worldwide youth movement to help Uganda.

3 TAKE YOUR PROJECTS ANYWHERE READY TO SHOW

If you have your videos in a portable format, you'll always have something to impress that agent you just happened to meet at the gym or that new crew member you're trying to recruit. The bottom line is that you can carry all of your video projects with you on an iPod, PSP, or other portable video player without the need for a computer, TV, or DVD player to show them off anytime, anywhere . . . and that's how guerrilla's roll.

4 | IT'S DIGITAL FILM SCHOOL

Filmmaking education isn't just established institutions with professors and formal classes, it's *anything* that helps you learn your craft. DVD extras and filmmaker commentaries are mini-film courses in themselves. Similarly, there are a growing number of podcasts (including the Down and Dirty DV podcast!) that cover the subject of filmmaking. Every month I watch or listen to a few hours of podcast content that helps keep me abreast of new equipment and technologies,

industry trends, tips and tricks, and generally how other filmmakers are dealing with the same issues I encounter. It's specialized education for free. Film school, workshops, and media all cost money. Right now the filmmaking podcasts are all free. That's a no-brainer.

5 | YOU CAN STILL GET IN ON THE GROUND FLOOR

The last stats I heard on podcasting (on a podcast ironically), said that only 10% of people surveyed even know what a podcast is. 10%! If you're thinking 10% is lame or why should you waste your time if there is only 10% penetration, then you're looking at it the wrong way. To me that figure means that this thing is just getting started. Podcasting today is like having an online business was in the early 90s—it's cutting edge and the field is still open enough to get attention because there isn't as much competition for eyeballs. That's the situation as I write this, but it's changing as we speak. Do you feel that draft in the room? Well that draft is coming from an open window of opportunity, baby! However, this window of wide open opportunity closes a little with every new and corporate-

sponsored podcast that hits the digital airwaves. If you're in now, God-willing, you'll be well positioned and established when the other 90% of filmmakers catch up in the coming years. Notable examples of film and media makers who have leveraged online attention to further their goals include the infamous "lonelygirl15," "Four Eyed Monsters," and the daily "Rocketboom" news and variety podcast.

FINDING AN AUDIENCE ONLINE

SUSAN BUICE AND ARIN CRUMLEY—
CO-DIRECTORS/PRODUCERS
(Four-Eyed Monsters Feature and Reality Video Podcast)

Susan: *Four-Eyed Monsters* is a film that we created that screened at Slamdance in 2005. As first-time filmmakers, this was our first film and our first major film festival, and we were really thinking, "Oh crap, we might get distribution and this is going to be ugly."

And we get here and I'm pretty sure no distributors came to our film, because it's not like we had an agent or anyone trying to get people in. It's not like our film was shot on 35 [mm]. It's not like we had anyone famous . . . So, no industry came to our film, which was completely understandable. That was something that after our first film festival, we discovered—if you didn't get distributed out of your first film festival round, you're not getting distributed, unless you do it a year later and go straight to DVD for a fraction of what you made the film for—even though you made the film low-budget.

So, having learned that, we were like, okay, we've taken this film on the film festival circuit and we know that there's an audience for it, because they love it and people are really responding to it. Just because *a distributor* doesn't think there's a big enough audience for it . . . what to them is a small audience would be huge for us. It would get us out of debt. It would pay for our next films. It's crazy! So, we thought, the film festival circuit's probably not the best place to find our audience either, being that our audience really is a younger generation of people that are on MySpace, that have these very personal profiles, where they're really exposing themselves.

Some people are calling it the Open Kimono. People are just opening up, their robes online and it's very expressive and that's what our work is like anyway. So, they get it. To them, it's not weird.

Susan: We've been filming everything that's been going on in our lives since getting into Slamdance. Basically, we thought with this video podcast, not only can we get people interested in us as people and our story, but we can get people interested in the way that we make film, in our visual aesthetic, and just in the story. And the people who are attracted to it are the people who like the film. And the people who don't like the video podcast don't need to waste their time watching our movie.

Arin: Because the video podcast is made very much in the same vein as the feature film. In a way, they're like these short films that have the same aesthetics and the same approach as the feature film. But, the interesting thing about them is that each episode ends with a slight question or a slight cliff-hanger or something encouraging the person to see the next episode. We tease the audience a little, and they all post us like, "Where's the next episode, where is it?"

Susan: It's so much fun. It's different than making the film. I don't know if filmmaking is actually a fun process. But, making the video podcast is really fun. And I love the interactiveness of the audience. They are constantly sending us videos, comments, written comments like they're constantly keeping us informed of how we're doing, what they want, and questions that they want answered.

Arin: And it sort of moves a little bit away from filmmaking honestly because it's more just media based communication. We put out our communication and they send back their communication. It's a feedback loop. The other thing that's really cool about the video podcast is that you know that they're watching it from 0 seconds at the beginning.

They're not gonna come in two minutes into the five-minute episode. There's no way technically that that can happen. So, it has that on-demand nature and that's actually a very empowering way to create.

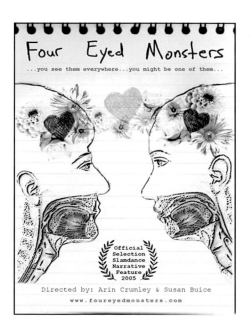

Think C.L.A.A.P. Before You Apply

Clout: All festivals are not created equal. Some are magnets for distributors and press and others are barely a blip on the industry radar screen. There are more industry players, perks, better networking, and better press coverage at the prestigious film fests. Making contacts for your current and future projects is a vital part of any long-term filmmaking strategy. Do your homework. Find out what caliber of industry folk are most likely to attend. Festival clout is the difference between an article in the *Hollywood Reporter* and the Skankville Gazette.

Location: Hustling your festival team and subject(s) downtown, a few states away, or all the way to Europe makes a big difference in cost, logistics, and how many people you can afford to bring with you. Less people means less promotion manpower.

Awards and Prizes: What types of awards might you win? Best Director? Best Foreign Film? Jury Award? And don't underestimate the attention-grabbing power of an Audience Award for best film. If you win what do you get? $30,000? (Doubtful.) A free rental or post-production package? The newest HD camera? A gift certificate to Red Lobster? Even digital guerrilla success has its rewards. And even if you don't win a single prize, remember that you beat out a bunch of people just to get nominated and you always have bragging rights!

Application Fee: Although there are festivals that are free to apply to, most film festivals have entry fees that range from $25 to $75. (And, no, you don't get your money back if your film is rejected.) Tack on the cost of mailing submissions and applying to just 10 festivals could easily run you well over 500 bucks! Apply to the festivals that will be most worthwhile for your project according to the goals of your festival strategy.

Perks: Will the festival cover airfare? A 5-star hotel room? Are there numerous events with free food and drinks? Is there a $500 goodie bag? Does the fest have a reputation for being *fun*? This industry is all about the perks, baby. The food, the drinks, the free tickets, the lavish parties, the celebrity access, the hotels. they all help take the sting out of your exhaustion, overwhelming debt, and battered ego. Even if your screening is half empty and you don't win a single award, you've still got some free stuff and a nice room with a view to enjoy. This part of the filmmaking experience is the 1% of what we do in the course of making a film that actually *is* glamorous. Enjoy it and take pictures.

PASSION, BUSINESS, & FILMMAKING

ADRIAN BELIC—CO-DIRECTOR/PRODUCER
(Gengis Blues, Beyond the Call)

And the way you nurture a film, the way you get allies on your side, is you go to festivals. And a lot of people think that festivals are about business, that's hawking yourself, that's being a salesperson. No, it's not. It's getting your *passion* out to the audience. I mean, I make films not for myself. I have a great time traveling around the world, but it's really hard to edit the film. So, I make films because I want the audience to see them.

At places like Sundance, they spend millions of dollars, every year, 365 days a year, to bring the world's top distributors here—business people, financiers, press people. And all I've got to do is show up, sleep on my friend's floor, and hustle from dawn to dusk, and all night long to get my film out to as many people as I can.

The other thing is to gain allies. We need to get allies, people who believe in our film and believe in *us*. And the only way that that happens is to go out. Some may call it business. I call it filmmaking. That's part of the whole filmmaking process. I spend three, four years making a film. To hell if I'm gonna let it just fall dead on the ground when I'm done! For me, it's about extending my passion. I just extend my passion through thinking of the film, and preproduction and production, and post, to distribution.

One of the things we realize is that, frankly, most people are lazy. You know how I know? Because, *I'm* lazy. So one of the things I try to do for distributors or pro-grammers or film festivals or the press is to make it as *easy* as it can be for them.

So, if we find out about a magazine that we want to get into, we learn something about that magazine, and then we try to figure out how to pitch our story to that magazine so that they'll pick it up. If there is a distributor that we want to get into, or some film festival, we learn a little bit about that film festival. What did they show last year? So, when we go and talk to that distributor, we actually know what the hell we're talking about.

Okay, you've poured your heart out into making your doc, it's finally finished, and you even got accepted into a few festivals. So, now it's time to sit back and let the accolades, awards, and applause roll in, right? Wrong! Now it's time to hustle just as hard as you did for all the other steps of the filmmaking process to make sure that people know about, see, and report about your film. Here's an overview of how to get the most out of a festival experience:

1. Do Your Homework

Any information that you can gather could give you an edge over the competition (or at least keep you from putting your foot in your mouth). So find out as much as you can about the particular festival you are attending. Read and print out all the info on their Web site. Look it up in the festival guides. Talk to past attendees and filmmakers. Try to figure out what films did well there and why. Find out what the audience responded to in the past. Research the programmers' tastes and stated festival goals.

2. Apply Early

Filmmakers are notorious procrastinators. However, this often isn't because we're irresponsible. It's because we're perfectionists and the guerrilla filmmaking process is such that things always seem to be twice as hard and take twice as long as we anticipated. However, with film festivals, procrastination is an ill-advised practice.

As someone who has organized a few festivals, I can tell you that the vast majority of entries come in during the *last few days* before the entry deadline. If your project is lumped in with all the rest of the last minute entries, it has less of a chance of standing out from the crowd. Weary festival organizers and screeners are more tempted to hit the fast forward or eject button at the first sign of flaws or boredom. So I strongly advise submitting your project several weeks before any deadline while the judges are still fresh and not glazed over from hours of viewing bad movies.

A more recent and revolutionary service for film festival applicants is Withoutabox.com. This Web site allows filmmakers to streamline the festival submission process by filling out and submitting one universal festival application and digital press kit to multiple film fests at once. According to their Web site, at last count there were more than 2000 participating film fests including many of the major festivals. This service is increasingly being embraced by the indie community, since it makes life easier for the festivals *and* the filmmakers.

Withoutabox.com simplifies the festival application process.

3. Put Together a Guerrilla Festival Team

You can't adequately promote your project all by yourself at a film festival. You need to enlist the help of your producers, crew members, friends, and family to help assemble promo materials then hit the festival streets and hang posters, hand out flyers, drum up press and interviews, pull wacky publicity stunts, and otherwise talk up, hype, and push your project. This is a great opportunity to bring your core filmmaking team back together for a celebratory reunion and one last hustle. If at all possible, try to bring the main subject(s) of your documentary. Audience and press are *much* more attracted to doc screenings where the actual subjects will be present and accessible. Inspiring or colorful subjects of well-received docs can become instant festival celebrities and easily double your promotion without even trying.

4. Put Together a Hot Press Kit and Promo Materials

There's crazy competition for eyeballs and attention at any film festival. Your posters, promotional materials, and trailer are the most important tools for luring audience members and press to your film. It helps if you have a decent budget, but creativity can help make up the difference. You'll need postcards, posters, a press release, video trailers, giveaways, production photos, and more. Originality, creativity, and grabbing attention counts more than your budget. You can do many ingenious things with paper alone. To take your guerrilla promotions to the next level, enlist some friends with advertising, design, or art backgrounds to come up with something that is cheap, clever, and, most important, *memorable*.

5. Get Your Hustle On

If you're a filmmaker with a film in a festival, you can't afford to be shy. You have to hustle to get butts in seats. You've gotta get out there, meet the festival attendees, and hype your film. Don't be a raving lunatic, but let anyone who will listen know about your film and when it's playing. A good-natured publicity stunt doesn't hurt either. The goal is to pack your screening to capacity and hopefully sell out. Get as many people handing out flyers as possible. Entertainment people hate to be "out of the loop." If there's a buzz, people want to know what it's about. Even if they don't actually see your project, the mere *buzz* created by full screenings, people discussing the project and looking at your clever handouts will create a positive impression and familiarity in their heads . . . "If people are talking about it, it must be good."

6. Mix at the Parties and Panels

The panels and parties are where people are most approachable and sociable. While many corporate business deals begin on the golf course, many film deals begin with a casual conversation over cocktails or at industry events. If you aren't likable, engaging, and pleasant to be around socially, who's going to seriously entertain the notion of entangling themselves with you in deals or projects that play out over months or even years? Oscar-nominated director, Adrian Belic of

The podcasting panel at Sundance.

Gengis Blues fame, summed it up best when he said, "Until people see your film, all they see is *you*." Given a choice, anyone would choose to work long-term with someone they enjoy being around rather than those they don't, so go to the parties and attend some filmmaking panels and let people know who you are and what you do. Filmmaking opportunities and alliances often start with a simple social conversation. So get out to those events and mix and mingle, even if it hurts.

7. Don't Just Network, Follow Up

Don't make the mistake of thinking that the only thing to be gained at a film festival is distribution and publicity. The cold truth is that a distribution deal is a long shot for most films at any festival, but it's far from the only prize. A single chance (or orchestrated) meeting could hold the key to your filmmaking future. Know this: Networking *is* the film and TV industry. Don't be intimidated by the word "networking." All it really means is meeting and connecting with people in your industry and trading info and resources. It's getting out there and putting yourself out there. The goal of networking is not to see how many people you can pitch your project to or hit up for favors. Networking is a two-way street. It's as much about what you can *give* as what you get. Lasting relationships are based on mutual giving whether it's trading advice, information, services, or connecting someone with one of your contacts. (Notice I didn't distinguish between "business" and "personal" relationships. The rules are one in the same.) If you genuinely connect and look to help other people, the rest will follow. If you're willing to help people, people will be willing to help you. People in this business can easily tell when you're desperate or just want to get something from them and it's a major turn off. Once you connect and you have a card, e-mail address, or phone number, you should follow up within two weeks tops. A short e-mail to say hello, point to an article, update them on your project, or asking what's going on with their project is sufficient. If you can meet up in person for lunch or coffee it's all the better. Once there's a human connection you will have another ally to help you achieve your future filmmaking goals.

HOW TO HUSTLE AT SUNDANCE

REBEKAH SINDORIS AND CHRISTIE PESICKA
(FilmTrix.com, *Paper Chasers, Paper Dolls, Rovin' Gamblers, Mr. Arizona*)

Rebekah: It's really good to go to the panels on any of the festivals—Slamdance or Sundance or any of the surrounding festivals. When you go to a panel discussion (and a lot of them are free) you get access to people afterwards. That is when people are very approachable. Read the publication about the people sitting on the panel. If you see any panelist that you want to talk to, you go afterwards with your business card and they're very approachable versus when they're in LA or New York or elsewhere.

I find my more valuable connections are earlier in the evening when there are more panels or earlier receptions. Because that's when you really talk more. They're a lot of fun and you never know who you're gonna meet . . . The panels are the most valuable resource, even if you don't see any movies. If you go to some panels up here and meet a couple of people who can help you fund your film or start your film, you've done better than most people.

So, I definitely recommend the panels. I recommend some of the receptions, the parties are great too, but go to some of the panels, especially the early evening ones, before everyone is out partying, because you'll be able to get some of your stuff out there and they will remember who you are.

Always write down on the back of people's business card who they are and where you met them, so you'll remember them. The most important part about all the connections you make up here is follow-up. Most people don't follow up. What good is a connection in a month or two if you don't follow up? Make sure you follow up or it's worthless . . .

Christie: If you don't have the money for a publicist, which can be tough, because truthfully, people spend more on publicity than they do their films. When you're talking about films being done for 10, 15, 20 thousand dollars, people are spending that on publicity just for a 10-day festival. So, how do you compete with them and get your film out there? You have to seek out shows like "Film Trix" (www.filmtrix.com) or Down and Dirty DV (www.DownAndDirtyDV.com) . . . Seek out people that really want to sit down and talk to you and hear what you have to say.

You want to make connections with some of the smaller shows, the smaller publications, that need you as much as you need them. Some people are seeking out Spielbergs and George Lucas' to get help . . . No, you need to find people who are on *your* level, who are going through the same thing who can help you. But, if you go to people who are kinda doing the same thing that you are doing, and maybe in a different area . . . If you can partner up with people like that, I think you're better off than trying to get a sound bite with a station that may or may not ever use it.

Rebekah: My recommendations on how to publicize your film if you don't have a lot of money and you're at a festival is to bring tons of DVDs, meet every distribution-type person you can. Go to the panels and Q&As . . . Talk to other filmmakers that have had success. Find out who their producer's reps are. Find out who is doing their distribution. Bring ton's of DVDs. Poster the town . . . Bring friends. Get a condo. Bunk up. It's not expensive if you book ahead of time. Get a bunch of people together. Some can sleep on the floor . . . It's not expensive if you do it that way. Get friends and family with you to help you spread the word. Set up your own screening if you want. It's a lot harder to do, but there are avenues. There are places where you can sign up for a screening time. Just really get to the people who are going to be able to help you sell it.

ANTHONY'S RECOMMENDED READS

The Shut Up and Shoot Documentary Guide is just a *starting point* for a film education. You've still got a long way to go to true guerrilla filmmaking enlightenment. First you must understand this: **Learning the craft of filmmaking is a life-long process**. (There's a reason why most of the people at the top of their game have gray hair—it takes that long to *master* it.)

Some things you read don't make sense until you shoot, but some things you screw up shooting don't make sense until you *read*. Guerrilla means maximizing your resources. And the number one resource that can help you make the most of any budget is knowledge. Whether you're in a film school, workshop, or self-teaching, you should begin building a filmmaking reference library. Here are some of my personal recommendations to help you get the ball rolling:

Bare Bones Camera Course for Film and Video
by Tom Schroeppel

I highly recommend this book to anyone new to cinematography. It's a self-published, underground classic not in too many stores but available online. True to its name, this book offers simple, clear, cartoon-illustrated instructions on the fundamentals of screen grammar and cinematography. I never fully "got" a lot of the things I read in other film books and heard in lectures until after I read this book. God bless Tom for finally explaining it to the rest of us.

What They Don't Teach You At Film School: 161 Strategies to Making Your Own Movie No Matter What
by Camille Landau and Tiara White

These smart women, who have obviously already been there and done that, have compiled a great collection of ultra-practical tips on the countless little things that frequently trip up filmmakers in the process. These are purely practical tips on the psychology, reality, and delicate daily minutia of filmmaking that you would only pick up from painful experience or by having the foresight to study a book of practical wisdom like this.

The Guerilla Film Makers Movie Blueprint
by Chris Jones

This is one the most practical and comprehensive film books I've ever read. It breaks down who does what, explains equipment packages, and lays out the filmmaking process step-by-step. It also features some very informative interviews from industry insiders who we don't usually hear too much from . . . and it's all in plain English. It's an invaluable reference guide for anyone making an indie feature.

Documentary Storytelling: Making Stronger and More Dramatic Nonfiction Films
by Sheila Curran Bernard

Now that you've got an overview of the process and a technical grasp of the genre, you need to dig deeper into the meaning and nuances of documentary. This book will help you understand the many visual, aural, and cerebral techniques and subtleties of telling a documentary story. It also features in-depth interviews with several notable names in docs.

Directing the Documentary
by Michael Rabiger

This is the definitive comprehensive text on documentary filmmaking. It's a bit thick, but it pretty much has to be to thoroughly cover all aspects of documentary filmmaking from history to theory to production practices. Includes student exercises.

Ultimate Film Festival Guide
by Chris Gore

Not many film books live up to their title, but this one really is the "ultimate" book on film festivals and festival strategy. Apart from the standard contact info and deadlines, Chris gives you tips on the flavor of each fest, self-promotion, and the application process. If you're planning on entering festivals, you should start with this book.

Television Production
by Gerald Millerson

This is the definitive book for the practices of television. From 3-camera shoots to blocking and editing, this book lays out and illustrates the entire world of TV production. The practices of TV are very similar but far from the same. If you want to work in "the little screen," you'll want to read this book.

The Documentary Filmmakers Handbook: A Guerilla Guide
by Genevieve Jolliffe

The latest entry in the guerrilla filmmaking handbook series turns the focus to docs. Heavy on interviews with industry insiders from directors to distributors and all the players in between, Genevieve shares detailed doc knowledge of the process that picks up where this book leaves off.

The IFILM Digital Video Filmmaker's Handbook
by Maxie Collier

From my fellow Down and Dirty filmmaker and good colleague, who was one of the very first authorities on DV filmmaking, this title gives beginning filmmakers an inspirational overview of the digital filmmaking process. It covers the creative and technical aspects and features a candid case study of the digital guerrilla documentary, *Paper Chasers*.

Development Girl: The Hollywood Virgin's Guide to Making It in the Movie Business
by Hadley Davis

If you have any inclination at all to work in the industry in any type of office setting, you can't afford not to read this humorous book, which chronicles the ins and outs of Hollywood workplace culture. Following Hadley's advice, you can avoid the most common newbie mistakes and go from Office Runner to Department Head in half the time.

Spike Lee's Gotta Have It
by Spike Lee

This is Spike's first film book and still my favorite of his series. It contains a script, interview, and diary of his struggle to make his first feature. While it's not about docs, it's a real study in the intense hustle, focus, and hard work it takes to pull off a low-budget indie.

Nuts and Bolts Filmmaking
by Dan Rahmel

If you're a DIY kinda filmmaker, then this is the text for you. It has instructions for building dozens of pieces of homemade equipment from dollies to lighting instruments.

How I Made a Hundred Movies in Hollywood and Never Lost a Dime
by Roger Corman

It's not about documentaries and I'm not even sure if this book is still in print, but it is a great autobiographical text by one of my idols, the B-film Godfather, Roger Corman. Before I was even born, Roger was keeping it Down and Dirty and cranking out quality films on ridiculously low budgets. Ron Howard, Martin Scorsese, and Francis Ford Coppola all started with Roger, and if they all had lessons to learn from him, so do we.

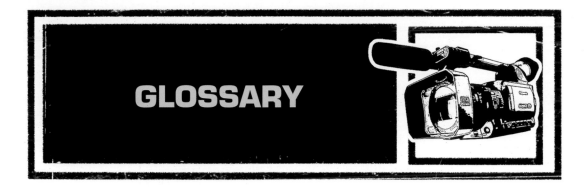

GLOSSARY

1-shot	A shot with only one person in frame.
3-point lighting	Traditional lighting set-up using three lights: key light, fill light, and hair light.
4-point lighting	Traditional lighting setup using four lights: key light, fill light, hair light, and background light.
Access	Your ability to get up close and inside the world of your subject. This is the golden ticket to documentary making.
ADR	Abbreviation for additional dialogue recording.
AGC	*See* Auto gain control.
Ambassador	Another term for a "stringer" or someone who acts as a liaison between your production and another community/culture. Someone who knows their way in the society you wish to film.
Amp	A unit that measures electricity. Most U.S. household circuits are 15 to 20 amps.
Anamorphic	A technique for capturing a 16 : 9 widescreen picture on a standard 4 : 3 aspect ratio camera. Uses an electronic process or a special lens that squeezes the 16 : 9 widescreen image into a 4 : 3 aspect ratio, which can be later unsqueezed in post-production.
Aperture ring	The spinning ring on a camera lens that controls exposure. (Prosumer camera models may have a small aperture dial instead of an aperture ring.)

Approach	How you choose to tell your documentary story. Using re-enactments, your style of camera work, narration, editing techniques, viewpoint, etc., are all parts of your overall approach.
Archival footage/photos	Any footage/photos that you use that weren't originally shot for your documentary. This includes news segments, movie clips, etc.
Aspect ratio	This is a ratio that simply refers to the shape of your image. In video there are two aspect ratios to choose from: 4 : 3 = standard TV, which is more square, and 16 : 9 = widescreen, which is more rectangular. The numbers represent a ratio of units of width : height.
Audience	These are the *people* you're actually making this film for. Don't ever forget about them.
Auto gain control	Commonly abbreviated as AGC, this is a camera feature that automatically adjusts sound levels for you.
Avid	One of the leading professional video editing programs available for PC and Mac.
Backlight	A light usually placed above left or right and behind your subject used to separate them from the background by using a rim of light to outline them. Also synonymous with a hair light, which is positioned the same but focused more on the hair.
Barn doors	The metal flaps mounted on the front of professional film lights that open and close to control the shape and amount of light. Barn doors help you keep the light only where you want it to go.
Blackwrap	Extra heavy-duty aluminum foil coated in a special heat-resistant black paint. This is used to shape and control light much like barn doors, but blackwrap can be quickly customized into an impromptu snoot, flag, or cookie.
Blown out	Overexposed video. This is the video kiss of death. If important parts of your video such as your subject's face or the entire background are blown out, it sucks to be you. Blown out white blotches in video simply can't be fixed in post. Use zebra stripes to help avoid this issue.
BNC	Video cable commonly used to connect cameras, monitors, projectors, and other A/V equipment.

Breakaway cables	Special sound cable that combines two XLR cables and a headphone extension cable into a single cable that connects between the camera and the mixer or microphone. There is a twist apart connector in the middle to allow camera people to quickly "breakaway" from sound people.
C-47s	Common ordinary wooden clothes pins. Used to secure gels to the barn doors of lights.
Character studies	Films whose content revolves around a specific character whose personality and presence drive the whole project.
Cheat	To move a prop or person to a new or staged position for a more favorable shot.
Chimera	Special heat-resistant tent-like housing for light instruments that provides soft evenly diffused light. Popular for interviews.
China ball (Chinaball)	*See* Chinese lantern.
Chinese lantern	Common round white household paper lanterns that produce soft warm light. Often used as soft key lights and as fill lights for interviews. Also known as China balls (Chinaballs).
Circuit breaker	An automatically operated electrical switch designed to protect an electrical circuit from damage caused by overload or short circuit.
Clapper board	Also known as a slate or clapboard, this item is used to mark the beginning or end of each take and provide info about the scene, but most importantly, the clapper board is used for syncing up visuals to sound by using the exact frame where the board claps as a visual and audio reference point in editing.
Closing down	*See* Stopping down.
Coaxial	Type of video cable used to connect cameras, decks, and monitors and other video equipment to each other. Most commonly recognized on your cable box, VCR, or TV.
Confessionals	A staple of personal docs and reality TV, the confessional is where subjects speak directly to the camera, often alone in a room, and share their private thoughts and confessions.

Contingency	This is all-purpose emergency money that is built into your budget. Industry standard is 15% set aside for contingency. Anything less than 10% is risky.
Cookie	A cut-out pattern used to cast interesting shadows that add texture to the background of scenes. A cookie may also mimic the pattern of light shining through a window, blinds, trees, etc.
Craft Services	The snacks, drinks, and sometimes food department on a film set. These people are responsible for keeping caffeine, snacks, and nourishment flowing at all times.
Crane	Piece of equipment used to raise a camera and/or camera operator to get high-angle shots and cool swooping camera moves.
Crop out	To adjust your frame by tightening a shot or recomposing, so that an undesirable element such as a sign or attention-starved jerk waving at the camera is no longer in the frame.
CTB gel	Abbreviation for color temperature blue. Use this gel on a tungsten (indoor) light source to make it appear the same color temperature as daylight.
CTO gel	Abbreviation for color temperature orange. Put this gel on a daylight-balanced light source to make it appear the same color temperature as tungsten (indoor) light.
Dailies	Refers to the footage shot the previous day (i.e., the crew's daily output). In an ideal world this footage is viewed daily by the director, cinematographer, and other invited crew members to make sure that everything is coming out okay and all necessary shots are being covered.
Dead Cat	Film slang for shaggy faux fur coverings used to block wind noise from boom mics. Also known as "windjammers."
Decibel	Abbreviation is dB. These units measure sound levels.
Depth-of-field	Abbreviation is d.o.f. A term that refers to how much of the area in front of and behind your subject is in focus at any given time. If your subject is in focus and the background and foreground is out of focus, then you have a shallow depth-of-field. If everything in the frame is in focus, then you have deep depth-of-field.

Digitize

To convert video into a digital format so that it can be edited. Done by hooking up a camera or tape deck to your computer and importing the video footage in a non-linear editing (NLE) program such as Final Cut Pro, iMovie, Premiere, or Avid.

Dimmer box

A small electrical accessory that uses a dial or sliding switch to adjust the brightness of any light instrument plugged into it.

Dolly

Any camera movement or piece of equipment that rolls the camera. If it has wheels and you put your camera on it to shoot a moving shot, then it's a dolly.

Dramatic readings

Storytelling convention where actors are used to read a document and/or portray the voice of a subject. Used to breathe life into letters, diaries, or other documents.

Dramatic zoom

The act of zooming in or out slowly on a subject to give dramatic emphasis to what is being said. These are generally done at the most important or compelling parts of an interview to bring the audience physically and emotionally closer to the subject.

Dutch angle

A shot tilted diagonally to visually communicate tension, edginess, energy, or wacky fun.

DV Rack

PC-only computer software that can record live footage directly to a hard drive via a laptop computer. Also has other features for image analysis and color correction.

End-roll

The term for the wise practice of letting the camera roll for an extra few seconds after each take, so that there is adequate room at the end of a scene for an editor to make a cut without losing the end of the take.

Equipment package

The entire list of equipment that you need to make a film. Includes your lights, camera, sound, and all the trimmings.

Filament

The tiny, thin, delicate spring that glows to produce the light inside light bulbs.

Fill light

A light whose function is to bring up the light level to fill in dark shadows so that details are visible on a subject's face or a lit scene. Fill light should be soft and even. Fill lights are often bounced off a wall or ceiling.

Firestore	A particular brand of small battery-powered camera-mountable hard drives that capture live video via Firewire as a DV camera records it. The captured video files are immediately ready to be edited, saving you tons of time digitizing and logging tapes.
Firewire 400/800	Also known as "IEEE 1394" and "iLink," these are super fast connections for transferring video data to or from a camera, computer, or hard drive. Firewire 800, used in computers and hard drives, is about twice as fast as Firewire 400 which transfers data at 400 MB/sec. (At the time of publication, DV cameras only use Firewire 400.)
Flood	To widen a beam of light so that it is less intense and more diffused and even. Focusable professional film lights have controls to allow you to flood or spot the light beam.
Fluorescent light	Long tubular mercury-vapor lights that use a ballast to regulate the flow of power. Professional fluorescent lights for filmmaking, such as KinoFlos, may come as tungsten or daylight-balanced. Note that many *household* and *industrial* fluorescent lights have an unattractive green or bluish tint and are more likely to flicker.
Frame line	The imaginary line that marks the top of a framed shot. If a boom mic drops below this line it will be in the shot.
Frame-within-a-frame	A shot composition that includes some other element of a scene, such as a doorway or window, that forms a second "frame" around a subject already in the camera's frame.
f-stop	F-stops are numbers that refer to the size of the hole that lets light into the lens, otherwise known as the aperture. It's counterintuitive, but the larger the f-stop number, the less light is allowed in the lens, the darker the image will be. The smaller the f-stop number, the brighter the image will be.
Gaffer's tape	Professional film industry tape, which is easy to rip by hand, but still very strong. It's also designed not to rip off paint or leave a sticky residue. An all-purpose must-have for any shoot.

Gain	This is just another word for "level." There are two types of gain—audio and video. Audio gain adjusts the volume level of audio signals. Video gain adjusts the voltage of the video signal to make an image brighter.
Gels	Transparent or translucent sheets of material used to color lights or correct the color of lights.
HDMI	Stands for High-definition multi-interface. A connection or cable that allows you to hook up video devices such as an HD camera and monitor to transmit high-quality, *high-definition* images. Look for these on high definition cameras, monitors, and TVs.
iMovie	Simple, easy-to-use, but powerful editing program that is bundled standard with Mac computers.
In-point	The starting time code point of a shot or edit.
Incandescent	An incandescent light passes electricity through a thin filament that heats up inside the vacuum of a bulb to provide light. Most household and professional film lights are incandescent. The other common type of lighting is fluorescent.
Insurance certificate	An insurance certificate is a representation of the insurance policy that covers a particular project or production company. At your request, your insurance company can issue certificates naming locations and equipment rental houses as "additional insured" as proof that they are also protected by your insurance policy.
Intensity	A term that simply refers to the quantity of light. Light intensity can be controlled in a number of ways including moving the light closer or farther, using ND or other light-reducing filters, or spotting or flooding the light beam.
Interview subjects	The people who will be interviewed for your project.
Jib	A mechanical arm balanced with a camera on one end and a counterweight and camera controls on the other end. Often mounted on tripod legs. Works similar to a seesaw, but the balance point is closer to the end with the controls, so that the camera is at the long end of the arm and can make sweeping vertical or horizontal moves.

Jump cuts	Refers to a cut made in editing where two shots of the same subject, but taken from different angles, are cut back-to-back to create a jarring "jump" in screen composition.
KinoFlo	Popular brand of professional fluorescent lights used in filmmaking. Known for their lightweight, soft even light, low power consumption, and low heat output.
Lavaliere (lav)	Small mics designed to be worn close to the body on the chest or neck. Because of their small size they can also be hidden on location to pick up sound in wide shots.
Location	Any real-life environment you shoot in not created specifically for film production such as an office, a park, or someone's home.
Location release	Legal agreement between a location owner and filmmaker that grants a filmmaker permission to shoot in and publicly show a location in their film. Also spells out any obligations to the location owner in the event of damage or injury.
Lock down	To secure a tripod's pan and tilt function so that the tripod doesn't move and keeps the shot on camera locked into place.
Log sheet	A form used to make notes about the location of scenes and quality of your footage. A log sheet typically includes information such as time code, scene description, length, and whether a shot was good or bad.
Logging	Going through all your footage to note the starting time code, contents, and other vital information that will be necessary for locating scenes and making decisions during editing. Usually written out in a log sheet.
Medium close-up (MCU)	A shot from the shoulders up.
Mini stereo connector	Another term for an 1/8" stereo sound connector like the one on your iPod. Commonly used for headphones and consumer-quality mics.
Monopod	Serves the same function as a tripod, but is made up of only a single extending and locking leg. Monopods are highly portable and easy to move and reset quickly.

Movie Magic Budgeting	A widely-used software program designed specifically for budgeting movies. MMB makes it easy to create, rearrange, and compare different versions of a budget. Gorilla Film Production Software also does the same thing.
Narration	The oral telling of a story. In documentary filmmaking narration is often laid in as a voice-over the picture.
Narrative filmmaking	Fictional filmmaking genre that tells a story. Narrative is almost always scripted, but can be improvised as well. If there are actors and a script, it's a narrative.
ND gel	Clear gray lighting gel used to cut down the intensity of lights without affecting color.
Noise	Video static and artifacts caused by using the camera's gain, digital zoom feature, or other electronic function that results in grainier, poorer image quality.
Non-linear editor (NLE)	Final Cut Pro, Avid, Premiere, and iMovie are all examples of popular NLEs.
On the D.L.	Short for "on the down low." Means to travel and shoot as low key as possible and not draw any unnecessary attention to yourself when shooting without permission or in hostile areas. Just keep it on the D.L.
Opening up the lens	To increase the camera's aperture so that more light comes into the lens to make the image brighter.
Out-point	The ending time code of a shot or edit.
Over-modulate	When sound levels are set so high that they distort, sound rumbly, or are unintelligible. Over-modulation can't be fixed in post-production. Avoid it at all costs.
Paper edit	A preliminary editing of a doc project by cutting and arranging sections of transcripts into the order they will appear in the film. You can then use this paper version of your project as a guide to create a rough cut.
Pick-up pattern	Outlines the direction(s) in which a microphone best captures and records sound. Common pick-up patterns are cardioid, hypercardioid, and omni.
Plan B	This is what you plan to do when your *first* idea doesn't work out. To be successful at guerrilla filmmaking you always need to have back-up plans when things don't work out . . . plans B, C, and D.

Playback	The act of viewing or listening to previously recorded video or audio.
Practical lights	Any lights that appear on-camera as part of your scene. They may or may not actually be contributing to the main lighting of your scene.
Preproduction	All the thought, preparation, planning, and budgeting that takes place before you start to shoot. The decisions that *most* impact the success of your film are all made during preproduction.
Pre-roll	Refers to the few seconds of tape that need to roll off before a camera or deck is up to proper recording speed.
Production insurance	Insurance that covers you and your crew from liabilities as a result of any property damage, loss, or personal death or injury caused by your production.
Production value	The professional look or polish of a production. Production value is affected by such factors as the quality of your lighting, video, audio, camerawork, sets, graphics, and number of mistakes. The term "putting your money on the screen" means raising production value wherever possible. It's the art of making 25 cents look like a dollar.
Raccoon eyes	The effect created when shooting subjects in bright daylight when the sun is high in the sky, which results in dark shadows in the subject's eye sockets.
Rate cards	A rental house or other vendor's price list.
RCA	Also, known as "phono." The very common yellow, white and red cables/connections used with video equipment: yellow = video, white = left, and red = right. Although color-coded, RCA cables are completely interchangeable as long as each end is plugged into the same color port.
Reaction shot	A shot showing how another participant is responding to an event. In interviews, this is the occasional shot of the interviewer responding to the subject. For a performance, a reaction shot would focus on audience members.
Re-enactments/recreations	A dramatic acting out of some significant event. May be performed by actors or the actual person involved in the original event. Often presented in documentary similar to flashbacks in narrative filmmaking. Re-enactments are common in crime, investigative, and historical documentaries.

Research
Any and all work you do to learn more about your subject as you prepare to shoot your documentary. Research encompasses reading books, surfing the Web, watching videos, visiting locations, talking to experts, etc. Research is doing *homework* on your subject and topic.

Reverse shot
Very similar to a reaction shot, a reverse shot is just the same action captured from the opposite angle to show a counter viewpoint.

Rule of thirds
Rule of composition that dictates if the screen is divided into thirds horizontally and vertically forming a tic-tac-toe pattern. Your subject should be framed so that they are positioned on the intersection of any two or more lines.

Run-and-gun
Guerrilla shooting style that generally refers to any hectic, unpredictable, fast, and unfolding shooting condition that requires you to cover a lot in a little time often at various locations. Local news and no-budget docs are almost always run-and gun-shooting situations.

Scene detection
The ability of some edit programs to automatically separate footage into video clips by detecting the time code when the record button was pressed to start each new shot.

Screen captions
Titles placed at the bottom of the frame to spell out dialogue or language subtitles.

Scrims
Specially fitted round metal screens of various thicknesses that come as full or half circles placed in front of a light to reduce intensity.

Shotgun
Another name for hypercardioid mics that have a very narrow pick-up pattern and only focus on sound in the direction they are pointed.

Shutter speed
This term refers to the amount of time the camera's shutter stays open to expose each frame of video. Shutter speed affects how motion is portrayed—sharp or blurry—and also affects how much light enters the lens in addition to the aperture.

Slate	This is a device used to synchronize picture and sound and mark particular scenes and takes recorded during production. Can be as simple as someone clapping their hands in front of the camera or as complicated as a battery-operated slate with electronic time code display. Also commonly used as a verb. Alternately known as a "clapper board," "clapboard," "marker," or "smart slate."
Snoots	Can-like cylindrical inserts that fit in front of lights to reduce the width of the beam to highlight a specific subject or object in a scene.
Society of Motion Picture and Television Engineers (SMPTE)	SMPTE (pronounced *simp-tee*) is a long-standing group of film and TV engineers who develop industry standards. Best known for their SMPTE color bar test pattern, which is used to adjust video colors on monitors.
Sound blankets	Thick, quilted mover's blankets used to dampen echoes caused by hard room surfaces. Can also be used to muffle unwanted noise. Any thick blanket, quilt, or other sound-absorbing material can serve as a sound blanket.
Speed	Term referring to the moment shortly after you press the record button when a camera has finished its pre-roll and reached the necessary speed to properly record video and audio signals.
Spill	Undesired light that is illuminating any area other than the targeted area is considered spill light. Barn doors, blackwrap, flags, and snoots are all used to control excess spill light.
Spot	To adjust a light's spot/flood control so that the light is at its narrowest, most intense beam.
SteadiCam	An industry standard and very expensive camera-stabilizing device used to get smooth fluid handheld camera shots. The high-end models require a trained operator. A trained SteadiCam operator can actually run with a SteadiCam and still get smooth footage. For DV filmmakers there is also a less pricey SteadiCam, Jr.
Sticks	Another word for tripod.
Stills	Refers to digital or filmed still photographs.

Stock footage	Stock footage is essentially any footage that wasn't originally shot for your documentary. It can be anything from scenic, establishing shots of a city to clips of old movies about your topic. Stock and archival footage houses sell historical and current video and film footage.
Stopping down	To make a shot darker by closing the lens aperture so that less light comes into the lens.
Surveillance video	Video that is recorded passively or secretly. Usually done from afar using telephoto lens or with hidden or unmanned cameras to capture criminal activity, unguarded moments, or daily activity in a given location.
S-video	Analog connection/cable used to transmit high-quality video signals between cameras, monitors, and videotape decks. Does not carry audio signal.
Take	Every time you call "cut" or start a shot or scene over again is considered a take. To successfully capture a single shot you may often do multiple takes.
Telephoto	The longest lens setting achieved by zooming all the way in to a subject or using a telephoto lens.
Time code	Time code is a digital signal recorded as a track on a DV tape that maintains consistent playback by digitally marking the precise time and tape position down to seconds and frames (1 second = 30 DV frames). This is what editing programs use to mark the exact start and stop points of an edit.
Transcript	The line-for-line written conversion of a videotaped interview or conversation into a "script." For doc filmmaking purposes transcripts should also denote the time code of interview questions and dialogue so they can be easily located during editing.
Tungsten	Light which has a filament and is orange in color temperature. Most quartz bulbs and standard household incandescent lights are tungsten.
USB/USB 2.0	USB is an abbreviation for Universal Serial Bus. These data cables/connectors are used to connect digital equipment such as cameras, computers, and hard drives. USB is fairly slow, but USB 2.0 is faster than Firewire.

Verbal release	Recording a subject giving you verbal permission to use their image in your project. This is a runner-up when you can't get a written release right then. These do *not* offer the legal protection of a signed talent release, but some verification is always better than none.
Warm cards	Pale green or blue "white cards" made to give your image a warmer look when you white-balance your camera on them instead of a pure white card.
Watts	A unit used to measure electricity. Typical household light bulbs are 40 to 150 watts. Professional film lights are typically 250 to 2000 watts or more.
White balance	A video camera function that adjusts your image to correct variations in color temperature. So white appears white on video.
White cards	A special pure white card used as a reference to set a camera's white-balance function to adjust for the lighting conditions on location. Pure white sheets of paper or crisp white T-shirts are a common substitute for white cards in the field.
Wild sound	The natural sound of a room or environment that is recorded to help you smooth out audio problems and recreate the original background noise and sound quality of the location during post-production.
Windjammer	This fuzzy faux fur covering goes over a zeppelin to dramatically help block wind noise when shooting outside. Also affectionately known as a "dead cat."
Wrap out	When everything is packed up and put back in place at the end of a shoot.
XLR	The most common high-quality sound cables/connectors used for professional sound applications. The connectors are three-pronged (male) or three-holed (female).
Zebra stripes	Zebra stripes are vibrating diagonal stripes that are superimposed on the overexposed parts of the image on a viewfinder or LCD screen to help you judge proper exposure. Zebra stripes are not recorded to tape.
Zeppelin	A blimp-like microphone housing designed to shield boom mics from wind noise.

INDEX

Anthony Q. Artis (*ant-nee kew art-iss*) originally hails from Baltimore, Maryland, and has made his home in New York City for most of the last 15 years where he has honed his skills as a straight-up digital guerrilla. Anthony is a graduate of New York University's Tisch School of the Arts. He has worked professionally in positions as diverse as producer, gaffer, cinematographer, special-FX makeup, sound mixer, and location manager, just to name a few.

Over the years, Anthony has crewed and produced a variety of television, documentary, and narrative projects. His feature films have screened at the Tribeca Film Festival, the IFP Market, Cinequest, and Slamdance and his television work has been broadcasted on MTV and The Education Channel. Most notably, he produced the feature film *Shelter*, which won first prize for Emerging Narratives at the 2003 IFP Market, an audience choice award at The Temecula International Film Festival, and a Special Jury Award at Cinequest, among other awards. He was also a segment producer on the popular MTV reality show, *Flipped*. Anthony can be *seen* in full guerrilla action as Associate Producer, Gaffer, and 2nd Unit DP in the feature documentary, *Paper Chasers*, which chronicles the hip-hop music industry and the down and dirty making of a low-budget guerrilla doc.

Through the years Anthony has organized numerous student film festivals and trained hundreds of aspiring guerrilla filmmakers for major institutions including New York University, New York City's famed LaGuardia High School for the Performing Arts, and Baltimore County Public Schools.

Anthony is presently the manager of the Film and TV Production Center at New York University's Tisch School of the Arts where he coordinates the technical training and production equipment for all film and TV students and teaches seminars in video lighting, camera work, and sound. Anthony is the producer and host of the Down and Dirty DV Podcast on iTunes and is currently producing an instructional series of guerrilla filmmaking books, DVDs, and boot camps. He remains an active guerrilla filmmaker, educator, consultant, and "artrepreneur." His web site is DownAndDirtyDV.com.

BOOK AND DVD CREDITS

Project Coordinator
Anthony Q. Artis
Associate Project Coordinators
Jenny Chun
Lisa Kjerulff
Nathan Kensinger
Meghan O'Hara
Jan Kardys
Project Consultant
Pete Chatmon
Additional Copy Editor
Darren C. Hackett
Interview Subjects
Adrian Belic
Alrick Brown
Susan Buice
John Canemaker
Arin Crumley
Christina DeHaven
Marion Lipschutz
Albert Maysles
Safiya McClinton
Christie Pesicka
Sam Pollard
Rose Rosenblatt
Micah Schaffer
Rebekah Sindoris
Featured Articles
Michelle Coe
Jon Harris
Rick Prelinger
Models
Marlyne Afflack
Sonya Artis
Tai Artis
Alisa Besher
Ori G. Carino
Dustin Chang
Eddie Cunha
Ina Franck
Sorayya Kassamali
Emily Konoppinski
Dorian Missick
Andrew Momsor
Frank Monteleone
Kathleen Monteleone
Estelle Newman
Hannah Schluder
Alec Strasser
Ella Strasser
Danielle Velkoff
Timothy Wong
Yekaterina Yakubov
Crew as Themselves

Videography for Photos
Fruto Corre
Ahmed Hawari
Freddie Jackson
Gary Jean
Rich Joneleit
Kian Najmabadi
Max Nova
Sophie Shepard
Additional Crew
Sean Charlesworth
Andrew Engbert
Maggie Langalinais
Kristin Wynn
DVD Authoring, Editing, and Animation
C. Daniel Shipp
DVD Trailer Editor
Greg Payton
DVD Music
B526 for Bshani Media Group
Maurice Carr
D&D Web site Design
Sarah Gallarello
Logo Design
Brian and Sarah Gallarello
Hand-Camera Graphic Design
Ian Kim
Additional Graphics
Sonya Artis
Canon
Core—The Education Channel
Death of Two Sons—Yimbe, Inc.
The Education of Shelby Knox—InCite
   Pictures
FourEyedMonsters.com
Glidecam
GoogleMaps
InvisibleChildren.com
JVC
Losmandy
Lowel Lighting
MapQuest.com
Panasonic
Paper Chasers—Son #1 Media
Sony
WithoutABox.com
Icons and Diagrams
T-ski's Ghetto Graphix

Interview Transcripts
Skye Dent—24/7 Transcriptions
Lisa Kjerulff
Kristin Wynn
Special Thanks
Sheril Antonio
Rob and Alyce Benevides
Maurice Carr
Cliff Charles
Evelyn Chatman
Christian City Church—Manhattan
Dave DiGioia
Yuri Densynko
Ralph DePalma
Double 7 Films
The Down and Dirty DV Nation
The Drumadics
Fritz Gerald
Julia Keydel
Brandon Kiggins
Lou LaVolpe
Rosanne Limoncelli
Jeremiah Newton
The NYU Film and TV Community
Damian Panitz
Student Filmmakers Magazine
The Treitley Family
Paul Yee
Inspiration and Motivation
Charles Blackwell
Pete Chatmon
Maxie Collier
Johnny Rice II
Bennie Randall *The Motivator*
The Original *Paper Chasers* Crew
My Production Center Family
My Family
Fat Joe
God

NO MORE EXCUSES...
SHUT UP AND SHOOT.

1.

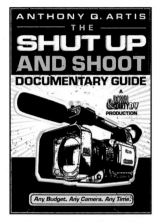

Read the Book.

2.

Buy the DVDs.

3.

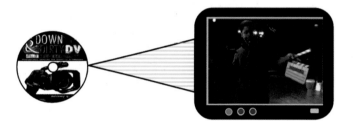

Make it happen.

DownAndDirtyDV.com
Any Budget. Any Camera. Any Time.